THE CITY & GUILDS TEXTBOOK

LEVEL 2 DIPLOMA IN

BUSINESS

ADMINISTRATION

THE CITY & GUILDS TEXTBOOK

LEVEL 2 DIPLOMA IN
BUSINESS ADMINISTRATION

VIC ASHLEY

SHEILA ASHLEY

City & Guilds

About City & Guilds

City & Guilds is the UK's leading provider of vocational qualifications, offering over 500 awards across a wide range of industries, and progressing from entry level to the highest levels of professional achievement. With over 8,500 centres in 100 countries, City & Guilds is recognised by employers worldwide for providing qualifications that offer proof of the skills they need to get the job done.

Equal opportunities

City & Guilds fully supports the principle of equal opportunities and we are committed to satisfying this principle in all our activities and published material. A copy of our equal opportunities policy statement is available on the City & Guilds website.

First edition 2015

ISBN 978 0 85193 252 1

Publisher: Charlie Evans

Development Editor: Claire Owen

Production Editor: Fiona Freel

Cover and text design by Design Deluxe

Typeset by Saxon Graphics, Derby

Printed in the UK by Cambrian Printers Ltd

British Library Cataloguing in Publication Data

A catalogue record is available from the British Library.

Publications

For information about or to order City & Guilds support materials, contact 0844 534 0000 or centresupport@cityandguilds.com. You can find more information about the materials we have available at www.cityandguild.com/bookshop.

Every effort has been made to ensure that the information contained in this publication is true and correct at the time of going to press. However, City & Guilds' products and services are subject to continuous development and improvement and the right is reserved to change products and services from time to time. City & Guilds cannot accept liability for loss or damage arising from the use of information in this publication.

City & Guilds
1 Giltspur Street
London EC1A 9DD

0844 543 0033
www.cityandguilds.com
publishingfeedback@cityandguilds.com

CONTENTS

ABOUT THE AUTHORS

Vic and Sheila Ashley are experienced authors in the business and education fields. They have published Business and Administration Student Handbooks at Levels 1, 2 and 3 through the Council for Administration (CfA), online resources for Retail and Business and Administration for the City & Guilds SmartScreen website (www.SmartScreen.co.uk) and workbooks supplying the knowledge and understanding for a range of qualifications available through www.aspect-training.com.

Vic has extensive retail experience, mainly with the Debenhams Group, and has spent 25 years working with awarding organisations including City & Guilds in a number of roles including consultant, lead verifier, regional verifier and external verifier. He is also the Chair of Examiners for the 14–19 Diploma in Retail Business for AQA – City & Guilds. Sheila has operated a successful catering business and acted as Centre Co-ordinator for her own training provider delivering Assessor and Verifier Awards, PTTLS, CTTLS and DTTLS.

We would like to thank the following people for their work on this textbook: Charlie Evans, Fiona Freel, Lucy Hyde, Claire Owen, Lynn Preston and Sylvia Sims.

HOW TO USE THIS TEXTBOOK

Welcome to your City & Guilds Level 2 Diploma in Business Administration textbook. It is designed to guide you through your Level 2 qualification and be a useful reference for you throughout your career.

Each chapter covers a unit from the 5528 Level 2 qualification, and covers everything you will need to understand in order to prepare for your assessments.

Throughout this textbook you will see the following features:

Assessment criteria

This section covers assessment criteria 1.1 and 1.2

ASSESSMENT CRITERIA – These highlight the assessment criteria coverage through each unit, so you can easily link your learning to what you need to know or do for each learning outcome.

Interactions

Communication between or joint activity involving two or more people

KEY TERM – Words in bold in the text are explained in the margin to aid your understanding. They also appear in the glossary at the back of the book.

ACTIVITY

List the different types of meetings that you have been involved in or are aware of within your organisation.

ACTIVITIES – These are suggested activities to help you learn and practise.

HANDY HINT

If you are uncertain what someone has said, ask them to repeat it.

HANDY HINTS – These are particularly useful tips that can assist you in the workplace or help you remember something important.

COMMON MISTAKE

Minutes do not, necessarily, have to record every word spoken at a meeting.

COMMON MISTAKES – These identify common mistakes to avoid.

CASE STUDIES – Each chapter ends with a case study describing situations you may encounter in your work.

CASE STUDY
CUSTOMER SERVICE

This case study concerns an unnamed hotel in South Korea. This is a true story and were it not for excellent customer service, the customer in question would have been in dire straits.

An author had to attend a business meeting in South Korea. He didn't know the area or the language. He took a two-hour taxi ride away from his airport, bound for a hotel in a remote region of the country.

When he arrived at his hotel he was informed that they had been overbooked and there was not a room for him. The author's hotel room had been pre-arranged, so an overbooked room left him virtually deserted in a foreign country.

The hotel manager appeared, and told the author he was sorry about the mistake. The manager went ahead and booked the author a room in another nearby hotel, then gave his taxi driver instructions to ensure that he made it to his room safely. The hotel manager took the time to understand the situation, and did everything he could to rectify it. The moral of this customer service case study is simple: where there is a crisis, there is an opportunity – you just have to make sure you know *how* to turn a bad experience into a good or great one.

TEST YOUR KNOWLEDGE QUESTIONS – At the end of every chapter are some questions designed to test your understanding of what you have learnt in that chapter. This can help with identifying further training or revision needed. You will find the suggested answers at the end of the book.

UNIT 222 (B&A 34): TEST YOUR KNOWLEDGE

Learning outcome 1: Understand the requirements of written and verbal business communication

1 Describe why different methods of communication are used.

2 Explain the purpose of communication.

3 Explain how you use body language in communicating at work.

4 Describe a situation in which verbal communication would be appropriate.

5 Describe a situation in which written communication would be appropriate.

MAPPING GRID

		Unit number													
		Unit 101 (B&A 4)	Unit 203 (B&A 15)	Unit 204 (B&A 16)	Unit 205 (B&A 17)	Unit 207 (B&A 19)	Unit 211 (B&A 23)	Unit 215 (B&A 27)	Unit 222 (B&A 34)	Unit 224 (B&A 36)	Unit 225 Unit 224 (B&A 37)	Unit 224 Unit 224 (B&A 38)	Unit 227 Unit 224 (B&A 39)	Unit 239 (M&L 1)	Unit 240 (M&L 2)
Unit number	Unit 101 (B&A 4)		★	★	★	★	★	★	★	★	★	★	★	★	
	Unit 203 (B&A 15)	★		★			★	★			★				
	Unit 204 (B&A 16)	★	★								★				
	Unit 205 (B&A 17)	★								★					
	Unit 207 (B&A 19)	★													
	Unit 211 (B&A 23)	★	★												
	Unit 215 (B&A 27)	★	★												
	Unit 222 (B&A 34)	★									★				
	Unit 224 (B&A 36)	★			★										

MAPPING GRID

	Unit number													
	Unit 101 (B&A 4)	Unit 203 (B&A 15)	Unit 204 (B&A 16)	Unit 205 (B&A 17)	Unit 207 (B&A 19)	Unit 211 (B&A 23)	Unit 215 (B&A 27)	Unit 222 (B&A 34)	Unit 224 (B&A 36)	Unit 225 Unit 224 (B&A 37)	Unit 224 Unit 224 (B&A 38)	Unit 227 Unit 224 (B&A 39)	Unit 239 (M&L 1)	Unit 240 (M&L 2)
Unit 224 Unit 224 (B&A 37)	★	★	★					★		▓				
Unit 226 Unit 224 (B&A 38)	★										▓			
Unit 224 Unit 224 (B&A 39)	★											▓		
Unit 239 (M&L 1)	★												▓	★
Unit 240 (M&L 2)	★												★	▓

CROSS-REFERENCING EVIDENCE

The table above indicates where it might be possible to cross-reference evidence. To use the table, look down the vertical axis, find the unit you have evidence for, and look across to find units that the evidence might cross-refer to, indicated with the symbol [star].

For instance, when you have collected evidence for Unit 204 (B&A 16), some of it might cross-refer to Units 203 (B&A 15) and 225 (B&A 37).

CAREER PLANNER

There are very few jobs for life in the current economy, so it is important that you plan your career. Look regularly at where you are now, where you would like to be in the short- and longer-term and how you can get there.

A short-term career plan focuses on a period of between one and five years. The most important aspect is to develop realistic goals and objectives. You need to narrow down your choices so that you can focus on the career that you really want and then carry out detailed research into that career. It may be a different career from the one you are currently employed in, or you may want to develop within your existing career.

The research will enable you to identify the qualifications needed to move into a new career or take the next step in your existing career. Compare the qualifications you already have with those identified by your research. If this indicates that you already have the necessary qualifications, you will be ready to look for opportunities to make the move into the position you want. If there is a significant gap, consider whether it is realistic to achieve the necessary qualifications in the short term. Look at obtaining further training, attending college (either on day release or in the evenings), or gaining additional experience, maybe in a voluntary role in your own time.

A long-term career plan focuses on the period beyond five years. As the workplace is rapidly changing, the competences you have now, or plan to gain in the short term, may not be appropriate in the future. There are fundamental skills that will always be in demand and you should concentrate on these for your long-term development. The skills that will always be in demand include verbal and written communication, computing, team leadership and team working, decision making, planning, organising, problem solving, and commitment to life-long learning.

Within the business and administration sector, qualifications can lead to career progression. With a level 2 qualification, typical job opportunities will include:

- administrator
- business support officer
- office junior
- receptionist
- junior legal secretary
- junior medical secretary
- medical receptionist.

With a Level 3 qualification, typical job opportunities will include:

- Administration officer – duties might range from helping to prepare financial statements to producing monthly management accounts. Other tasks you will be likely to take on include:
  - budgeting
  - raising invoices
  - managing ledgers
  - processing expenses
  - preparing VAT returns.

- Bookkeeper – you will help prepare the profit and loss sheets for the annual accounts. Other tasks you will be likely to take on include:
  - balancing accounts
  - processing sales invoices, receipts and payments
  - VAT returns
  - checking bank statements
  - dealing with financial paperwork and filing.

- Office supervisor – this role is demanding. Your daily tasks may well include:
  - balancing budgets
  - arranging travel, meetings and appointments
  - ordering stationery and equipment
  - supervising and monitoring staff
  - discussing problems
  - reporting to management
  - reviewing and implementing the company's health and safety policy
  - arranging training.

- Personal assistant – you will be helping your manager organise their working life so they always know where they need to be and what they're doing. Your duties will include tasks such as:
  - typing up minutes
  - organising diaries
  - fielding calls
  - managing junior staff
  - organising travel arrangements
  - researching projects, writing reports or managing budgets (once you have more experience and training).

- Purchase ledger clerk – you may have sole control over payments or work as part of a much bigger purchase ledger team. Purchase ledger clerks are expected to be able to:
  - code and check invoices
  - work out VAT payments

- pay out money via BACS or by cheque
- check and reconcile supplier statements
- file invoices and statements
- deal with purchase enquiries
- process staff expenses.

- Sales ledger clerk – your responsibility is to ensure that money owed to a company is accounted and invoiced for. Your main duties will include:
  - setting up new clients
  - producing invoices
  - banking and reconciliation
  - running off turnover statements
  - chasing up outstanding debts
  - checking VAT has been included on invoices
  - providing creditors with VAT receipts.

The possibilities for progression within the business administration sector really are exciting, with a wide range of careers available including:

- accountant
- advertising account executive
- banker: investment or commercial
- banking manager
- buyer (industrial or retail)
- company secretary
- commodity broker
- distribution/logistics manager
- insurance underwriter
- IT consultant
- management consultant
- marketing executive
- market research executive
- human resources manager
- public relations account executive
- recruitment consultant
- retail manager
- sales executive
- stockbroker
- systems analyst.

Whatever career path you embark upon, this textbook will help you take the first steps.

ACKNOWLEDGEMENTS

City & Guilds would like to sincerely thank the following:

For invaluable subject knowledge and expertise
Lynn Preston and Sylvia Sims

For freelance editorial support
Lucy Hyde

Picture credits
Every effort has been made to acknowledge all copyright holders as below and the publishers will, if notified, correct any errors in future editions.

Front cover: © Tetra Images/Corbis
Back cover: Shutterstock – © Creativa, © Goodluz, © Pressmaster, © racorn.
iStock: © micha360 p198; © Neustockimages p226; **Shutterstock:** © 2xSamara.com p116; © 3DProfi p93; © aastock p225; © AD Hunter p80; © Adam Gregor204; © Adriano Castelli p219; © Akos Nagy p54; © Alexandr Makarov p42; © alexford p269; © Andrew Horwitz p220; © Angel_Vasilev77 p135; © antb p241; © auremar pp 17, 147, 186; © Avesun p42; © baloon111 p35; © Beth Swanson p103; © bikeriderlondon p30; © bogdanhoda p274; © Brad Wynnyk p43; © CandyBox Images pp205, 236; © Creativa p77; © cristovao p272; © d_arts p155; © dotshock p224; © Dragon Images p21; © EdBockStock p208; © EDHAR pp 109, 144; © Elena11 p221; © Ensuper p177; © evievee09 57; © fiphoto p96; © FooTToo p263; © FrameAngel p262; © Frank Gaertner p134; © Gines Valera Marin p155; © Glovatskiy p107; © Golden Pixels LLC p213; © Goodluz pp 118, 132, 181, 199, 236; © graphixmania p72; © Grounder p73; © g-stockstudio p112; © Hurst Photo p22; © hxdbzxy pp 183, 267; © imageshunter p52; © Iryna Rasko p9; © Jakub Zak p245; © JMiks p178; © Kheng Guan Toh p122; © Kzenon p29; © Laurens Parsons Photography p270; © legenda p3; © Lightspring p173; © littleny p222; © Lucky Business p143; © Maksym Bondarchuk p40; © marekuliasz p154; © Marie C Fields p171; © Martin Good p97; © mast3r p8; © mhatzapa p154; © Monkey Business Images pp 4, 5, 14, 25, 169, 185, 199, 215, 257; © ostill p238; © OtnaYdur p69; © pio3 p217; © Pixsooz p78; © Piyato p90; © Plukhin p220; © pmphoto p156; © polat p179; © Pressmaster pp 16, 76, 125, 127, 151, 157, 158, 192; © racorn pp 1, 149, 195, 196, 229; © Radoslaw Korga p38; © Robyn Mackenzie p187; © Rtimages 251; © Samo Trebizan 253; © Sebastian Kaulitzki p259; © Sergey Nivens p207; © shooarts p161; © smuay p202; © Sophie James p221; © StockLite pp 16, 124, 129, 141, 210; © Svetlana Lukienko p163; © Syda Productions p19; © terekhov igor p114; © trekandshoot p273; © Wade Vaillancourt p44; © wavebreakmedia pp 62, 80, 211, 231, 243; © Wilm Ihlenfeld p167; © wizdata1 p66; © Zerbor p85.

MANDATORY UNITS

CHAPTER 1

UNIT 222 (B&A 34) COMMUNICATION IN A BUSINESS ENVIRONMENT

A survey of recruiters from the largest employers identifies communication skills as the single most important factor in selecting managers. Whatever role you have, in any organisation, you will need to communicate – with customers, suppliers or colleagues. No one works entirely in isolation. All communication has a purpose, either to generate actions or to pass on or request information. Effective communication achieves its purpose by generating the desired effect without the message losing clarity during the process.

Communication, whether written or verbal, has to follow certain conventions (customary ways in which things are done within an organisation) if it is to be understood – this is the role of language in communication. Spelling, punctuation and grammar contribute greatly to the communication of ideas. If the receiver of the message is unable to understand it, the message will not have the desired effect.

In this unit you will cover the following learning outcomes:

1 understand the requirements of written and verbal business communication

2 be able to produce written business communications

3 be able to communicate verbally in business environments.

Interactions

Communication between or joint activity involving two or more people

Motivate

To make somebody feel enthusiastic, interested, and committed to something

ACTIVITIES

- Research the structure of a formal report.
- Research the layout of a business letter.
- Research the layout of emails used in your organisation.

BUSINESS COMMUNICATION

It is important to understand the communication needs of colleagues. These will include knowing what business the organisation is in, who the customers are, specific details about products or services, where forms are located and who to see when there is a problem. They also need the practical skills required to do their job well and the **interactions** that give them a sense of belonging and self-worth, such as being listened to, respected, trusted and valued.

Communicating in a business environment always has a purpose: this is to send a message to an individual or group of people in order to request action, inform, teach, persuade, **motivate** or inspire. Communication is a process, which must be understood if it is to be effective and misunderstanding and confusion are to be avoided.

According to communications theories, the process consists of the:

- Sender – the person sending the communication. You need to be clear what you want to communicate, who to, how and why.
- Message – the information you want to communicate must be clear and not capable of being misunderstood.
- Encoding – putting the message into a form that can be understood. You need to understand your audience and their level of knowledge of the subject, avoiding mistaken assumptions that may arise as a result of missing information or cultural issues.
- Channel – the method of sending the message. Channels may be written, for instance letters, emails, memos or reports, or verbal, for instance presentations or face-to-face meetings.

You will need to communicate with people through a range of channels, such as face-to-face meetings

- Decoding – reading or hearing the message. The message can be misunderstood through a lack of knowledge, a poorly worded message or not enough time being given to considering its meaning.

- Audience – the individual reading or hearing the message. Even if the message is sent to a group, it is received by individuals, each of whom has to understand the message. Individuals receiving the message may have pre-conceived ideas which will affect their interpretation of the message, so the sender will need to take these into consideration when encoding it.

- Feedback – the response which you, as the sender, get from the receiver. You will be able to gauge from the feedback whether the receiver has understood the message. This will tell you if your communication has been effective and, if not, give you the opportunity to send a further message to correct any misunderstanding.

- Context – the exterior factors that affect the effective communication of the message. These could be language, culture, organisational culture, etc.

- Intended outcomes – the desired result of the communication.

Think about how your audience will receive the message

COMMUNICATION SYSTEMS

Different methods of communication include:

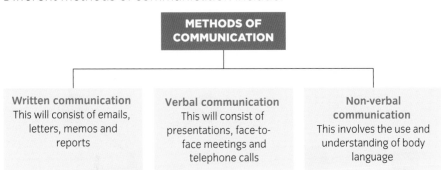

METHODS OF COMMUNICATION

Written communication	Verbal communication	Non-verbal communication
This will consist of emails, letters, memos and reports	This will consist of presentations, face-to-face meetings and telephone calls	This involves the use and understanding of body language

Each method will be used in different circumstances. More formal communication is likely to need written communication while verbal communication will often be appropriate to informal situations. Non-verbal communication is, of course, used whenever two or more people are together. The common thread is the passing of information from the sender to the receiver in a form that is clearly understood. The method of communication you choose will depend on the urgency and complexity of the information being communicated. You will also need to adapt your communications for different audiences, both internal and external.

There are several patterns of communication:

- The 'chain' represents the **hierarchical** pattern that characterises strictly formal information flow, 'from the top down', in military and some types of business organisation.
- The 'wheel' is found in a typical autocratic organisation, meaning one-man rule and limited employee participation.
- 'The star or all-channel network' allows free flow of communication in a group, encouraging all of its members to become involved in group decision processes.
- 'The Y pattern' is a more complicated arrangement where the group is separated into three and the group members can communicate with the other members of the group through the leader.
- The 'circle' is where the sender can communicate only with the group members next to him/her. Other group members can't receive the sender's message.

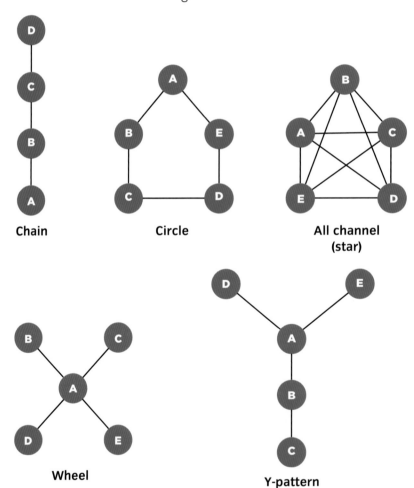

Chain   Circle   All channel (star)

Wheel   Y-pattern

The structure of communications within an organisation will have a significant influence on the accuracy of decisions, the speed with which they can be reached, and the satisfaction of the people involved. In networks in which the responsibility for initiating and passing along messages is shared more evenly among the members, better communications will be achieved.

WRITTEN COMMUNICATION

Assessment criteria

This section covers assessment criteria 1.3, 2.1, 2.2, 2.3, 2.4, 2.5 and 2.6

Written communication in a business environment consists of emails, letters, memos, agendas, minutes, notices and reports. Electronic communication can combine different media such as text, graphics, sound and video. This can produce more meaningful communication relevant to your particular audience. Because it is interactive, it can engage the audience in two-way communications.

While each form of written communication has its own conventions, they all require you to use the three main elements of written communication.

STRUCTURE

The first element is structure, which refers to the way that you lay out the content. To organise the structure of your communication, think about what you want the receiver to understand from your message.

Identify the key points and facts that you are trying to **convey** and put them into a logical order. Make sure you start with a powerful introduction, as this will create a positive first impression.

Convey

To communicate or express something

Use headings, sub-headings and bullet points to help the receiver identify the main points of the message, and write in short sentences and paragraphs. Each paragraph should start with a main point, followed by supporting information.

HANDY HINT

Keep it short and simple (KISS)

End the communication with a conclusion or a recommendation or by restating the main point of the message, depending on the purpose of communicating. The last paragraph is the one the receiver will remember longest, so don't use it to waffle on after you have made your main point.

STYLE AND TONE

The second element is style and tone, which refer to the way you write. All business communication should be concise, simple, direct and **lucid**. Sentences should contain no more than thirty words, and paragraphs should be no more than ten lines long.

Lucid

Clear and easily understood

Written communication in general, but particularly letters, should be kept as short as possible while containing all the necessary information. If people receive a lot of letters, they will tend to look to see who the letter is from, and read it if it is short. If it looks too long, they will put it aside and read it when they have time. An effective business letter should consist of no more than three paragraphs of four or five lines per paragraph.

There are standard conventions for writing a formal business letter

Broadsheet

A newspaper that is printed in a large format and is associated with serious journalism

Tabloid

A small-format popular newspaper with a simple style, many photographs, and sometimes an emphasis on sensational stories

You need to consider how much information and how much detail should be included, and how formal the message is. This will depend to a great extent on the audience the message is for. If you are writing an article for a **broadsheet** newspaper, you would use a different style from an article on the same subject in a **tabloid**.

Write positively – if you have to advise your customers of a price increase, point out the excellent value your product or service still is, and remind them of the benefits it has over your competitors. The exception might be when you have had to deal with a disciplinary or performance issue with a team member. After initially discussing the situation verbally you will have to record the outcome formally in writing.

The first sentence of any communication should be interesting, to capture the interest of the receiver. The majority of the letter should relate to the receiver – people are always more interested in themselves than in you – they want to know what the benefit will be to them, so use 'you', 'your' and 'yours' as much as possible.

Jargon

Language that is used by a group or profession, especially words and phrases which are not understood or used by other people

Jargon and abbreviations should be avoided unless they will definitely be understood by the receiver, or are explained within the communication. Short, familiar words should be used rather than obscure, complex words. Active words should be used – say 'I think…' rather than 'it is thought…' – and use single words rather than phrases – say 'now' not 'at this point in time'.

When communicating on behalf of colleagues or your line manager, it is important to keep them informed of your progress in meeting any deadline they may have given you. If you are experiencing difficulties you will be able to alert them to the need to plan for any effect a delay in communication may cause.

CONTENT

The third element is content, which refers, obviously, to what you are writing about. The information you need to communicate may have come from a variety of sources, including your own research and information which has been passed to you for the specific purpose of communicating it to a wider audience. You need to think through what your message is, making sure your objective is clear. Check that you have made your essential points clearly and developed your argument logically. Make the content positive and constructive and don't allow detail to obscure the main issues.

Don't write for the sake of writing – people are busy and don't have time to read unnecessary messages. Do, on the other hand, write to congratulate or praise people who deserve it. This may seem unnecessary, on the face of it, but will mean a lot to the recipient. They may have worked very hard to achieve the promotion or the successful sales pitch, and it is worth the time to let them know you appreciate it.

Use plain English. This will allow the receiver to understand exactly what you mean. Plain English is written clearly and concisely so the reader can take the required action.

Government departments, banks, insurance companies and local councils have moved towards the use of plain English in order to provide clear communication, rather than **missives** that impress or confuse their clients or customers. The simple rules for writing plain English are to write in short sentences, use everyday words, use personal words such as 'I', 'we' and 'you', and write as concisely and directly as possible.

Customers expect to be treated with respect, and using plain English when writing to them is one way to do this. Before you send your message, read it and think how you would feel if you received it. If your reaction is the one you intend, then send it; if not, rewrite it.

Receiving a letter of congratulations can mean a lot to the recipient

Missive

A letter or other written communication, often formal or legal communication

SPELLING, PUNCTUATION AND GRAMMAR

Spelling, punctuation and grammar are all vital to effective communication. A badly spelt, badly punctuated, ungrammatical message will give a very poor impression to your colleagues if used internally and of the whole organisation if used in communication with customers, clients or suppliers. The ironic thing is that even people whose own English is poor can recognise when yours is.

PUNCTUATION

Poor spelling, punctuation and grammar can totally alter the meaning of your message, possibly with serious consequences. A misplaced or omitted comma can completely change the meaning of a sentence. Consider the following which lists the ingredients of a salad:

> **HANDY HINTS**
>
> Consider the writing rules of George Orwell:
>
> - Never use a long word where a short one will do.
> - If it is possible to cut a word out, cut it out.
> - Never use the passive voice.
> - Never use jargon if you can think of an everyday equivalent.

'Tomatoes, onions, goats, cheese.' The addition of a comma after the word 'goats' and the omission of the apostrophe from the 'goats' cheese' have made it an entirely different dish.

There are lots of punctuation marks that you will need to know how to use correctly if your text is to be completely accurate, but the most important are:

- Full stops – these are used at the end of sentences or to indicate an abbreviation, such as 'etc'.
- Commas – these are used to separate individual words in a list, or to indicate where a pause is intended in a sentence.
- Apostrophes – these are used to indicate a missing letter ('he's' meaning 'he is') or that something belongs to someone ('St. John's Wood', 'The King's Head').

GRAMMAR

Practise spelling words correctly – remember some word processing programmes use American English rather than UK English as their basic dictionary. They will indicate a word is misspelt when it is actually correct and correct when it is actually incorrect, so check this and alter the settings if you can.

As well as improving your spelling it is important to improve your knowledge of the meanings of words; there are a number of words in the English language which are commonly misused: learn their meaning and you will not confuse them.

Commonly misused words	
Accept	Except
Advice	Advise
Affect	Effect
Ambivalent	Indifferent
Disinterested	Indifferent
Disinterested	Uninterested
Eligible	Illegible
Enervating	Energising
Ensure	Insure
Farther	Further

Commonly misused words	
Fewer	Less
Meddle	Medal
Personal	Personnel
Practice	Practise
Principal	Principle
Stationary	Stationery
Than	Then
There	Their or they're
Your	You're

GRAMMAR

The third part of language that you need to understand is the correct use of grammar. Again, there are far too many rules of grammar to cover in a book like this, but the key parts of speech to understand are:

Key parts of speech	
Nouns	These are the names of people, places or things, such as 'laptop', 'medal', 'James' or 'Norwich'.
Pronouns	These are used to replace nouns to avoid repetition, for example 'he', 'she', 'his' or 'theirs'.
Verbs	These are used to indicate action or being, such as 'to be', 'to type' or 'to watch'.
Adverbs	These describe a verb, such as 'to type *accurately*' or 'to watch *closely*'. They usually end in 'ly'.
Adjectives	These describe a noun, such as '*new* laptop', '*gold* medal', '*handsome* James' or '*beautiful* Norwich'

Parts of speech are joined together into sentences, and sentences are joined together into paragraphs. Sentences should express a single thought; paragraphs should link together sentences on a single topic.

The basic parts of a sentence are the subject, the verb, and often, but not always the object. The subject is usually a noun. The verb usually follows the subject and identifies an action or a state of being. An object receives the action and usually follows the verb. A common way of expanding the basic sentence is with modifiers, words that add to the meanings of other words. The simplest modifiers are adjectives and adverbs. Adjectives modify nouns, while adverbs modify verbs, adjectives, and other adverbs. Like adjectives and adverbs, prepositional phrases add meaning to the nouns and verbs in sentences. A prepositional phrase has two basic parts: a preposition plus a noun or a pronoun that serves as the object of the preposition.

There are four basic sentence structures in English:

- A simple sentence, which is a sentence with just one independent clause, eg 'Peter coughed'.
- A compound sentence contains at least two independent clauses, eg 'Peter coughed and Ahmed sneezed'.
- A complex sentence contains an independent clause and at least one dependent clause, eg 'Ahmed sneezed when Peter coughed'.
- A compound-complex sentence contains two or more independent clauses and at least one dependent clause, eg 'Peter coughed and Ahmed sneezed when someone spilled pepper near their seats'.

INTERNET ETIQUETTE

If you are communicating over the internet, a form of convention known as 'netiquette' has developed. This requires you to:

- treat your readers with the kind of respect you would expect from them
- not harass or insult people – your readers or others
- respect copyrights
- not overuse CAPITAL LETTERS
- not send **spam**
- tell the truth
- use correct grammar and punctuation
- not use inappropriate language
- research your facts
- acknowledge your sources.

Spam

An unsolicited, often commercial, message transmitted through the internet as a mass mailing to a large number of recipients

ACTIVITIES

Correct the following:

Google survises go offlion in China

Google sez It's serch ingen and uther internet survises have bin cutt of form mutch of China jus as the countrys rewling party pick new leeders.

Data posted on Googles website show it's survises in China becaime largely inaxessable form around 5pm locle tyme inn Beijing.

A Google spookswomen said the company found no problem in I'ts own compooter or network that wood disrupt It's survises inn China.

That razed the posabilaty that Chinas Commnist Party desided to block Googles survises at a polaticily sensitif tyme.

Googles surch ingines, email and other survises have bin perodicly unavalable in China sinse 2010. That were when Google desided to stop censering it's surch ressults to remove websites what Chinas goverment found objecshunnjable.

Correctly punctuate the following paragraph:

if you fly economy listen up results from the most comprehensive survey ever. into seat sizes has just been revealed and amethyst. Flyaway, and Getaway, airlines have tied at first place we love both. airlines for having top notch customer service in any case and this. news will only sweeten the experience while airlines such as scottish airways have been improving. their food offerings and check in speed it languishes. in 21st place for legroom unsurprisingly frillfreeair is. in 24th place for having a seat width of 16 inches but at least the airline can gloat. at the fact that it has beaten lazyjet in the legroom category which came second, from last frillfreeair had 30 inches; while lazyjet was 29 inches, the worst airline for legroom is Cattleair

VERBAL COMMUNICATION

Assessment criteria

This section covers assessment criteria 1.4, 3.1, 3.2, 3.3, 3.4, 3.5 and 3.6

Verbal communication includes making presentations, using the telephone, speaking to people one-to-one and holding discussions with two or more people. The principles of effective verbal communication are the same:

- Speak clearly – if you are nervous about the situation, you will speak more quickly than if you are relaxed, and this will make it more difficult for people to understand you. Make sure you have prepared (at least mentally) what you want to say, stick to the point and avoid waffling or unnecessarily repeating yourself. If possible, give examples that your audience will be able to relate to in support of your arguments.

- Speak properly – consider the culture, background and level of understanding of your audience and use English correctly. If your levels of grammar and vocabulary come across as below those expected by your audience you will be seen as lazy, undereducated or, at worst, disrespectful if it is perceived that you are '**dumbing down**' your delivery. In an increasingly global workplace, it is more important than ever to speak English well if you are to be understood by people who have learnt it as a foreign language.

Dumbing down

The deliberate diminishment of the intellectual level of the content of schooling and education, of literature and cinema, and of news

All types of oral communication must be clear and easy to understand

- Speak thoughtfully – consider your audience and the effect your message may have on them. Remember to make a conversation about the people you are speaking to rather than about you, wherever possible. People much prefer talking about themselves – it is everyone's favourite subject. Ask questions and show interest in the answers. Try to remember personal details so that next time you speak to them you can ask how their husband/wife/child/dog is. This will encourage dialogue, and give you the opening you need to get your message across. Everybody prefers working with people they like, so make people like you.

- Speak sincerely – if you think someone has made a particularly good effort, tell them so. Show interest in your colleagues by congratulating them, but be careful not to be insincere – people can tell if you are saying 'well done' while thinking 'lucky so-and-so'. Avoid personal remarks, as comments on a colleague's physical attributes, for instance, can be misunderstood and lead to a variety of problems.

- Speak confidently – if you don't believe what you are saying you shouldn't be surprised if no one else does. You can demonstrate confidence in what you are saying through the way you speak. Think about pace, pitch and volume of your voice – although this doesn't mean shout at your audience. Stand upright and make eye contact, but don't stare, it is very **disconcerting**.

Disconcerting

Making somebody feel ill at ease, slightly confused, or taken aback

Remember that just because you understand what you are saying, it doesn't mean the person you are speaking to understands. They will hear what you say against a background of their own experiences and opinions which might completely alter the meaning.

Only ten per cent of what you say is actually received by the listener. Try to avoid using jargon and abbreviations which might not be familiar to them or long difficult words which you might think will impress them but in fact will only obscure the point you are trying to make.

If the purpose of your verbal communication is to resolve a problem, remember that the best way to get answers from people is to ask questions. If you start by stating the problem and ask for opinions or suggestions you will get a more balanced response than if you start with your solution to the problem and ask if people agree with it.

If you are dealing with poor performance or behaviour, ask for their side of the story before you make a decision on how you are going to handle the situation; you may be surprised to find that the actual problem is completely different from what you imagine it to be.

LISTENING

Remember that hearing and listening are not the same. We all hear lots of things we don't listen to. Listening is a conscious activity aimed at understanding what you hear. Unfortunately, even when we listen we don't necessarily hear. People speak at up to 175 words per minute, but we are able to listen intelligently at up to 800 words per minute, so there is a lot of spare capacity, which we usually fill by thinking about something else.

There are seven levels of listening, these are:

Seven levels of listening	
Passive listening	You are not really listening at all, simply hearing background noise.
Pretend listening	You are giving all the outward signs of listening, nodding, smiling, saying 'of course', but you are really thinking about something else.
Selective listening	You have already made up your mind what your response is going to be, so have stopped listening.
Misunderstood listening	You are hearing what you want to hear, not what is actually being said.
Active listening	You are listening, understanding feelings and gathering facts.

Active listening means you are listening, understanding feelings and gathering facts

Seven levels of listening	
Empathic listening	You are understanding feelings and checking facts, with the speaker's purpose in mind.
Facilitative listening	You are listening with the speaker's purpose uppermost.

In a business environment, you need to be listening at or above the 'active' level. In many conversations, nobody is listening; everybody is simply taking turns to speak. Everybody is more interested in giving their own views than in listening to those of other people. At the same time, we all want to be listened to and understood.

Active listening requires you to:

- stop what you are doing
- look at the speaker
- let others speak
- be interested in what is being said
- ask open-ended questions to clarify what you hear
- spend more time listening than talking
- not finish the speaker's sentences
- not interrupt
- avoid answering questions with questions
- plan your response after the speaker has finished, not while they are talking
- only give your own opinions after you have heard the speaker's.

When you have listened actively to what is being said, summarise it in your own words so the speaker can confirm that you have understood it.

HANDY HINT

When a person is speaking, do not interrupt. Not all conversations are about winning an argument or making a point. Communication is as much about listening as it is about talking.

NON-VERBAL COMMUNICATION

An important part of verbal communication is, strangely enough, non-verbal communication; what we say without speaking. Body language is an extremely complex subject, which even the acknowledged experts disagree about, but there are some simple clues which you give off all the time, and which you can learn to read in others. The primary elements of body language are usually listed as:

- Face – the most obvious source of expression; your face can smile, frown, show anger, show disgust or show disbelief. Smiling is used to indicate friendliness, happiness or non-threatening behaviour.

Smiling indicates friendliness, happiness or non-threatening behaviour

- Eyes – perhaps more difficult to control than your facial expression, your eyes can make or avoid contact with other people, look 'shifty' or express sympathy. Eye contact is an indication of interest or concern.

- Posture – the way you hold your head, the way you stand, folding your arms all express your feelings towards other people. Standing erect and leaning forward means that you are approachable.

- Gestures – we all know and understand basic gestures such as a wave hello (or goodbye), but there is a whole language of gestures – and just to confuse the issue further, they differ between different nationalities and cultures. Speaking without gestures gives the impression of being uncomfortable with what you are saying.

The gestures you use convey a message

- Voice – while what you say is verbal communication, how you say it – tone, volume, pace, pitch, rhythm and **inflection** – is non-verbal. Vary these six elements and you will avoid being boring, dull and monotonous.

- Movement – the way you move gives off messages: moving towards someone may be friendly or threatening; moving away may be submissive or dismissive. Try not to invade others' personal space.

You can use combinations of these elements to deliver or interpret non-verbal messages. Make sure your words match your tone and your body language. Look at the person you are speaking to or, if you are speaking to a group, look at each of them in turn unless you are directing a comment or question to one individual.

ACTIVITY

Research body language and the meaning of facial expressions, positive gestures, etc.

COMMON MISTAKE

If the message has not been understood, saying it again more loudly will not help.

HANDY HINT

While it is often difficult to be sure that someone is telling the truth simply by listening to the words, if you watch their body language closely you will get vital clues.

Inflection

A change in the pitch or tone of the voice

CONFIRM UNDERSTANDING

Be clear about what you are saying, but don't over-complicate it with too much detail. Look for signs of confusion and ask the listeners if they are following what you are saying. Give them the chance to comment or ask questions – remember that verbal communication should always be two-way. If you just wanted to get your point across, without comment or discussion, you could have written to them. It is important to confirm they have understood correctly what you wanted to communicate.

HANDY HINT

Speaking to elderly people as if they were children is extremely disrespectful – remember they have already been your age, while you have no experience of being theirs.

ACTIVITY

Ask a colleague to help with this activity. Ask them to read aloud a newspaper article. Then ask them to read it aloud again, but to make some changes. Each time a change is read out, you must interrupt them and tell them the change that has been made. This requires you to listen carefully and remember important information and details.

ACTIVITY

Ask a colleague to make a note of any negative comments that you make over a period of a week, without making you aware when they are doing it. At the end of the week ask them to share the comments with you. Answer the following questions:

- Are you inclined to use negative statements?
- How frequently do you use them?
- Are they necessary?
- Can you avoid them?
- Is it easy to replace them with positive statements?
- What are you planning to do to eliminate them?

James Rowe is a salesman for Aspect Pharmaceuticals. He is leaving for work when he receives a letter from his sales manager, criticising his sales performance, his approach, his organisation and his planning.

James is frustrated by the tone of the letter, as he feels there are reasons for his performance which his manager is either unaware of, or has failed to take into account. Instead of going to the appointment he had, he waits at home until the office opens, and rings to speak to his manager.

He is told his manager is out of the office and won't be back that day. James goes to his first sales call, is late arriving, and fails to make a sale. He spends the rest of the day thinking about how he is going to handle his boss's criticism, and fails to make a single sale.

The next morning he rings again and makes an appointment to see his manager that afternoon. His manager is surprised to hear how badly the letter has affected James' morale – he had intended to improve James' results by pointing out where he thought he was going wrong. After a full and frank discussion, James goes back to selling with a new determination and finds his sales figures improving gradually as he takes on board the advice he was given.

UNIT 222 (B&A 34): TEST YOUR KNOWLEDGE

Learning outcome 1: Understand the requirements of written and verbal business communication

1 Describe why different methods of communication are used.

2 Explain the purpose of communication.

3 Explain how you use body language in communicating at work.

4 Describe a situation in which verbal communication would be appropriate.

5 Describe a situation in which written communication would be appropriate.

Learning outcome 2: Be able to produce written business communications

1 Explain the importance of checking written communication before sending it.

2 Describe the appropriate tone to use in a letter responding to a customer complaint.

3 Explain why accurate grammar, spelling and punctuation are important.

4 Explain the importance of using plain English.

5 Explain why it is important to meet deadlines.

Learning outcome 3: Be able to communicate verbally in business environments

1 Describe why active listening is important.

2 Explain the importance of summarising verbal communication.

3 Describe the use of tone of voice in effective communication.

4 Explain the importance of presenting information clearly.

5 Explain the importance of confirming that the audience has understood.

UNIT 224 (B&A 36) PRINCIPLES OF PROVIDING ADMINISTRATIVE SERVICES

Over three million people currently work in business and administration roles in the United Kingdom, and millions more work in positions that require some administration skills. The future success of businesses depends on staff having professional administration skills. Recent developments in business have been towards more horizontal management with less administrative support available within teams and an expectation that staff will carry out their own administration. If you are not employed as an administrator but do not have access to administrative support and are expected to carry out your own administration as part of your job, you need to know what you're doing.

In this unit you will cover the following learning outcomes:

1 understand the organisation and administration of meetings
2 understand the organisation of travel and accommodation
3 understand how to manage diary systems
4 understand how to use office equipment
5 understand the use of mail services in a business context
6 understand customer service in a business environment.

THE ADMINISTRATION OF MEETINGS

People working in all businesses get involved in meetings, some informal and others formal. Many meetings will be internal, attended only by people who work for the same organisation, for instance:

- Board meetings – the directors of the company meet regularly to discuss the general running of the organisation.

- Management meetings – the managers meet to discuss the day-to-day running of the organisation. The purpose of the meeting is to decide how the strategy agreed by the board is to be implemented.

- Committee meetings – these range from official public committees such as parish councils to things like social club committees or the health and safety committee within the organisation.

A shareholders' meeting

Some meetings will be external, attended by people who work for the organisation along with other people, for instance:

- Annual general meetings (AGMs) – public limited companies are required to hold a meeting at least once a year where all shareholders are invited to attend. Their purpose is to give shareholders the opportunity to question directors and vote on resolutions. Private limited companies are no longer obliged to hold AGMs, but are able to hold shareholder meetings if they wish to and meetings can be instituted by the directors at any time, or by members representing 10% of voting shares (5% if it is more than 12 months since the members met). Companies may still need to hold a meeting in certain circumstances, since they will not be able to dismiss a director or an auditor before the end of their term of office by written resolution. Since the AGM requirement has been abolished, private company meetings now all require 14-days' notice unless the articles say otherwise. Meetings can be held at short notice as long as there is 90% agreement to do so by members (although the articles can specify a higher percentage up to but not exceeding 95%).

- Extraordinary general meetings – additional meetings can be called if the holders of at least 10% of the shares require them. Their purpose is to discuss issues that have arisen since the last annual general meeting that can't wait until the next, for example dismissal of the chief executive officer or management.

Attendance at some meetings is mandatory, but meetings where people have a choice whether to attend or not can attract a disappointing turnout. In order to **optimise** the number of people attending:

Optimise

Make something such as a method or process as good or as effective as possible

- Set an end time (and stick to it). More people will attend your meetings if they are confident they can fit it in to their busy schedule.

- Make the objective of the meeting clear. If anyone in the meeting does not understand the purpose of a meeting, they won't come back. Set an objective in advance and repeat it, writing the meeting objective at the top of the agenda.

- Explain why this specific meeting is important. People understand that meetings in general are important but they need to be informed what's special about this particular meeting.

- Focus on the **engagement** of existing attendees first, and then seek new ones. Getting people interested and contributing is more important than getting new people to attend. Ensure that everyone who attends feels their presence at the meeting has contributed in some way. In a small meeting this might mean everyone introducing themselves and giving a point of view. In a larger meeting this might include getting everyone to vote on some issue or other.

Engagement

The feeling of being involved in a particular activity

- Keep reminding people. While your meeting might be the most important thing happening from your point of view, for the attendees it is often just one thing in a very busy schedule. Send meeting reminders by email or text message. Don't be afraid to remind people that the event is still on: they rarely mind! An old marketing adage called the 'Rule of Seven' states that people need to hear your message seven times before they take action!

- Keep your structure the same each meeting. Maintaining a structure for each meeting helps people engage with it because they know what to expect each time.

- Understand and explain the benefits of attendance for the attendees. It might be clear to you why you need a meeting but very often the benefit is not clear for the attendees. Spend some time to **articulate** what's in it for them.

Articulate

To express thoughts, ideas, or feelings coherently

ORGANISING MEETINGS

All meetings will need planning and organising, and in most cases notice being sent to attendees, an agenda, a chairperson's agenda, minutes, reports, briefings and correspondence. They will usually need:

- a chairperson, who is responsible for making sure that the meeting is conducted correctly
- a secretary, who is responsible for recording the meeting
- in some cases a treasurer, who is responsible for reporting on financial issues.

There will also be resources such as audio/visual equipment, pens, pencils and paper, or refreshments to organise. As far in advance of the meeting as possible send out invitations to attend. At this time also send a map showing the location of the meeting, car parks and the nearest railway station together with directions to the venue. A week before the meeting send an agenda and copies of any meeting papers to those who indicated they would be attending.

The agenda of a meeting sets out in a logical order what is to be discussed at the meeting. It is important to have an agenda so that the object of the meeting is met or can be reviewed afterwards if it is not met. The first three items in an agenda are usually apologies for absence, the minutes of the last meeting and matters arising. The last two items are always any other business (AOB) and the date of the next meeting. The actual business of the meeting is sandwiched between the first three and the last two items. Copies of any documents needed are sent with the agenda.

In many cases the chairperson will have been involved in the initial planning of the meeting and will be well aware of its purpose, but there will be occasions when they will need to be briefed on the particular stances or viewpoints of the attendees.

Meetings also require recording, so that attendees know what future actions were agreed, who is to carry them out, and to what timescales. The record of the meeting is known as the minutes. The level of recording will depend on the type of meeting. The more formal the meeting, the more detailed the notes that must be kept. The most formal meetings will require minutes to be taken and signed by the chairperson as a true record. There are various ways in which minutes can be taken including:

- Verbatim – everything is recorded word for word.
- Narrative – a summary of the meeting including discussions and conclusions. Formal resolutions are recorded verbatim.

- Resolution – a resolution is a motion which has been voted on and passed. Details of the proposer and seconder are recorded with a verbatim recording of the resolution.

Minutes are a written record of what took place at a meeting, and whichever form is used they must contain everything of importance. They must be written in a **neutral** fashion and always in the past tense. If you are responsible for taking the minutes:

- write too much rather than too little, you can always edit later.
- record what is said and agreed. This may not follow the agenda.
- encourage the chairperson to stick to the agenda.
- listen actively.
- cross-reference anything that refers to previous meetings.
- record the names and times of late arrivals and early departures.
- record the names of the proposer and seconder of formal resolutions.
- record details of any opposing view to the majority.
- record who is responsible for all agreed actions and the target date.
- record the agreed date, time and place of the next meeting.
- include a list of attendees.
- ensure that all attendees, and those whose apologies for absence were noted, receive a copy of the minutes.

When you have typed up the minutes, take them to the chairperson to approve. Make any necessary amendments and distribute the minutes as soon as possible and before the agreed deadline. Keep a copy for the file. Check through the action points to see if any papers were to be forwarded following the meeting and make sure these are enclosed. You may also need to send copies of papers distributed at the meeting to those who submitted their apologies.

Neutral

Belonging to, favouring, or assisting no side in a dispute, contest, or controversy

COMMON MISTAKE

Minutes do not, necessarily, have to record every word spoken at a meeting.

HANDY HINT

If you are uncertain what someone has said, ask them to repeat it.

The chairperson is responsible for making sure that the meeting is conducted correctly

After distributing the minutes, you may receive requests to alter the contents. These must always be referred to the chairperson. If amendments are agreed, produce an amended set of minutes and circulate those. If the chairperson is unwilling to have the minutes amended, you will need to advise the attendee accordingly and they will have to raise the matter at the next meeting. If the meeting is subject to the requirements of the Companies Act, minutes must be retained for at least ten years.

Meetings that are usually less formal may not require all of the above documentation. These may include:

- Departmental meetings – these may include the sales department, the production department, the customer service department, the design department or the accounts department each discussing the issues that affect them directly. At these meetings information will be cascaded from the management.

- Team meetings – their purpose is to discuss issues, consider tactics and inform the staff of issues that will affect them.

- Progress meetings – these are used in projects to inform members of the project team of tasks that have been completed and those that are still outstanding.

- Briefings – these are normally used to pass information on a topic or situation to the attendees, as opposed to a meeting where ideas are exchanged and decisions made.

- One-to-one meetings – this covers all communication between a member of staff and another person, but generally one-to-one meetings refer to meetings between you and your line manager. They are usually intended to be more informal than a review meeting and a chance to talk with your manager away from distractions.

Information that you will still need for these more informal meetings includes:

- The date, time and duration of the meeting – delegates will need to know the start and finish times to arrange transport.

- Venue – delegates will need to know where the meeting is being held.

- Delegates – people like to know who else is attending.

- Catering and accommodation – will attendees require lunch, tea and coffee or overnight accommodation?

- Equipment required – not only a list of requirements, but who is supplying it.

- Special requirements – do any of the attendees have special dietary requirements, accommodation needs or access issues?

ACTIVITY

List the different types of meetings that you have been involved in or are aware of within your organisation.

ACTIVITY

Attend and take minutes at a meeting.

Some meetings are held remotely, as people are working from remote offices and satellite locations. In these situations, a video conference or telephone conference may be the best solution. These will need as much organising as face-to-face meetings:

- Circulate an agenda to all the participants and ask them to submit any problems at least three days prior to the meeting.

- Email any information needed to participate in the meeting at least one week prior to the meeting.

- There can be problems with sound and video delay on remote meetings, so it is critical to maintain professional courtesy.

- Address one issue at a time, and ask all participants whether they are satisfied that the issue has been addressed before the meeting moves on.

- Review the information presented at the meeting before calling the meeting to a close.

- Allow for a question and answer session at the end of the meeting.

ORGANISING TRAVEL AND ACCOMMODATION

Assessment criteria

This section covers assessment criteria 2.1, 2.2 and 2.3

If you are to organise travel and accommodation for your colleagues, you will need to confirm:

- Details of the people travelling – not just the number of people but, if they are travelling abroad, their names as they appear on their passport, their passport number, the country of issue and their date of birth.

- Where they are travelling from and to – remember that they may not be travelling directly from their starting point to their finishing point.

- Their required departure and arrival times.

- The class of travel and accommodation required – air travel may be first class, business class, club class or economy; rail travel may be first class or standard class; accommodation may be anything from a guest house to a five star hotel.

- Their documentation requirements – they may need train tickets, air tickets, hotel reservations, **visas**, car hire information or directions.

- Special requirements – they may have mobility issues, special dietary requirements or need access to facilities such as wireless connectivity or an interpreter.

COMMON MISTAKE

Many people book travel and accommodation through travel agents although it is actually often cheaper to do it online.

Visa

An official endorsement in a passport authorising the bearer to enter or leave, and travel in or through, a specific country or region

Consulate

The office of a government official living in a foreign city to promote the commercial interests of the official's own state and protect its citizens

Useful sources of information when planning business travel include travel agencies, **consulates**, timetables, hotel guides, maps, directories and the internet. Travel tickets can be purchased via the internet and paid for using a company credit card or purchased through a travel agent who will invoice the company. Look for the most cost effective tickets as major discounts can be achieved by booking as far in advance as possible.

TRAVEL

Depending on the destination, you will have a choice between travelling by road, sea, rail and air. Take into account the overall cost, the cost of the traveller's time and the traveller's personal preferences. When considering road travel, take into account:

- the number of travellers and the number of vehicles they would need
- availability of parking at the destination
- overall time required
- the effect of the length of the journey on the driver.

When considering sea travel, take into account:

- convenience of the departure port
- convenience of the destination port
- reliability of the ferry service
- risk of delays due to bad weather
- additional time for check-in.

When considering rail travel, take into account:

- convenience of the departure railway station
- convenience of the destination railway station
- travelling time
- number of changes
- reliability of the train service
- whether luggage and equipment can be easily transported.

When considering air travel, take into account:

- convenience of the departure airport
- convenience of the destination airport
- reliability of the air service
- additional time for check-in and luggage retrieval.

Hotels offer different options which should also be discussed with the traveller. These include:

- Full board – the price of accommodation includes all meals.

- Half board – the price of accommodation includes breakfast and dinner, but not lunch.

- Bed and breakfast – the price of accommodation includes breakfast but not dinner or lunch.

ACCOMMODATION

Some organisations have arrangements with hotel groups that provide reduced room rates. Where these exist they should be used. An alternative to hotel accommodation becoming more common in large organisations is the use of serviced apartments. There are different types:

- The extended stay hotel or 'aparthotel', which generally offers a 24-hour reception, is located in a city centre and attempts to give the guest a 'home away from home' feeling, within a hotel-like environment. Some extended stay properties have been built as an annex to existing four- or five-star hotels, and the guests in the apartments can make use of the hotel's facilities at no extra charge.

- Corporate housing offers residential properties that have been upgraded for shorter-term rentals and packaged together with services such as cleaning, utility charges, local taxes, telephone and television for stays of 30 days or more. They can be in city centres but are more often than not on the outskirts of town, within easy access to main business areas.

Having a kitchen means that the client can opt for eating in instead of eating out and so make an instant saving. Other benefits of a serviced apartment include added space to work, more privacy and more comfort.

A traveller arriving at a hotel

Whether booking hotels or serviced apartments, it is important that reservations are confirmed before the traveller departs, to avoid difficulties on arrival. Remember to take into account any organisational policy on standard of travel and accommodation to be used. In selecting potential suppliers and in comparing quotations, the purchasing department will consider financial restrictions, available budget, organisational policies and equality of opportunity.

Considerations other than price should be taken into account when selecting from the potential suppliers that can meet your organisation's specifications for organising travel and accommodation:

- Suitability. Will the product or service actually meet the requirements of the user?

- Discounts. Often there will be deals to be made if bulk orders are placed with a supplier, either for large quantities of single items or a number of different items.

- Delivery and after-sales service charges. Take care that there are no hidden charges that make the purchase price appear lower.

- Reliability and reputation. The old maxim 'you get what you pay for' is still often true. A reputable brand is often worth paying extra for.

PLANNING THE ITINERARY

Plan the journey and prepare the **itinerary** taking into account:

- Time and climatic differences between their departure point and their destination. Remember that departure and arrival times will be shown in terms of local time.

- Time and budget available. The cheapest form of transport is not necessarily the most cost effective.

The precise steps to take in planning an itinerary will depend on the type of trip planned, but as an example, for a business trip involving meetings with clients, the steps would be:

- Schedule the itinerary at least a month in advance so that you can get reasonable rate quotes and the exact arrangements you need.

- Call the business contacts to schedule any meetings before you start setting travel plans. (This step may already have been taken by the traveller themselves, but you will need this information.)

- Book the transport required for the trip. Schedule arrival one to two days before the first business meeting if possible, to allow time for the traveller to rest and go over their plans for the trip.

- Arrange a rental car or book a car to pick the traveller up at the airport if needed.

- Book a hotel and contact the hotel ahead of time to book meeting rooms if needed. Check the hotel has an internet connection, wake-

Itinerary

A plan for a journey listing different places in the order in which they are to be visited

up service and any other details needed for a successful and pleasant business trip.

- Ask the travellers if they would consider sharing a hotel room to save money.

- Create a written itinerary based on the plans made. List all of your important appointments, including the dates, times and locations in order of their occurrence.

- Use an online map program, such as www.mapquest.com, which allows you to set up a series of stops within one search, and print directions to guide the travellers through the trip.

- Check the weather forecast for the dates of your trip ahead of time in that location so they can pack accordingly.

- Confirm all meetings and trip arrangements a few days before the trip. Print the written business itinerary and directions and give them to the traveller to pack in their case along with their laptop.

A table or spreadsheet like the example below may help to make sure that the itinerary you have prepared gives the traveller all the information they need in a convenient format.

Date	Depart from	Depart time	Destination	Arrival time	Destination address	Tel. number	Travel time	Comments

Some forms of travel are available at different classes, subject to different pricing structures. Sea travel in the past was available with different facilities ranging from first class, with all the luxury of five star hotel accommodation, to steerage, which was extremely basic. While this range can still be found on cruise ships, most business travel will take place on ferries, where the choice will usually range from having a private cabin to a reserved seat.

Air travel offers a wide range of classes of travel, which are given different names by different airlines. As an example, British Airways offer:

ACTIVITY

Select a destination abroad that interests you and plan a journey and itinerary for a visit.

- Economy class, which includes complimentary newspapers on most flights, hot breakfast, tea and coffee on early morning flights, free snacks and hot and cold drinks on all flights.
- Premium economy, which offers more privacy, space and comfort in a smaller, secluded cabin.
- Business class, offering lounge access, delicious meals and drinks, extra space to work or relax and flat beds on long haul flights.
- First class, with dedicated service, exceptional comfort, luxurious lounges and on-board fine dining.

Rail travel in the UK usually offers two classes:

- Standard class, which offers a seat, and reservations on some services.
- First class, which offers larger, more comfortable seats with extra legroom, spacious tables from which to work, complimentary newspapers and complimentary refreshments served at your seat on selected services.

You will need to provide travellers going abroad with information on requirements for:

- Passports. Everybody travelling abroad must hold a valid passport. In many cases the passport must be valid for six months beyond the expected return date, so it is important to check this.
- Visas. Many countries also require visitors to have a visa permitting entry for a specific purpose, such as holidays, study, business, etc. Failure to supply the correct visa can result in the visitor being refused entry to the country.
- Health certificates. Some countries require visitors to have certificates showing that they have been vaccinated against certain diseases. As this requirement changes regularly, it is important to check the government website www.gov.uk for the latest information.
- Travel insurance. Medical travel insurance provides medical coverage during the trip. Travellers should check their own health insurance policy to see what coverage they have already. Many people find that their own policies restrict coverage to a limited geographic area, and cover emergencies only outside of that area. Plans differ in their requirements for coverage. Many medical insurance plans have a **pre-existing** condition period. In this case, you will not be covered for an illness or injury for which you are seeking treatment if you were advised to see a doctor for the condition, had symptoms or were taking medication for the condition within a defined length of time. Medical Evacuation Travel Insurance Plans evacuate ill or injured people to a nearby medical facility and back to their home. Requirements are generally that the injury or illness is sudden and unexpected.

Air travel with probably be used for overseas trips

Pre-existing

Something that already existed

- Driving licences. Travellers who intend to drive during their journey must have a valid driving licence. Check that a UK driving licence is valid in the country of destination.

- Car insurance. Valid insurance will be needed if driving abroad. This can be purchased as part of a car hire package, but this isn't always the most economical, so check with your organisation's insurance company, if you have one, or the individual's insurer may be able to help. There are other legal requirements for driving abroad which differ from country to country – even within Europe, as shown below, so again, check these before the journey.

> **ACTIVITY**
>
> For the journey you planned in the previous activity, check the need for travel documentation and the best way to cover day-to-day expenses.

	Austria	Belgium	France	Germany	Italy	Holland	Switzerland	Spain
GB sticker	C	C	C	C	C	C	C	C
Headlight beam converter	C	C	C	C	C	C	C	C
Warning triangle	C	C	R	R	C	R	C	C
High visibility jacket	C	C				C		C
First aid box	C	R		R				
On the spot fines	YES	YES	YES	YES	YES	YES	YES	YES

C = COMPULSORY R = RECOMMENDED

- Credit cards and foreign currency. The traveller abroad will have day-to-day expenses, which they will need to meet either by charging a credit card or by using the currency of the country they are in. Many organisations have credit cards which they authorise certain of their staff to use, but these, and the individual's credit cards, will often have **punitive** charges or interest rates for transactions carried out abroad, so it is important to check on these before the visit takes place. Foreign currency can be bought from a wide range of financial institutions, travel agents and **bureaux de change**, but the rates offered will vary, often considerably, and even from minute to minute, so again it is important to take care to get the best possible rate. When the traveller returns, they may have some foreign currency left over. A decision will have to be made whether to change this back into **sterling,** which will be at a less favourable rate than when it was bought, or to keep it in a safe place for the next person visiting a country where it can be used.

> **Punitive**
>
> Causing great difficulty or hardship
>
> **Bureau de change**
>
> An office, often found in a bank, which allows consumers to exchange one currency for another. The bureau de change charges a commission for the currency exchange service.
>
> **Sterling**
>
> The currency in pounds and pence used in the United Kingdom

Having confirmed the itinerary with the traveller you will then be able to book accommodation, travel tickets and car hire as required.

On completion of the journey, you will need to keep records of the travel and accommodation details including booking documents and receipts in order to:

- Account for costs incurred and paid for directly by the organisation for auditing purposes.

- Meet expense claims from the traveller for costs incurred and paid for by them.

- Use the information for future reference if a similar journey needs to be planned.

MANAGING DIARY SYSTEMS

The main purpose of keeping a diary is to record events that are planned to happen in the future. It would be impossible, for most people, to remember everything they have agreed to do on or by a given date, every meeting they have agreed to attend and every appointment they have made. Using a diary effectively avoids those embarrassing moments when you receive a phone call from your boss asking why you are not at the meeting at Head Office which has been scheduled for three months, or the cancellation of an order because you forgot to send the details which had been requested just before you went home and you promised to forward on the following day.

TYPES OF DIARY SYSTEM

There are many different types of diary system available, but these can be basically divided into paper or electronic diary systems. Paper diaries may be bound books, with one day a page, two pages per day or a whole week showing over two days, or loose-leaf time management systems which can be used for many years rather than being replaced at the end of each year, as bound diaries usually are.

Electronic diaries have many of the same features as paper diaries, but have the advantage of being easier to update and easier to allow access to colleagues who may need to share the information. If a number of people need the information contained in a diary system **simultaneously**, an electronic system is probably more efficient. It allows anybody who is authorised to make and amend entries, and the entries will be available to all authorised users immediately.

Diary systems can be either paper-based or electronic

Until the development of portable electronic equipment, one of the disadvantages of electronic diary systems was that you couldn't easily take them with you. This led to people using a **hybrid** system, with an electronic diary on their computer giving access to colleagues and a paper diary which they carried with them to record any information received while away from their desk. The risk with this method is that unless information is updated regularly from one system to the other, you can find yourself double-booking an appointment or over-promising the tasks that you are able to complete by a required deadline.

Electronic diary systems have the advantage of increased security. While paper diaries have to be locked up to keep the information confidential, electronic diaries can be protected by passwords or by **encryption**. In addition, information can be downloaded onto removable media such as a disk and the disk placed in a secure area. They can also be programmed to give an audible or visual warning when an event is imminent. For instance at 9am each morning, the diary appointments for the following day can come up on screen to remind you and those involved.

Whether using a paper diary or an electronic system, it is important that all the relevant information is obtained if you are asked to make an entry into the diary or amend an existing one. The date and time of an appointment or meeting is not enough on its own; the location and duration are equally important.

HANDY HINT

If keeping a paper diary, make entries in pencil; it is much easier to make changes.

Hybrid

A system made up of a mixture of paper and electronic systems

COMMON MISTAKE

Keeping two diaries and failing to synchronise them can lead to double-booking or over-promising tasks you are able to complete in a given time.

Encryption

The conversion of computer data and messages into something incomprehensible using a key, so that only a holder of the matching key can reconvert them

ACTIVITY

Give an example of when you have had to make a change to your diary which has caused a problem and how you overcame the problem.

PRIORITISING AND MANAGING DIARY TASKS

When making bookings of people or facilities in your diary system, you must be able to prioritise requests, understanding the difference between urgent and important issues.

Urgent tasks are, generally, those that have an immediate (or even passed) deadline. They may not have a significant impact on your overall workload but they have become urgent because you knew they needed doing but kept putting them off.

Important tasks, on the other hand, may not have a deadline or, if they do, it may be some time ahead. What they will have is a major impact on your work, especially if you don't complete them. Some tasks, of course, are both urgent and important. If, for instance, you have to get a report in the post by the end of the day or lose a major customer's business, it is both urgent and important that you complete it before the post goes.

Urgency of tasks is based on deadlines; importance is based on the impact which completing or not completing them will have.

Covey's Time Management Matrix divides tasks into urgent or non-urgent on one axis and important or non-important on the other. This divides all tasks into four quadrants:

- Quadrant 1 – urgent and important
- Quadrant 2 – not urgent but important
- Quadrant 3 – urgent but not important
- Quadrant 4 – not urgent and not important

Tasks in quadrant 1 should, obviously, be top priority and be completed at all costs. Tasks in quadrant 2 tend to be delayed, because they are not urgent, while quadrant 3 tasks are given priority because they are urgent. When prioritising your own tasks, try to do quadrant 3 tasks before those in quadrant 2, but allocate less time to them. Tasks in quadrant 4 should only be given time if all other tasks have been dealt with.

There are some simple habits which, if developed, and most importantly followed, will make your management of a diary system much more effective. You need to develop a method of managing your time and your diary which works for you, but the crucial elements of your method must be that it enables you to record all the necessary information, prioritise requests and balance the needs of everybody involved.

The first habit to develop is making sure the diary for the following day is written up before you go home. When you arrive for work each day you should have everything ready and set up to allow not only you, but anyone whose appointments you are responsible for, to have an effective day, free from the stress of constantly trying to catch up.

HANDY HINTS

- Do the task you least look forward to first; it will be out of the way and off your mind.
- Give important tasks more time than tasks that are urgent, but not so important.

HANDY HINT

Remember that stress is caused by NOT doing things much more than by things you have done.

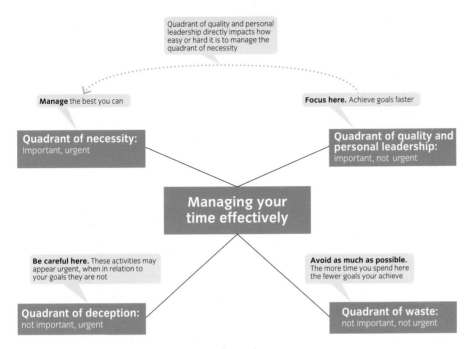

Quadrant of quality and personal leadership directly impacts how easy or hard it is to manage the quadrant of necessity

Manage the best you can

Focus here. Achieve goals faster

Quadrant of necessity:
Important, urgent

Quadrant of quality and personal leadership:
important, not urgent

Managing your time effectively

Be careful here. These activities may appear urgent, when in relation to your goals they are not

Avoid as much as possible. The more time you spend here the fewer goals your achieve

Quadrant of deception:
not important, urgent

Quadrant of waste:
not important, not urgent

Source: Stephen R. Covey (1999), *First Things First*, Simon & Schuster Ltd.

When you make an entry in your diary, put in all the information, even if the event is taking place the next day. Don't fall into the trap of thinking you will remember – treat every entry as if it is for an event happening a year from now. Enter the time and place of the meeting or appointment, details of any contact names and numbers, and don't forget to put in the diary for earlier dates enough time for any preparation that is needed. Devise a colour code for different types of event so that you can see at a glance when important meetings are happening.

Use your diary as a to-do list, and use simple tricks to make the most effective use of your time. Put activities into an order which allows you to move naturally from one activity to the next. If you have a time allocated to start a task, get in the habit of starting five minutes early – the extra few minutes will be a great stress-reliever. Block activities such as telephone calls together, and avoid making calls at lunch times, when the person you are calling will probably not be available.

Leave gaps in your diary for unexpected requests or over-running meetings or activities. If these don't happen, the thinking time the gaps will provide will be invaluable. Do this for anyone you are scheduling appointments for, too. They will welcome the chance to recover from and reflect on one meeting before dashing to the next. Don't forget to leave time for getting from one meeting to the next, especially if this involves travelling from one site to another. If you (or your boss) are always the ones travelling to a regular meeting, see if you can negotiate for the meetings to alternate between sites, so that sometimes others are travelling to you.

COMMON MISTAKE

Allowing yourself to be distracted by a new request – unless it is really urgent, add it to your to-do list and deal with it in its turn.

Don't forget to leave time for getting from one meeting to the next

Commercially sensitive

Information that an organisation would not like to be in the public domain as it may give an advantage to a competitor

If you think there may be a problem with you (or your boss) getting to a meeting on time, find out when the agenda item that requires your input is scheduled, and advise in advance that you may be late for the start of the meeting but will arrive for your item.

In some organisations, meetings are scheduled which, in reality, are unnecessary or unproductive. If you are in a position to make decisions on the need for meetings, ask yourself if a face-to-face meeting is the best way for all involved to spend their time; could a video conference or telephone conference achieve the same results?

If a regular meeting cannot be replaced entirely, see if it can be reduced in length or frequency. If you, or your boss, leave a meeting feeling that you have not contributed to it, or learned anything from it, consider declining the invitation in future.

It probably goes without saying that it is absolutely vital that your diary system is kept up to date at all times and that the information recorded is correct. This is even more crucial if more than one person has access to it, and could schedule something entirely unaware that it clashes with another event because you haven't got around to entering the details. Similarly, it is important to communicate any changes to everybody affected as soon as you are made aware of the need to make alterations to your schedule. Add the date and time to the notification of any changes so that you can trace the sequence of events should there be any dispute at a later date.

Updating your diary and making sure everybody involved is made aware of any changes resulting from new requests, will avoid the problems which can arise.

DIARY SECURITY AND CONFIDENTIALITY

The final habit to cultivate is appreciating the need for security and confidentiality when using your diary system. Information contained may be personal, in which case it is covered by the Data Protection Act, or it may be **commercially sensitive**, giving an advantage to a competitor if it falls into the wrong hands.

The principles of the Data Protection Act state that information shall be processed fairly and lawfully and, in particular, shall not be processed unless:

- obtained only for one or more specified and lawful purposes
- adequate, relevant and not excessive
- accurate and kept up to date
- not kept for longer than is necessary for that purpose or those purposes
- processed in accordance with the rights of data subjects under the act

- appropriate measures are taken against unauthorised or unlawful processing of personal data and against accidental loss or destruction of, or damage to, personal data.

Information shall also not be transferred to a country outside the European Economic Area unless that country ensures an adequate level of protection.

USING OFFICE EQUIPMENT

Office equipment ranges from paper clips to multi-functional photocopiers. Every office, in every organisation, will have a different selection of equipment in use. It would be practically impossible to list every piece of equipment that you might come across in your career, especially as technology is advancing at a rapid pace and new equipment is regularly being introduced.

We have restricted the information in this chapter to the most common equipment:

- telephones
- computer hardware including monitors, keyboards and mice
- printers
- photocopiers
- binding machines
- fax machines
- scanners
- shredders
- franking machines
- laminators.

TELEPHONES

The basic purpose of a telephone is to make and receive calls, but most office telephone systems may have many more features including:

- Automatic transfer, which allows you to programme the phone to forward incoming calls to another number if your line is engaged, is not answered after a pre-set number of rings or you are away from your desk.
- Call holding, which allows you to put the caller on hold while you answer another phone or make an outgoing call. Some phones will allow you to pick up the original call on another phone.
- Call pickup, which allows you to pick up on your phone a call coming in on another phone.

- Call transfer, which allows you to transfer a call to another phone.
- Call waiting, which lets you know that there is another incoming call when you are using the phone.
- Caller ID, which displays the name or telephone number of the person calling.
- Conference calling, which allows three or more people to hold a telephone conversation.
- Last number redial, which allows you to redial the last number you dialled by pushing one button.
- Menu, which gives the caller a number of options allowing their call to be routed to the correct person.
- Message waiting indicator, which tells you there is a message in your mailbox.
- Ring again, which tells you when a number that you have found engaged has become free.
- Speed dialling, which allows you to dial a frequently called number by programming the number to dial by pushing one button.
- Voicemail, which allows callers to record a message that can be retrieved later.

Many organisations now provide employees with mobile phones so that they can stay in touch while on the move or if they frequently work from home.

COMPUTER HARDWARE

Computers are used to produce documents, produce spreadsheets, send and receive emails and connect to the internet, as well as operating software which makes them capable of anything from playing games to landing a man on the moon. The basic hardware involved consists of a processor, which processes data; a monitor, which allows you to see data on the screen; a keyboard, which enables you to input data and a mouse which enables you to navigate around the screen. In a laptop computer or tablet all of these are contained in one piece of equipment. Computers are often linked together with other computers to form networks, which can share files.

PRINTERS

The basic purpose of a printer is to produce hard copies of the data from the computer. There are different types of printer which have different features:

- Inkjet printers can produce a wide range of documents including complex colour documents such as photographs.
- Laser printers can print off text documents at high speed but cannot print photographs.

HANDY HINT

Static electricity can destroy computer chips, so touch metal with your finger occasionally when cleaning the computer to dispel static build-up.

A multi-functional printer

The features of printers will vary, including their ability to print in black and white or colour, produce draft and high quality copies, the speed at which copies are produced and the ability to switch automatically to energy-saving mode. Many printers will incorporate some of the features of scanners, photocopiers and fax machines. Printers can be networked so that they will accept instructions from a number of separate computers.

PHOTOCOPIERS

Modern photocopiers have features such as:

- Automatic document feeders which allow you to copy multi-page documents.

- Reverse automatic document feeders which allow you to copy both sides of multi-page documents.

- Duplex copying which allows you to print on both sides of the copy paper.

- Sorting capability which allows you to sort the copies of multi-page documents.

- Finishing capability which allows you to staple, hole punch, bind or fold copies.

- Faxing capability which allows you to send and receive multi-page faxes.

- Automatic resizing which allows you to enlarge or reduce the size of copies.

- Scan and network print which allows you to use the photocopier as a network printer for a number of computers.

- Document management which allows you to scan documents to computer files or directly to an email address.

- Image and document editing which allows you to edit documents while copying them or add automatic page numbering, a date stamp or annotations such as 'confidential' or 'duplicate'. Some photocopies can rotate scanned images to match the paper.

- Automatic shut-off which turns off the copier if it has not been used for a set period of time, saving energy and decreasing wear.

- Security or PIN codes which allow you to prevent unauthorised use and to analyse use by different users.

A binding machine

A fax machine

Digitise

Convert an image, graph, or other data into digital form for processing on a computer

BINDING MACHINES

The basic purpose of a binding machine is to convert loose leaf documents into bound books. There are various types of binding machine:

Channel binding machines, which produce professionally-bound documents in 15 seconds or less by compressing the documents inside a folder. Documents can be bound and unbound up to three times, so binding errors or updates can easily be corrected.

Wire binding machines, which punch holes through the documents and insert wire binders through the holes.

Plastic comb binding machines, which work in the same way as wire binding machines but insert plastic combs through the holes, enabling thicker books to be produced.

FAX MACHINES

The basic purpose of a fax machine is to transmit copies of documents and photographs from one location to another. The original is fed into the sender's fax machine, the telephone number of the receiver's fax machine is dialled and a copy of the document is printed by the receiver's fax machine. Most fax machines incorporate a telephone handset, while other equipment such as printers, scanners, photocopiers and computers often incorporate fax facilities.

Fax machines can send copies to multiple locations simultaneously. Many will include speed dialling, group dialling which allows the machine to contact a number of receiving machines simultaneously and distinctive caller tones so that you can recognise whether a voice call or a fax is incoming.

SCANNERS

The basic purpose of a scanner is to convert hard-copy text into computer files which can be edited and stored. Many scanners can scan slides and photographic negatives as well as paper. Most scanners include software which will enable you to edit images and convert words into text documents that can be edited, making it possible to **digitise** typewritten documents.

There are several different types of scanners. There are flatbed scanners, where you lift the top to place the document on the glass; paper-fed scanners where you can put several documents in at once and feed them through and hand-held scanners for scanning a page at a time. Scanners are basically used to copy graphics, print, articles or images from the scanner to a computer.

SHREDDERS

The basic purpose of a shredder is to destroy documents for security purposes. There are different types of shredder which provide different levels of security. Strip- and ribbon-cut shredders turn documents into long strips of paper; these can potentially be sorted out and stuck back together, so the security level is relatively low. Cross-cut shredders turn documents into small squares, while diamond cut shredders turn documents into diamond shaped pieces, which greatly improves their security level.

Additional features available on some shredders include:

A shredder

- Auto-start, which starts the shredder automatically when paper is fed into the slot.

- Auto-stop, which stops the shredder automatically if paper jams in the slot.

- Motor reverse, which allows you to reverse the paper out of the shredder if it jams.

- Thermal safety switches, which automatically cut off the shredder if it overheats.

- CD slot, which allows you to shred CDs and DVDs.

- Credit card slot, which allows you to shred credit cards. These should not be used with strip- and ribbon-cut shredders as the personal information may still be readable.

- Paper clip and staple slot, which shreds paper clips and staples without damaging the cutters.

COMMON MISTAKE

Trying to shred too many sheets of paper at once

FRANKING MACHINES

The basic purpose of a franking machine is to pay for postage without the need for postage stamps. Following the increase in postage prices in April 2012, the discounts offered by Royal Mail to users of franking machines were increased to up to 38% compared with using stamps.

The features of new electronic franking machines include the option to top up the machine by phone or online, integrated scales ensuring the correct postage is calculated, automatic date change so the correct date is always shown on your post and the option to add a business logo or advertising message to letters and packages.

COMMON MISTAKE

Putting envelopes through a franking machine and missing the envelope with the imprint

HANDY HINT

Check the franking machine value has been returned to zero or is set to the correct amount.

LAMINATORS

These **encapsulate** documents such as business cards, ID cards, telephone lists and photos inside plastic pouches to protect them from damage. The features of laminators include carrier-free operation, a reverse button and auto power-save to shut them off when not in use.

Encapsulate

To enclose something completely

You will see from the descriptions of the equipment that, in many cases, their functions overlap. Printers can photocopy, fax machines incorporate telephones, and photocopiers can scan documents. When choosing the equipment to use for a particular task you need to consider:

- Could the equipment be required for other tasks? For instance if you produce 1,000 copies of a document on a printer rather than a photocopier you can't use the printer for anything else meanwhile.
- Could somebody else need to use the equipment? For instance, if you use a photocopier to scan documents are you preventing somebody else using the photocopier?
- Are you using the most economical piece of equipment? For instance calls on mobile phones are often more expensive than calls on landlines.
- The quality of the finished product. For instance, for internal use a document stapled together may be sufficient while you may need to use a binder to produce the same document for a customer.

Although many pieces of equipment are multi-functional, it is important not to use equipment for purposes for which it is not designed. Using a knife to remove staples or scissors to remove screws is not only dangerous, it is also likely to damage the equipment and **invalidate** the guarantee.

Invalidate

To deprive something of its legal force or value, for example by failing to comply with some terms and conditions.

USING EQUIPMENT

Every new piece of equipment will come with manufacturer's instructions. All the equipment in the office should have an instruction manual, although these may be difficult to find. It is a good idea to read through the manual and familiarise yourself with its features and operating systems before using any equipment that you have never used before.

The most important reason to follow manufacturers' instructions when using equipment is to ensure the safety of yourself and your colleagues. Equipment such as trimmers and guillotines have blades which could seriously injure people if the equipment is misused; equipment such as laminators use heat in their operation which could cause burns. Following the guidelines also avoids damaging the equipment. If you feed paper with paper clips and staples attached into a shredder that doesn't have a paper clip and staple slot, you will damage the cutters. If you damage the equipment through failing to follow the manufacturer's instruction, you will invalidate the guarantee and your organisation will have to pay for the repairs.

In addition to the manufacturer's instructions there will be organisational instructions about using some equipment. For instance, you will probably not be allowed to make personal telephone calls on the office phone, put personal mail through the franking machine or use the printer to print things you have downloaded about your hobby. This is because this misuse costs the organisation money. Other organisational instructions will also be in place to protect the resources. If you fail to follow these instructions you may not be covered by insurance in case of accident or damage to the equipment and you may face disciplinary action as a result.

Each piece of equipment will have health and safety procedures to follow if the equipment is to be used safely. These procedures can also be found in the manufacturer's instructions. Some procedures will apply to all equipment. For instance, whenever you use any electrical equipment you need to be aware of any exposed wires, damage to the equipment which might make it possible for you to come into contact with live parts, or signs of overheating. The most obvious sign of overheating is smoke coming from the equipment, but you should also be aware of any smell of hot metal, or paper coming from a photocopier feeling unusually hot.

Some equipment will have particular dangers. For instance, you should never use a photocopier with the lid open because the bright light used can irritate your eyes. Simple equipment such as scissors, staplers and even pens and pencils can cause injury. When using trimmers and guillotines make sure the guard is in place. Always use staple removers and keep sharp objects like scissors in a drawer or with the point downwards. When using computer screens make sure the screen is at a distance from your eye that allows you to focus easily. The top of the screen should be below eye level and the bottom of the screen should be able to be read without moving your head too much.

One of the more common health and safety problems found in an office environment is **repetitive strain injury (RSI).** The risk of RSI can be reduced by the use of workstations that allow you to feel more comfortable when using a keyboard or mouse. There is equipment available to reduce risks such as **ergonomically** designed keyboards and mice, wrist rests to keep your hands at the correct angle and foot rests to keep your posture correct. You should have regular breaks from these tasks, not necessarily breaks from work but periods when you do something different.

A major risk to the health of people working in an office comes from the fact that the equipment they use is not kept clean and hygienic. Where equipment is used by several different people, it can be a major source of infection. Whenever you speak on a telephone, you spray droplets onto the equipment. Using a keyboard or a mouse with unwashed hands spreads germs from your hands onto the equipment and then onto the hands of anybody else who uses it.

Repetitive strain injury (RSI)

An injury of the musculoskeletal and nervous systems that may be caused by repetitive tasks, forceful exertions, vibrations, pressing against hard surfaces and sustained or awkward positions

Ergonomic

Designed for maximum comfort, efficiency, safety and ease of use, especially in the workplace

Cross-contamination

The passing of bacteria or other harmful substances indirectly from one person to another

Computers will need to be cleaned on a regular basis

Optical

An instrument or device that is sensitive to light

Clean, hygienic office equipment significantly reduces **cross-contamination** which can lead to headaches, nausea and eyestrain. The equipment will also last longer as a build-up of dust and dirt is largely responsible for overheating, data corruption and computer crashes. Exterior surfaces of equipment and desktops can be cleaned using a lint-free cloth sprayed with anti-static cleaner. Glass monitors and screens should be wiped down with a lint-free cloth dampened with distilled water, as this does not contain particles that can scratch the glass.

Cleaning electronic equipment requires a certain amount of care as the use of any liquid or spray on a keyboard, for instance, would be extremely dangerous. Commercial screen cleaners are designed to remove dirt without scratching or streaking the surface. It is important to use the right cleaner for the right surface as some are specifically designed for particular uses such as laptop screens.

Computers, as they are probably the most-used pieces of equipment in the office, will need cleaning on a more frequent basis. The computer base unit will collect dust. A build-up of dust on the fan at the back of the case is an indication that the base unit needs cleaning. Unplug the system and carefully remove the case. Be aware, some organisations will not allow you to remove the case as they will have technicians who will be responsible for this. Clean the dust out with a mini-vacuum cleaner or a normal vacuum cleaner with a small nozzle attachment.

Keyboards will become sticky and full of dust. Turn the keyboard upside down and use a compressed air duster between and under the keys to push the dust out. If you don't have a compressed air duster, use a mini-vacuum cleaner to pull the dust out. Wipe the keys with a damp clean cloth or a cotton swab.

If a non-**optical** mouse sticks it probably needs cleaning. Turn the computer off and unplug the mouse. Open the housing that covers the tracking ball, and remove the tracking ball and clean it with an electrical cleaner or soap and water, but make sure any cleaner you use has no lubricant in it. Remove dust from the inside of the housing with a damp cotton swab or tweezers. Dirty mouse mats will affect the performance of both optical and non-optical mice. Keep them clean with a soft damp cloth.

By following manufacturers' instructions, organisational instructions and keeping equipment clean and hygienic you will greatly reduce the risks of health and safety problems within the office. Remember to take care with any cleaners used. Some will contain toxic substances and will need to be stored carefully. In some organisations, cleaning of equipment can only be carried out by technicians or staff authorised to carry out these tasks. This should not, however, prevent you from keeping your work area clean and tidy and carrying out basic hygiene procedures.

USING RESOURCES EFFICIENTLY

When using equipment, you will be making use of a variety of resources, some more obvious than others. Resources involved include not only the **consumables** such as paper and ink but also the electricity used and the time of everybody involved. The resource which is often overlooked is time. If you have to repeat a task because you have made an error in using the equipment, the time taken in duplicating the effort is time you will not be able to use in carrying out some other task. Remember, time is finite and once used cannot be recovered.

Consumables

Items that are intended to be discarded after use

Waste will increase the cost of operating the organisation. This will reduce **profit** for commercial organisations and leave less money available for charitable or public organisations to spend on other items such as salaries, pensions, staff welfare or improving working conditions. Wasting resources makes it more difficult to justify buying new equipment, as the projected costs based on the running costs of the existing equipment will be higher.

Profit

The difference between sales and expenses

Throwing away things wastes resources. It wastes the raw materials and energy used in making the items and it wastes money. Reducing waste means less environmental impact, fewer resources and less energy used, and it saves money:

- Use both sides of the paper. Whenever possible use double-sided photocopying – and make sure that all staff regularly using photocopiers know how to do this. Better still, set the photocopier to default to double-sided printing.

- Have a policy that photocopiers and printers always reset to single copy printing after someone has used them, and check anyway before using them.

- Put scrap pieces of paper together to make a notepad, use them for notes to colleagues too.

- Re-use envelopes for internal circulation and, if possible, externally with a re-use sticker.

- Regularly check computerised mailing lists and remove duplicates and out-of-date addresses.

- Review the need for computer print-outs from time to time. It is all too easy to go on printing out a regular 50-page report for the same ten people who have received it for the last two years – do they all still need it? Do any of them need it?

- Keep a pile of good quality A4 scrap paper next to the printer for rough or trial copies. Out-of-date headed paper is ideal for this purpose.

- Use the smallest piece of paper appropriate to the task. For example, photocopy A3 documents to A4 size, use A5 size cover sheets for faxes, or just send one A4 page if the message is short.

HANDY HINTS

Learning the features of equipment will help you use it more efficiently.

- Re-use wallet folders, hanging file dividers and other storage items.

- Review procedures that require regular circulation of forms and memos, and consider how many can be eliminated.

- Large numbers of fasteners are used in offices, such as paper clips, drawing pins and staples. Some of these can be re-used, but staples cannot. Even though they do not constitute a major part of the waste from offices, it is noteworthy that, in aggregate, they amount to a significant loss of resources. It has been calculated that if everyone in UK offices saved one staple a day that would be 72 tonnes of metal saved a year.

- Before producing multiple copies on a photocopier or printer, make one copy on the lowest quality available so that you can check for errors and layout. This will avoid the need to throw away large quantities of paper.

- Check long runs of printing regularly for ink running out. If one colour runs out, the whole run will need to be re-printed from the point where it ran out, wasting paper, ink and time.

- Print draft quality whenever acceptable. This will save on the use of ink.

- Check before you shred documents that they really are not needed. This will avoid the need to recreate the document at a cost of paper, ink and time.

- Use franking machines carefully. Even the most sophisticated franking machine cannot prevent you franking 2nd class mail at 1st class prices if you forget to change the settings. You need to weigh packages accurately and check the postage correctly. When you finish using the franking machine, set it back to zero.

- When using paper drills, hole punches, paper trimmers or guillotines check that the paper is correctly positioned before operating on a quantity of paper. If the paper is incorrectly positioned or moves during operation, it may have to be thrown away.

- When laminating, position the original document carefully, especially if it's not easily reproduced. It is very difficult to remove a document from the plastic film, so an irreplaceable document may be destroyed, as well as the cost of the laminate and the heat being wasted.

- Turn off electrical equipment when it is not in use to save energy. Some equipment has a standby mode which uses less power than operational mode.

- Keep telephone conversations as short as possible without being abrupt with customers or clients. Calls cost money and are charged by the minute. Check the number you are calling before you make the call, as wrong numbers also get charged.

- If you have both mobile and landline telephones, check which is cheaper to use for different types of calls.

It is very easy to think that it doesn't matter very much if you waste resources when you are using equipment at work. After all, throwing away a sheet of paper because you have printed a document on it and then found a mistake costs practically nothing doesn't it? However, if everybody in the organisation throws away a sheet of paper every day, the total cost over a year will be significant.

DEALING WITH PROBLEMS

The most common problem with office equipment will be connected to the fact that it needs electrical power in order to work. So, when it stops working, the first thing to check should always be that it has power. Is it plugged in? Is it switched on? Taking these simple steps will avoid the embarrassment of calling in a repair man only for him to plug the machine in, switch it on and send you a bill. When you have checked that the equipment is receiving power, try switching it off and switching it on again.

If the electricity supply is not the problem, you will need to investigate further.

Computers will stop performing the tasks required. If they will not connect to the internet or the printer or scanner, there may be a problem with the wireless router. Sometimes they will give you an error message which will help you to deal with the problem. If you are technically proficient enough, you may be able to deal with the error by following links or by using a search engine to find a solution. Otherwise, you can contact an IT helpline, which may be internal or external. This will put you in touch with an expert who will talk you through the solution.

Router

A piece of equipment or software that finds the best way of sending information between any two networks

USB

Universal serial bus: a way of connecting a printer, keyboard, or other piece of equipment to a computer using a special cable and without having to turn the computer off and on again

Printers have two different types of problem: electronic and mechanical. Electronic problems will arise when the printer is unable to connect successfully with the computer. If the printer is wireless you will need to check the **router** is working correctly. If the printer is connected to the computer by a **USB** cable you will need to check the connections at both ends. Printers will have mechanical problems similar to those experienced by photocopiers.

Photocopiers are probably the pieces of office equipment most prone to having mechanical problems. These will usually be paper jams which can be solved by carefully removing the trapped paper so that small pieces do not remain trapped and cause further jams. The other common problem is that the ink runs out before the run is completed. This can be prevented by regularly checking that ink cartridges are not nearing the end of their working life.

Shredders can suffer from paper jams or overheating. Paper jams are caused by attempting to shred too many sheets of paper at once or by staples catching in the cutters. If the shredder has a reverse mode, reverse the paper out of the shredder carefully and re-insert fewer sheets. If a staple has become jammed between the cutters, it will not reverse out and you will need to remove the staple. In this case, switch off the shredder before poking anything between the cutters. Overheating is caused by the motor overworking trying to cope with too heavy a load. Switch the shredder off and allow it to cool down and use it more responsibly. Overheating may cause a blown fuse, stopping the shredder working.

It is important not to attempt to deal with equipment problems that are beyond your experience. A botched repair attempt can create much greater problems which may require expensive repairs and may invalidate the manufacturer's guarantee. The manufacturer's instruction manual will often give a troubleshooting guide. Your organisation's procedures must be followed. It is particularly important that you do not attempt to make any repairs to franking machines, as government regulations prohibit franking machine owners from dealing with any technical problem without the guidance of an accredited Royal Mail engineer.

ACTIVITY

- List the equipment in use in your workplace. Indicate those you have been trained to use.

- Think about the uses you put equipment to regularly. Is there another piece of equipment that would do the job more efficiently?

- Look at all the equipment in your office. Plan what alternative equipment you could use if it broke down when you needed it urgently.

- Find the instruction manuals for the equipment in your office and create a library of them, making sure everyone knows where it is. If manuals are missing, see if you can download them or obtain copies from the manufacturer.

- Choose one piece of equipment and create a check list which could be used to make sure that waste is reduced to a minimum when using the equipment.

- Make a list of contact details in the event of problems with equipment that needs help. Include both internal and external contacts.

- Keep a work diary for the period of three months, recording the equipment problems that have occurred and how they were dealt with.

USING MAIL SERVICES

Assessment criteria

This section covers assessment criteria 5.1, 5.2, 5.3 and 5.4

DEALING WITH INCOMING MAIL

Incoming mail will include:

- mail delivered by the post office
- mail delivered by a courier company
- mail hand-delivered
- internal mail
- faxes.

Incoming mail may be dealt with by the mail room in larger organisations, or by administrators in smaller organisations. Many organisations have specific guidelines for handling incoming mail, for instance:

- Dealing with enclosures. These are items enclosed in addition to the main document in the envelope, for example, a cheque. If enclosures are not attached to the main document, use a paper clip or put the document and the enclosure in a clear plastic wallet before you pass them on to the intended internal recipient.

- Stamping incoming post with the date. Many organisations, particularly legal firms, banks and insurance companies stamp all incoming mail with the date it is received. This provides evidence of receipt of important documents. The date is usually stamped in the same place on every document for consistency, for example in the top right hand corner so that it can be seen easily when needed. Some organisations require a separate log to record payments received in the post.

- Entering details in an incoming post book. This lists the type of mail received, when, how the mail arrived (for example, by hand or by post) and who it was distributed to internally.

- Confidentiality. Customer and employee information may be disclosed in documents and letters you receive and open and you will be need to demonstrate **discretion** and **diplomacy** in your handling of incoming mail.

- Whether mail should be opened before being distributed or passed to the recipient unopened if the recipient is named on the envelope.

- Handling mail that is clearly marked 'For the attention of', 'Personal', 'Confidential', 'Private' or 'Urgent'.

- Dealing with cash or valuables received to safeguard the person opening the mail.

It is important that mail received is dealt with swiftly, kept safely and distributed promptly to the correct person. It will be related to the

Discretion

The ability to keep sensitive information secret and the power to make decisions sensitively on the basis of one's knowledge

Diplomacy

Skill and tact in dealing with other people

business of the organisation, and staff could be waiting for replies, payments, orders and other responses which may be urgent.

Dealing efficiently with incoming mail is particularly important when payments or important documents are involved. For example, some organisations may receive payments from customers by cheque in the post. Others such as solicitors may rely on legal contracts being sent and received by post. If incoming mail is handled slowly or not given sufficient priority, there could be serious consequences. A delay in paying cheques into the bank could have a serious effect on the organisation's **cash flow**, while failing to handle incoming orders or contracts promptly could lead to a loss of business, so distributing the post should be a priority.

In order to distribute the mail efficiently you will need to understand the structure of the organisation, people's names and their roles, the purpose of teams and departments and their location in the building. After opening incoming mail it will need to be sorted to facilitate distribution. There are a number of different ways the mail could be sorted:

- name, for example 'Mrs. J. Watling'
- role, for example 'Warehouse Manager'
- department, for example 'Accounts'
- location, for example 'Floor 3'

Over recent years there have been a number of security alerts due to suspicious-looking incoming mail received by organisations, some of which have been potentially dangerous. In a few extreme cases, the results have been very dangerous where the envelope or package has contained explosives or poisonous substances.

Cash flow

The cash flow of a business is the movement of money into and out of it. Also used to describe the funds in a company's bank account that allow them to carry out their day-to-day business operations such as payment for supplies and staff salaries.

Do not open suspicious-looking packages

Many organisations will have put in place safety precautions to be taken by staff when dealing with incoming mail, including:

- Ensuring that staff understand what a suspicious piece of mail might look like.

- Being alert for any envelopes or packages with suspicious features.

- Handling incoming mail in a designated area. Access to the mailroom should be restricted to authorised people or those monitored in and out to ensure that the general public and other staff do not have easy access to the mail and that it cannot be tampered with.

- Protecting your hands. Some organisations insist that their mail handlers wear protective gloves to avoid skin contact with potentially harmful substances present in mail items. A letter opener should be used to open mail.

The Royal Mail has issued the following guidance on recognising suspicious items:

- Dimensions: a letter bomb is unlikely to be less than 3 mm (1/8 inch) thick, or weigh less than 43 grams (1½ ounces).

- Balance/weight: is the packet evenly balanced? Lopsided packages should be treated with suspicion. Packages that are disproportionately heavy for their size could contain an **improvised explosive device (IED)**.

- Holes or stains: packages with grease stains or pin holes in the wrapping should be treated as suspect.

- Smell: some explosive materials smell of marzipan or almonds.

- Noise: ticking or hissing sounds may indicate the presence of an explosive device.

- The flap: is the wrapping completely stuck down? Small gaps left at the end of the flap might indicate a suspect item.

- Type of envelope: experience has shown that postal bombs are usually found in 'Jiffy' bags or similar types of envelope.

- Packaging and postage: has an excessive amount of wrapping or sealing material been used or has an excessive amount of postage been paid to avoid any possibility of delay or enquiry due to underpayment?

- Contents: if, in addition to other indicators (balance, weight, packaging etc) the appearance suggests that the package could contain a book or video cassette it should be treated as a possible postal bomb or IED. If a powdery, granular or sand-like substance, residue or liquid can be seen on the outside of the item or leaking from it, the item should be treated as suspect.

- Markings: restrictive endorsements such as 'Personal' or 'Confidential' may indicate a suspicious item.

> **HANDY HINT**
>
> When opening the mail, care should be taken as the contents of envelopes could be easily damaged, particularly if you are using a letter-opening knife.

> **Improvised explosive device (IED)**
>
> A simple bomb that someone, especially a terrorist or guerrilla, has made themselves

> **HANDY HINT**
>
> After opening an envelope to remove the contents, double check that ALL contents have been removed.

If you have found a suspicious item, the Royal Mail's advice is:

- If you in are in the mailroom or an office, set it down carefully on the nearest flat horizontal surface or, if available, place it in a purpose-built suspect package container.

- Warn everyone in the immediate vicinity and clear the surrounding area to a 20-metre radius around the item.

- Notify your immediate supervisor who will, if necessary, contact the police and seek assistance from the local security staff.

- If you find a suspicious item while outside the mailroom or office, warn members of the public in the vicinity and set the item down carefully.

- If the item is in a post box, do not clear the box, and arrange it to be sealed. Seek immediate police assistance by the most convenient means and contact your supervisor.

- If you are asked by a member of the public to take back an item which they have had delivered and are suspicious of the contents, they must be advised to contact the police. On no account accept the item.

- Wash your hands as soon as possible if in contact with a suspect substance.

Do not:

- drop, shake or throw the item away

- attempt to open a package

- bend or flex the package in an attempt to ascertain the contents

- immerse the package in sand or water

- place it under a sandbag or other heavy object

- place the package in any container other than the one specifically designed for this purpose

- handle the package any more than is absolutely necessary.

Other problems that may be faced in handling incoming mail include mail that arrives damaged or with missing contents. These should still be sorted and checked in following the organisation's usual process. Damaged or missing enclosures should be noted in the register if there is one, or if not a note pinned to the document describing the problem, signed and dated by the person that opened the item. Ideally it should be taken straight to the recipient so they can decide what action, if any, to take.

Junk mail, sometimes called unsolicited mail, meaning it has not been requested and is unwanted, is received both physically and electronically these days. Junk mail that arrives in the post usually consists of flyers, advertisements, brochures, letters and postcards. They are sent out to thousands of organisations without being

You may have to deal with problems such as damaged mail

HANDY HINTS

- Mail marked 'URGENT' should be opened immediately and given priority.
- Mail marked 'PERSONAL' should not be opened but should be handed straight to the addressee.
- Letters and documents that have enclosures with them usually have the word 'Enclosure' or 'ENC' at the foot of the document.
- Mail marked 'PRIVATE & CONFIDENTIAL' or 'CONFIDENTIAL' should never be opened. It should be handed straight to the addressee.

ACTIVITY

Identify the types of documents that are faxed to your organisation.

requested. Junk mail is normally addressed to the organisation or **generically**, for example 'The Manager', and is usually trying to sell products or services to the company. Most junk mail items of this nature are discarded and thrown away. Junk mail is wasteful and can be harmful to the environment, due to the amount of paper, effort and processes involved in producing and delivering it.

There are a number of steps that can be taken to reduce the amount of unsolicited mail received:

- 'Door-to-door opt-out' – Royal Mail distributes between 25% and 50% of all unaddressed junk mail. To stop unsolicited leaflets delivered by the postman you can register with Royal Mail's 'Door-to-door opt-out'. To register you first need to request an opt-out form by sending an email to optout@royalmail.com or by phoning 01865 796 988.

- 'Your Choice Preference Scheme' – there's a second opt-out service for unaddressed junk mail, the 'Your choice preference scheme for unaddressed mail'. Registering will stop leaflets distributed by members of the Direct Marketing Association. It's unlikely to stop more than a handful of leaflets per year, but registering is free. You need to order an opt-out pack before you can sign up by sending an email to yourchoice@dma.org.uk.

- Letterbox stickers. Roughly half of all the leaflets in your post box aren't covered by the opt-out schemes. Putting a 'No Junk Mail' sign on your door is the only way to stop unaddressed mail that's not distributed by Royal Mail or members of the Junk Mail Association.

- Mailing Preference Service – signing up to the Mailing Preference Service can reduce unsolicited, addressed junk mail. You can also use the service to register a previous occupant's name at your current address. You can register online but the scheme is not as effective as it claims to be. Only members of the Direct Marketing Association have to check if you're registered, and the scheme doesn't allow you to stop mailings addressed 'To the occupier'.

- You can ask junk mailers to stop sending you junk mail by contacting them directly. You can do so informally via telephone or email, or you can make a formal request by sending a 'data protection notice'. A data protection notice is a legally binding demand made with reference to Article 11 of the Data Protection Act 1998. Any organisation based in the UK has to stop sending you (addressed) junk mail if you send them such a notice. It's a very effective way to stop mailings from organisations that ignore informal requests.

- Some junk mail is impossible to stop. Adverts addressed 'To the occupier', for example, aren't covered by the Mailing Preference Service and can't be stopped with a data protection notice. Your only option is to send it back to the offender. Similarly, you might

Generic

Relating to or suitable for a range or class of similar things

ACTIVITY

Draw an organisation chart showing your organisational structure and the names, roles and responsibilities and locations of individuals and teams. List the different types of incoming mail each receives on a daily basis.

want to return leaflets from organisations that insist on pushing adverts through your door – even if you're registered with the two opt-out schemes for leaflets and have a 'No Junk Mail' sign on your door. You don't have to put up with such rude junk mailers, you can simply stick the leaflet in an unstamped envelope, address it to the offender and drop it in your nearest pillar box.

DEALING WITH OUTGOING MAIL

Just as there are procedures for processing incoming mail in an organisation, there will be guidelines about how to deal with outgoing mail. Outgoing mail may be external, sent to people and organisations outside the organisation, or internal. Internal mail may be sent to people in the same organisation but at different locations, for instance a different region or country, or to colleagues in a different part of the building.

In most organisations, outgoing mail has to be ready towards the end of the afternoon. This allows the mailroom time to prepare the mail for despatch by checking that packages and envelopes are secure and clearly addressed before the correct postage is applied. Daily post in most organisations is taken to the post office but in some cases, the post office or courier will collect the prepared post from the organisation's premises. Most organisations will seek the most cost effective way to get their mail delivered. There are a range of organisations in addition to Royal Mail that offer competitively priced postal services, including courier services to collect packages and other items and arrange delivery.

While Royal Mail has limitations and restrictions to the size and weight of the parcels they are able to take on for delivery, couriers can deliver extremely large or heavy packages and may offer same-day delivery in case of really urgent mail. Couriers will deliver just about any sized package, including extremely fragile or large and bulky ones. International couriers accept international deliveries, medical couriers work with the medical trade and gift couriers deal exclusively with gifts, while some couriers will take on all of these different types.

Some larger organisations, such as local authorities with departments in several buildings in the same town or area, will have their own postal arrangements for delivering mail between buildings by hand, using their own vehicles.

Outgoing mail may be collected from the various departments throughout the building or brought to the mailroom to be dealt with. There is usually a deadline and all departments are made aware of the latest time for the daily post to be ready for dispatch.

Once collected, the mail then has to be prepared. The items have to be weighed and the size taken into account for the correct postage to be applied. Parcels need to be packaged securely as they will be handled several times during delivery, being loaded on and off vehicles, conveyor belts and even aircraft.

Regular mail will be posted by first or second class post. This will not include valuable packets or parcels needing insurance or 'signed for' supplements to be paid. Urgent, registered and recorded mail will require special preparation:

- Urgent mail is usually despatched by first class postage, special delivery or courier. A label is normally applied to the front of the envelope or package to highlight the fact that the item should be given priority.

- Items of value are usually sent by special delivery as the postage cost of this service includes insurance. These items require a signature by the recipient to verify they have received them.

- 'Recorded signed for' is similar to special delivery but items are not insured. A signature is required upon receipt and the speed of delivery can be second or first class.

Postage and delivery rates are subject to frequent changes, so keeping up to date with this information is important when dealing with outgoing mail. The choice of service to be used will depend on the weight, size, cost and urgency. If using Royal Mail the following are available for delivery within the UK:

- First class mail – Royal Mail aim to deliver the next working day.

- Second class mail – Royal Mail aim to deliver within three working days.

- Special Delivery 9am guarantees delivery by 9am the next working day or your money back, has a maximum weight of 2kg and offers compensation up to £2500 for loss or damage.

- Special Delivery next day guarantees delivery by 1pm the next working day or your money back, has a maximum weight of 10kg and offers compensation up to £2500 for loss or damage.

- Standard parcel – Royal Mail aims to deliver within five days.

- Recorded signed for – this provides a signature from the recipient to prove delivery.

First and second class mail is divided into:

- Letters which are a maximum of 240mm x 165mm x 5mm and weigh no more than 100g

- Large letters which are a maximum of 353mm x 250mm x 25mm and weigh no more than 750g

- Packets which are larger than the maximum for large letters and are priced according to their weight, with a maximum for second class of 1kg

HANDY HINT

'Signed for' means the letter or packet has to be signed for by the recipient when delivered to confirm they have received it safely. There is usually a small supplement payable in addition to the normal postage costs for this service paid at the time of posting.

ACTIVITY

If your organisation doesn't have its outgoing mail collected by the post office, investigate whether this could be arranged and what benefits there would be.

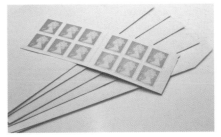

First class post

- Small parcels size 1 which can measure up to 45cm x 35cm x 8cm
- Small parcels size 2 which can measure up to 35cm x 25cm x 16cm
- Medium parcels which can measure up to 61cm x 46cm x 46cm
- Large parcels which can measure up to length 1.5m, length and girth combined 3m, weight up to 30kg.

Overseas mail can be sent using:

- Air mail – all letters to Europe must be sent by air mail. Letters to the rest of the world can be sent by air mail, as can small packets to a maximum weight of 2kg, apart from books and pamphlets which have a maximum weight of 5kg.
- Surface mail – mail travels by land and sea rather than by air and therefore takes considerably longer. Weight limits are the same as for air mail.
- Airsure – mail is sent on the earliest available flight, receives priority handling and compensation up to £500 is available. Delivery can be confirmed via the Royal Mail website.
- International signed for – this provides a signature from the recipient to prove delivery.

Each service has prices based on size and weight, so it is important to check with the sender which service is required. Usually a postage book is kept to record the details of packages and parcels sent, including who the parcel is being sent to, which service it is being sent by and the date it was sent. Mail consisting of envelopes is usually recorded in bulk, for example '150 letters at 60p, sent first class'.

The organisation may have a stock of postage stamps to be applied to outgoing letters, but if dealing with large volumes of mail daily they may have a franking machine, which the postal clerk will operate.

Operating a franking machine is relatively simple. Although machines will differ in the exact way they are operated, reading the manual will give all the information needed. Basically, franking machines are operated by:

1 Placing the letter or parcel onto the scales.
2 Determining whether the letter or parcel is to be sent first or second class, etc. Larger machines with built-in scales will decide the price.
3 Feeding the envelope into the machine, facing upwards, where it will be automatically franked. Larger machines will feed the mail in bundles automatically. For larger packets, you may print off a franking label to affix to the parcel, to avoid parcel printing being **illegible** or the parcel itself becoming creased or damaged.

The benefits of using a franking machine include:

- Discounts from Royal Mail, which have dramatically increased because handling franked items is a lot cheaper than issuing

ACTIVITY

You have a package containing items to the value of £327 which weighs 13kg and must be delivered by the next day to a location in the UK. Investigate the different options and calculate the cost.

Illegible

Impossible or very difficult to read

stamps and processing stamped mail. In order to encourage more businesses to use franking machines, Royal Mail offer big discounts on postal charges for customers who frank their post.

- Presenting a professional image – the organisation's franked stamp can be **customised** to contain your organisation's logo and promotional text or other business messages. Franking your mail gives you the opportunity to advertise new services, promotions and new offers. Using a franking machine that offers text messaging allows the organisation to change the message on a daily basis.

- Avoiding overstamping – a franking machine with an **integral** scale will ensure the correct postage is dialled in to the machine and franked.

- Avoiding understamping – Royal Mail used to charge the sender if postal items were understamped. Now they deliver the item to the recipient's receiving office and ask the recipient to pick up the item and pay the difference plus a handling fee. If an organisation accidentally understamps mail, it causes inconvenience to its customers and also costs them money. With a franking machine, it is easy to get the correct postage every time and avoid the embarrassment of understamping.

- Time-saving and convenience – stamps will run out at the most inconvenient time and trips to the post office for more stamps are not only time-consuming but also tiresome. Franking machines can be topped up online 24 hours a day, seven days a week and even when the post office is shut you will never run out of postage. Mail items can be easily weighed and correct postage applied. Batches of letters can be quickly passed through the franking machine and dispatched.

- **Accountability** and recording **expenditure** – for organisations wanting to keep track of postage across departments, most franking machines allow for multiple department accounts to be set up and reported on. This can help keep control of costs.

Collecting and preparing the mail for dispatch requires organisation and good time management. Problems could occur with the process if:

- staff overrun the deadline set for having their outgoing mail ready

- there is an unexpected amount of outgoing post to be processed

- supplies in the post room run low.

Customised

Altered to fit somebody's requirements

Integral

Part of something larger and not separate from it

Accountability

Responsibility to somebody or for something

Expenditure

The amount of money spent

CUSTOMER SERVICE IN A BUSINESS ENVIRONMENT

REACHING DIFFERENT TYPES OF CUSTOMER

An internal customer is anyone in the organisation who relies on a product or service from someone else in the same organisation. The major difference between internal and external customers is that generally the internal customer does not have a choice of suppliers. It is as important to deliver excellent customer service to internal customers as it is to external customers. The service given to your colleagues will have an impact on the service they are able to provide to their external customers.

The common feature of internal customers is that they receive a service from others within the organisation, for example Human Resources or IT departments. In supply chain situations there may be more employees supporting internal customers than dealing with external customers. External customers are customers who don't work for the organisation which is supplying the products or services they are purchasing. Providing customer service to both internal and external customers involves giving them what they want and need.

Delivering excellent customer service to external customers is a vital part of any organisation's procedures. The survival of commercial organisations depends on their ability to generate income through providing products and services to existing and new customers. Turning customers into repeat customers through meeting or exceeding their expectations will introduce new customers as they hear good reports about the organisation. Dealing promptly with customers' problems and complaints will turn them into positive experiences for the customer and increase the likelihood of them using your services again, rather than decreasing it.

A type of customer that is often overlooked is the prospective customer. This is anyone who has not yet purchased goods or services from the organisation, but might in the future. Lists of prospective customers can be created through business networking and research, or can be purchased. Developing your own list will take longer than buying one, but it is more likely to fit your longer-term marketing strategy.

It is also important to remember that all visitors to your organisation, whether callers or tradespeople, who are not existing customers, are prospective customers. The way their enquiries are handled will impact on whether they become customers in the future.

THE IMPACT OF POOR CUSTOMER SERVICE

While poor customer service when dealing with an internal customer can lead to a breakdown in your working relationship with that colleague, failing to meet an external customer's needs can ruin the organisation's reputation and lose it the customer's business. It is said that seven out of ten customers who switch to a competitor do so because of poor service, rather than **price differentials**. Good customer service results in the customer receiving their desired expectation of service. While this type of service is regarded in a positive light, it is the least memorable. Organisations aim for excellent customer service, because this produces customers who feel that not only were their expectations met, but that they were valued. A customer with this type of service will tell at least eight other people**.**

The purpose of meeting and exceeding the expectations of customers is to bring them back to the organisation as repeat customers. Promotions and low prices will help to bring in new customers but only exceptional customer service will make them return and pass on to their friends and colleagues how well they were treated, creating more new potential customers.

It is more profitable, in the longer term, to create good customer relationships than to make a quick sale. Remember that customers pay your wages and those of everybody else in your organisation: no customers, no sales; no sales, no job. Customers will return to organisations whose people make an effort to form a relationship of loyalty and trust with them. They need to feel confident that their problems are going to be dealt with positively and not with a 'don't care' attitude.

Price differential

A difference in the prices of two products or of the same product in different places

COMMON MISTAKE

Customers will not buy from you just because you open your doors and invite them to.

THE GOLDEN RULES OF CUSTOMER SERVICE

There are seven golden rules to dealing with customers:

GOLDEN RULE NUMBER 1

Stay in close contact with your customers. Find out what they want. It is easy to assume you know what customers want without checking. Don't give customers what you want them to have, or what you think they should want: find out what they need. Tell customers what is happening. If you have to increase your prices, tell them and tell them why. Don't hope they won't notice, because they will, and they will be annoyed that you have tried to deceive them. Most customers will react reasonably to bad news as long as they are kept informed, and those who react unreasonably would do so whether you told them or not.

It's important to create good customer relationships

GOLDEN RULE NUMBER 2

Make it easy for your customers to contact you. Always answer phone calls. Customers do not want to speak to a recorded message, they want contact with a human being, so make sure someone is available during business hours to answer the phone. If a customer has to leave a message, call them back as soon as possible. If you put it off, another organisation will have responded to their problem and you will have lost a customer. If your contact with customers is over the internet, respond to their emails promptly and fully. Make sure your website is user-friendly and easy to navigate. Not every customer will be a computer geek: many will be nervous and uncertain and, if they encounter difficulties, will go elsewhere.

GOLDEN RULE NUMBER 3

Be helpful. Sometimes a customer needs something that won't immediately lead to a sale, but the organisation that provides them with the help needed will be the one they return to when they do make a purchase. If a customer asks for advice such as 'where is the nearest post office?' give them it with a smile and as much detail as possible. If they ask where they can find a particular product, don't just tell them, show them. Even better, wait to see if they need any further help or advice when you have shown them.

GOLDEN RULE NUMBER 4

Don't overpromise and under-deliver. If you tell a customer something is going to happen, you must be sure it is going to and you must make sure that it does. It is much better to tell them that delivery will be next week and you will confirm which day when you know for sure than to confidently state that delivery will be on Tuesday. When delivery turns out to be on Wednesday the customer in the first case will be pleased, in the second case disappointed.

GOLDEN RULE NUMBER 5

Give your customers more than they expect and reward them often. Whether you give them a coupon giving a discount on a future purchase, a complimentary product such as a packet of washing powder with a new washing machine or simply service that goes beyond their expectations, they will be delighted and sure to come back again.

GOLDEN RULE NUMBER 6

Understand and work to your organisation's quality standards. These will ensure that every customer receives a high standard of workmanship in the products they buy or a high level of professionalism in the service provided. Quality standards may be internally agreed or may be set by external bodies such as:

- The International Organisation for Standardisation. The ISO 9000 family of standards is related to quality management systems and designed to help organisations ensure that they meet the needs of customers while meeting statutory and regulatory requirements related to the products.

- NEBOSH (National Examination Board in Occupational Safety and Health), a UK-based independent examination board delivering vocational qualifications in health, safety and environmental practice and management.

- Investors in People (IIP). The standard framework is structured around four key principles:
  - Commitment – commitment to invest in people to achieve goals.
  - Planning – planning how skills, individuals and teams are to be developed to achieve these goals.
  - Action – taking action to develop and use necessary skills in a well-defined and continuing programme directly tied to business objectives.

○ Evaluation – evaluating the outcomes of training and development for individuals' progress towards goals, the value achieved and future needs.

One of the most important quality standards is meeting agreed timescales. Often a customer needs the product or service from you in order to deliver a product or service to their customer, so any delay will have a knock-on effect.

GOLDEN RULE NUMBER 7

Follow golden rules numbers 1 to 6. A good salesperson can sell anything to anyone – once. Your approach to customer service will decide whether the customer comes back for more. Salespeople need to remember they will be judged by what they do, not what they say they will do. Make sure you have all the information necessary to answer customers' queries and the authority necessary to deal with customers' problems without having to refer to someone more senior.

Don't make negative comments about customers, they are the most important factor in the organisation's success and as such deserve to be treated with respect at all times. Similarly, don't make negative comments about the organisation in front of customers. This gives a poor impression of the organisation and may discourage customers from returning.

UNDERSTANDING WHAT YOU CAN OFFER YOUR CUSTOMERS

Your organisation may provide customers with products, services or both. It is important to understand the differences between products and services. Products are tangible and can be touched, consumed and owned by the customer. Examples are clothing and computers. Both are real things that people can touch. Services, on the other hand, are things that one person does for another. Examples would be fixing a customer's computer when it is not working or laundering their clothes. Services are intangible because they are not something the customer can physically grasp. Products are usually first produced, then sold and then consumed; services are first sold, then produced and consumed simultaneously. The sale of a product may provide the opportunity to sell a service, for instance helpline facilities following the sale of a computer.

Every successful organisation will have either a unique selling point (USP) or a unique service offer (USO) or, possibly, both. A unique selling point sets the organisation's products or services apart from those of their competitors. For example:

- packaging
- performance

- market perception
- quality
- availability
- meeting deadlines.

A unique service offer is something which sets the organisation apart from its competitors by the service which they provide. For example an estate agency may offer a free website-listing service which is not offered by its competitors or a pharmacy may offer a prescription collection service. Unique service offers are directly related to the reasons customers use the products or services of an organisation.

It is crucial to understand the unique selling point or unique service offer so that you can emphasise these to customers in your dealings with them. Your organisation will be selling products and services, but your customers will be buying benefits and solutions. When you are trying to sell products and services, it is important that you understand the differences between features and benefits. Features describe what a product or service is or has, but benefits describe what it does for the customer. Customers may explain their needs in terms of features, but they make buying decisions based on benefits. For example, they may say they want a leather three-piece suite, but they will buy it because it is easy to keep clean and reflects their view of their lifestyle.

In every organisation the products and services supplied will regularly change. You may, for example, be giving advice on unemployment benefits and the criteria for eligibility may change. Because of this you must make sure that you regularly update your knowledge in order to give the best possible advice. It is important that you know more about the products and services you are supplying than your customers. Information can be obtained from:

- colleagues and internal departments
- the internet or intranet
- catalogues, brochures and price lists
- training sessions
- organisational product and service information or literature
- feedback from customers.

Keep your knowledge of the organisation's products and services up to date – it is very frustrating to customers to be told all about a fantastic deal which exactly meets their needs, only to find out that the product or service was discontinued last week. This will be worse than not having told them about it at all, as they will now know what they are missing.

ACTIVITY

Find out what your organisation's USP or USO is. Write an explanation of how it is used to promote the organisation.

ACTIVITY

Carry out a survey of your customers' opinions of the service provided by your organisation or department. Analyse the results and make suggestions for improvements.

HANDY HINT

When composing questionnaires, there are two types of question, open questions and closed questions, and you need to be clear which you want to use and when.

HANDY HINT

If you don't know, ask.

CASE STUDY
CUSTOMER SERVICE

This case study concerns an unnamed hotel in South Korea. This is a true story and were it not for excellent customer service, the customer in question would have been in dire straits.

An author had to attend a business meeting in South Korea. He didn't know the area or the language. He took a two-hour taxi ride away from his airport, bound for a hotel in a remote region of the country.

When he arrived at his hotel he was informed that they had been overbooked and there was not a room for him. The author's hotel room had been pre-arranged, so an overbooked room left him virtually deserted in a foreign country.

The hotel manager appeared, and told the author he was sorry about the mistake. The manager went ahead and booked the author a room in another nearby hotel, then gave his taxi driver instructions to ensure that he made it to his room safely. The hotel manager took the time to understand the situation, and did everything he could to rectify it. The moral of this customer service case study is simple: where there is a crisis, there is an opportunity – you just have to make sure you know *how* to turn a bad experience into a good or great one.

UNIT 224 (B&A 36): TEST YOUR KNOWLEDGE

Learning outcome 1: Understand the organisation and administration of meetings

1 Describe two differences between a formal meeting and an informal meeting.

2 Explain why it is necessary to plan for meetings.

3 Describe two procedures involved in organising meetings.

Learning outcome 2: Understand the organisation of travel and accommodation

1 List three different types of travel.

2 Explain why it is important to confirm instructions for travel.

3 Explain two reasons for keeping records of business travel.

Learning outcome 3: Understand how to manage diary systems

1 Explain two advantages and disadvantages of:

   a   A paper diary

   b   An electronic diary system.

2 State three pieces of information which would be essential in order to successfully record a meeting in a diary system.

3 Describe how you communicate changes to arrangements, ensuring that everyone who needs to be advised is contacted in a timely manner.

Learning outcome 4: Understand how to use office equipment

1 Explain why it is advisable to get quotations before placing an equipment order.

2 Describe your organisation's ordering procedures.

3 State the two basic uses of the telephone.

4 Explain which pieces of equipment would be used to create 400 copies of a double-sided document, four colours, collated and bound. Why would these pieces of equipment be chosen?

UNIT 224 (B&A 36): TEST YOUR KNOWLEDGE

Learning outcome 5: Understand the use of mail services in a business context

1 What type of mail do some organisations not like the mail clerk to open?

2 Why is dispatching outgoing mail treated urgently in most organisations?

3 Why might an organisation use a courier service to deliver mail items rather than Royal Mail?

Learning outcome 6: Understand customer service in a business environment

1 Explain what is meant by an external customer.

2 Describe the products and services provided to internal customers by your own organisation.

3 Explain why it is important to meet or exceed the expectations of customers.

4 Describe the quality standards used in your organisation to provide customer service.

CHAPTER 3

UNIT 225 (B&A 37) PRINCIPLES OF BUSINESS DOCUMENT PRODUCTION AND INFORMATION MANAGEMENT

When preparing new documents, you need to understand their purpose, readership, content, style and format as well as the deadline for completion. The first impression a potential customer receives of your organisation from a document they receive may be the deciding factor in whether they do business with you or not, and first impressions are made in 30 seconds or less.

One of the most interesting aspects of working in administration is being asked to research information. You will need to agree the objectives and deadlines for researching the information, identify and agree the best sources of information and the methods of recording and storing the information once you have found it.

In this unit you will cover the following learning outcomes:

1 understand how to prepare business documents
2 understand the distribution of business documents
3 understand how information is managed in business organisations.

PREPARATION OF BUSINESS DOCUMENTS

When designing and producing documents, remember that whether for internal or external use, documents are visual. They make an impression on the reader or user based on the way they look, so you must give a great deal of thought to their format and their layout.

When preparing documents, it is important to:

- Use a consistent format. There is a huge variety of fonts available, and all of them can be used in different sizes and colours, together with italicising, bolding or using capital letters. However, most documents will benefit from using no more than two different fonts. In particular, long documents should remain similar in general look and feel throughout as too much variation will confuse the reader.

- Use different sizes of font and bold letters for headings and subheadings to make the document easier to navigate. For instance, if the main text is in a font size of 12, a subheading could be size 14 and a main heading size 16. Use a combination of serif fonts and sans serif fonts. Serif fonts such as Times New Roman have accents at the edge of each character. While they are highly readable over large blocks of text, they can be overpowering in large sizes. Sans serif fonts such as Tahoma can be used for headings and subheadings. They have no accents at the edge of each character. They are very readable at large sizes but become unreadable over large blocks of text.

- Only create a design element that has a purpose. The design of your documents should help your content make its point, not overwhelm it. If in doubt, remember less is more.

- Think about spacing. People find it very difficult to read documents that are crammed full of text. Use white space to separate paragraphs and as margins. Use visual aids such as photographs, diagrams, graphs and charts to break up large blocks of text and make the document page more visually appealing

- Use colours. Colours attract the reader's attention and are useful in directing the eye to a particularly important point. Remember to use colour sparingly, however, and not to make your documents look like the product of a small child's art class. There are some colours whose use is traditional, such as red when indicating a negative in financial figures, and these conventions should be adhered to, or the reader may be confused.

- Use bullet points to summarise information and numbered lists to explain sequences of events or activities. Remember to be consistent when creating lists.

TYPES OF BUSINESS DOCUMENTS

Any list of types of documents that may be produced would be almost endless. The most common include:

When producing memos, remember that they will only be used internally, so the size and quality of paper can be reduced in comparison to a letterhead. Memos can usually be printed on A5 paper, headed with the word 'Memo' and simply a template of 'To', 'From', 'Date' and 'Subject'.

Letters are used for formally communicating information, normally externally. They should:

- be clearly structured and well presented – reflect image of organisation
- follow standard conventions as relevant, for example the use of 'Dear Sir' at the beginning and the use of 'Yours faithfully' together, or the use of 'Dear Mr Xxxxx' and 'Yours sincerely' together
- be accurate
- follow house styles if relevant/required

When producing letterheads, you need to consider:

- the paper colour
- the text colour
- the size and font of the text
- the positioning of the organisation's logo

- The positioning of the organisation's name and address, website, email address, telephone number, fax number, VAT registration number and company registration number.

A letterhead should reflect corporate identity

ACTIVITY

Look at a letter that you have received that did not impress you. Discuss with your supervisor the impression that it gives of the organisation that sent it.

Succinct

Expressed with brevity and clarity, with no wasted words

When producing reports, remember that a written report should provide information and facts as **succinctly** as possible. A formal report will contain the following:

- A title that reflects the subject of the report.
- A table of contents if the report is more than 10 pages long.
- An executive summary. This is written last and summarises the essential points of the report, including the conclusions as briefly as possible. It should be able to be read in isolation, allowing the reader to decide whether it is necessary to read the whole report.
- An introduction explaining why the report has been written, giving background information and explaining the method of investigation used.
- Main text where the findings of the report are listed under sections and subsections. Each section will refer to a different topic and describe, analyse, interpret and evaluate the data. Only proven facts should be used, not opinions at this stage.
- Conclusion, which should sum up the main points. Opinions can be expressed if the evidence to support them is given in the main text. This may lead to recommendations.

- Recommendations for improvements or actions based on the conclusions.
- Bibliography listing the publications cited in the report or referred to when putting it together.
- Appendix containing material which is referred to in the report which requires greater detail.

Producing minutes is explained in detail in Chapter 9 (Unit 205, B&A 17).

When producing invoices, there are a number of pieces of information which must be included:

- the client's or customer's name and address
- your organisation's name, address, telephone number and email address
- when you expect payment and by what method
- an invoice number.

COMPANY NAME: ADDRESS: PHONE:	**INVOICE**
INVOICE NR.:	DATE:

| TO:
NAME:
COMPANY NAME:
ADDRESS:
PHONE: | SHIP TO:
NAME:
COMPANY NAME:
ADDRESS:
PHONE: |

COMMENTS / SPECIAL INSTRUCTIONS:

QUANTITY	DESCRIPTION	UNIT PRICE	TOTAL

SUBTOTAL:
SALES TAX:
SHIPPING & HANDLING:
TOTAL DUE:

AUTHORIZED SIGNATURE

Make all cheques payable to:
Payment is due within 30 days.
If you have any questions concerning this invoice, contact:
Thank you for your business!

An example of an invoice

When producing forms, you again need to consider the demographics of the people who will be filling them in. If they are for internal use there will be an opportunity for training to be provided, so less information may need to be given on the form itself and some jargon may be acceptable. When designing forms for completion by customers or the general public, it is important to remember they may only ever complete the form once, so they will have no previous experience to fall back on, and will find jargon or technical language confusing. In this case, notes explaining how to fill the form in should appear at the beginning. Other design tips when creating forms are:

- use tick boxes wherever possible
- signature boxes need to be a minimum of 2½ inches × ¾ inch (60mm × 20mm)
- address boxes should be at least five lines
- written answer boxes should allow a ¼ inch (6mm) space between lines.

Poorly designed forms can affect the efficiency of the organisation and its reputation with customers, clients and the general public. Take the time to produce them well and you can improve the organisation's image, reputation and performance.

When producing templates, you are usually looking to create a master which can be used in a mail merge. This allows you to create personalised letters and pre-addressed envelopes or mailing labels for mass mailings from a word processing document which contains fixed text, which will be the same in each output document, and variables, which act as placeholders that are replaced by text from the data source.

The data source is typically a spreadsheet or a database which has a field or column for each variable in the template. When the mail merge is run, the word processing system creates an output document for each row in the database, using the fixed text exactly as it appears in the template, but substituting the data variables in the template with the values from the matching columns.

DOCUMENT VERSION CONTROL

When amending forms or documents that already exist, it is important to use a system of document version control, which is a process by which different drafts and versions of a document or record are managed. Basically version control is a tool which tracks a series of draft documents which end in a final version. It provides an audit trail for the revision and update of these finalised versions.

Version control clearly identifies the development of the document. It allows you for example to retain and identify the:

ACTIVITY

Collect samples of forms used in your organisation. Check whether they conform to the standards described in this chapter. If not, make suggestions to the appropriate person to amend them

---

COMMON MISTAKE

It is easy to forget to take a break from your keyboard when you are busy. You will be more productive if you take regular breaks than if you try to work for long periods.

- first draft which was submitted to someone for comment
- draft which was created as a result of comments
- versions that went back and forth for further comment
- final version which was signed off.

It is also useful where you are working on a document with others. Changes made by different individuals at different times can thus be clearly identified. Having such versions identified and easily accessible allows the development of the document to be easily understood. It allows a return to previous versions to determine when decisions on content were made.

Version control should be used where more than one version of a document exists, or where this is likely to be the case in the future, and can be achieved by adding a number at the end of a file title. Each successive draft of a document is numbered sequentially from 0.1, 0.2, 0.3… until a finalised version is complete. This would be titled Version 1.0. If version 1.0 is to be revised, drafts would be numbered as 1.1, 1.2… until Version 2.0 is complete.

In addition to adding the version number to the end of the file title, it should also be displayed within the document. The version number should appear on any document title page, and also in the header or footer of each page. To ensure against the accidental loss of final versions of records, a **read-only tag** can also be applied. Should any changes to this document be made, the user will be prompted to save the file with a new title. It should also be decided who is responsible for authorising changes made to the document.

Read-only tag

Users are unable to change the content without saving the file with a new title

INFORMATION AND COMMUNICATIONS TECHNOLOGY (ICT)

The resources needed to produce business documents may include a printer, paper and envelopes. The best quality paper and envelopes should be used for documents intended for use outside the organisation. Lower quality stationery can be used for internal documents.

There is a range of technology available for inputting, formatting and editing text. This includes:

- The keyboard and mouse – these are the most common pieces of hardware used for inputting text and are widely available as they are supplied with most computers. The downsides are that they can be relatively slow and prone to errors if your keyboarding skills are not good.

- Voice recognition software – this allows you to convert speech directly into text, avoiding spelling errors or keyboarding mistakes. The downsides are that, except for very expensive systems, the input can be inaccurate, and most will use American spellings and will struggle with regional accents. It is also unsuitable for a noisy office environment.

- Scanners and optical character recognition (OCR) software – these allow you to scan printed documents and convert them to text. The downsides are that inexpensive systems can be inaccurate and the original document being scanned must be very clear and in a suitable font.

- Simple text editors – these allow basic editing and corrections. The downsides are that there are very few **enhancements** available, often underline and bold only, and the size of files that can be saved is small.

- Word processing software – this allows a much higher level of editing, correction and text enhancement with a wide choice of fonts and colours. The downside is that the file size is often large because of the formatting details.

- Desktop publishing software – this allows you to create page layouts with text, graphics and photos. The downside is the software can be expensive for small-scale printing

- Presentation graphics software – this allows you to give presentations and slideshows. The downside is the system requirements involved.

- Spreadsheet software – this allows you to store data in a grid of horizontal rows and vertical columns. The downside is their vulnerability to human error such as missed negative signs and misaligned rows.

- Database software – this allows you to store electronic information. The downside is that whenever a database is opened to retrieve or update information, it is vulnerable to loss.

- Financial software – this allows you to automate routine accounting tasks, to establish controls and to create financial reports. The downside is that information in an accounting system is only as valid as the information put into the system.

A combination of the technology listed may be used to produce different types of documents, but most will be produced using word processing software or with desktop publishing software if a more professionally designed look is required.

Text and non-text can be integrated by inserting pictures, graphs and clip art. There are a variety of different features that can be used in programs such as Microsoft Word. Other applications such as Excel and PowerPoint help with integrating text and non-text in spreadsheets and slides.

Enhancement

The increase of the clarity, degree of detail, or another quality of an electronic image by using a computer program

An employee using desktop publishing software

ACTIVITIES

- Research the benefits of obtaining any resources listed above which your organisation does not currently use. Write a short report detailing reasons for investing in them.
- Identify the software packages used in your workplace. Research the use of those that you are not familiar with.
- Look through the menus on your word processing package and familiarise yourself with the use of each function.

AGREEING THE BRIEF

Before starting to produce documents, it is important to understand exactly what is required. You will need to liaise closely with the user or department that requires the document to agree the purpose of the document and the content, style and quality that is required. In some organisations, there is a manager or even a department responsible for checking that all documentation meets the organisation's standards and uses the agreed **house style**. In these organisations, new or amended documents must be approved before being put into use.

The benefits of agreeing the purpose, content and style for the contents of documents are that documents are standardised across the organisation and there are no poorly designed or poorly produced documents giving a bad impression of the organisation to customers or clients.

House style

A set of rules concerning spellings, layout, typography, etc

A variety of different features can be used in programs such as Microsoft Word

It is also important to agree a deadline for the design and production of the document. A fabulous, award-winning brochure giving details of an event in August is completely worthless if it is not completed until mid-September. It may be necessary to research the information needed to complete the document. The research may be carried out internally, by checking on facts and figures, or externally. External research will mostly be carried out on the internet, using search engines such as Google or Bing.

In the case of promotional material, for instance, it is important that prices and descriptions of products and services are accurate and up to date. You will also need to clarify the format of the document and the resources needed to complete it by the required deadline. When you have gathered the necessary information, you will be able to organise it to create the most effective document in the most efficient way.

CHECKING THE DOCUMENT

When the document is complete, it is important that it is proofread for spelling, grammar and punctuation as well as correctness. Remember that spell-checking facilities on your computer will only find some errors; it cannot tell whether you meant to say 'its' or 'it's', or correct common typing errors such as 'form' for 'from' or 'then' for 'than', for instance. Check that it is set to English (UK) rather than English (US) or it will insist on changing words like 'organisation' to 'organization'. While proofreading will find spelling mistakes, it will not find errors of fact, so it is important to check issues such as model number, prices, etc as errors can lead to confusion and loss of business. Be particularly careful when checking numbers, dates, times and amounts.

All documents should be proofread once complete

Another important aspect to bear in mind when checking documents is confidentiality. Care must be taken not to include any information which is **commercially sensitive** in documentation which will be available to people outside the organisation. Any document must comply with the principles of the Data Protection Act, the Copyright, Designs and Patents Act and intellectual property rights, which include copyright, trademarks, patents, industrial design rights, trade dress and trade secrets.

Under UK law copyright material sent over the internet is generally protected in the same way as material in other media. You cannot distribute or download material that others have placed on the internet without the permission of the owners of the rights in the material unless copyright exceptions apply. Although the law may be different in other countries, meaning copyright material may have been put on the internet in other countries without infringing copyright there, it could still be illegal to use that material without permission in the UK.

The Data Protection Act covers personal data which relates to a living individual who can be identified from the data or from the data combined with other information in the possession of the **data controller**. There are eight principles of information handling outlined in the act. These say that data must:

- be fairly and lawfully processed
- be processed for limited purposes
- be adequate, relevant and not excessive
- be accurate and up to date
- not be kept for longer than is necessary
- be processed in line with the rights of the data subject
- be secure
- not be transferred to other countries without adequate protection.

Data controller

The person who decides the purpose for which personal data is to be processed

ACTIVITY

Research the Data Protection Act and the Copyright, Designs and Patents Act and consider how they apply to documents you produce.

DISTRIBUTING BUSINESS DOCUMENTS

Assessment criteria

This section covers assessment criteria 2.2

When the document that you have produced is complete and has been checked for accuracy, it will need to be distributed to its authorised readers. It may be necessary to protect documents with passwords or by marking them as confidential for security reasons. Distribution channels may be internal or external and include:

- Email – this has the benefit of speed of distribution but the disadvantage that the recipient will not necessarily be aware of the email until they open their browser.

- Post – this has the benefit of distributing hard copies of documents to recipients without the need for them to print off their own copies, but the disadvantage of sometimes being slow to be delivered.

- Courier – this has the benefits of the post, plus overcoming the issue of speed of delivery, but can be expensive in comparison, especially if delivery is to multiple recipients.

- By hand – cheapest and fastest for small numbers of internal recipients. If external, this is basically a courier.

Stationery such as letterheads, reports, minutes, invoices and memos will be made available to those members of staff who need them. Usually the only restrictions on this type of document might be that business cards should be passed directly to the person named on them.

Promotional material such as catalogues, brochures and leaflets may be for general distribution to the general public, customers or potential customers. These may be distributed as printed documents or electronically as email attachments. If they are to be distributed to a specific list of customers, you will need access to a distribution list in order to send them to everyone who should get them and to avoid sending them to anyone who your organisation doesn't want to receive them.

Forms may be for use by particular departments or for general use. For instance, purchase orders will be specific to the purchasing department in organisations which have one, but in smaller organisations may be used by a number of departments, while invoices may be used by the sales department or the accounts department.

An email distribution list provides an easy way to send messages to a group of people. For instance, if you regularly send messages to the marketing team, you can create a distribution list called 'Marketing team' that contains the names of the members of the marketing team. A message sent to this distribution list goes to all recipients listed in the distribution list. You can easily add and delete names in a distribution list, send it to others, and print it.

> **HANDY HINT**
>
> Keep distribution lists up to date as a priority – sending communications to people who no longer need them or, worse, failing to send communications to people who do need them, can be very annoying.

A customer reading

An example of a brochure

For hard copy documents, there may be a distribution list which is used for all instances of similar documents such as catalogues being produced. It is important that this is kept up to date, with new recipients added, recipients deleted who are no longer relevant and addresses being amended when information is received. Individual one-off documents such as memos will have a specific distribution list for use on only the one occasion.

Final documents will need to be produced in the medium which is appropriate to the reader. The most effective method of communication will vary from organisation to organisation. For example, some organisations may use written communication for tangible goals such as making directives clear, while others will use email to help simplify communication with employees. For some, motivational messages may be better delivered through verbal communications, while for organisations whose staff is largely telecommuting or spread out throughout the country, email is a more reliable and consistent method of communication.

MANAGING BUSINESS INFORMATION

When you are asked to find information, the person making the request will have an objective in mind and a deadline for receiving the information. It is important that you understand what these are. Once you understand the objective and the deadline involved, you will be able to identify whether you are carrying out primary or secondary research. These are explored in greater depth in Chapter 11 (Unit 211, B&A 23).

The types of information found in business organisations include:

- Customer information such as names, addresses, contact details, agreed terms and conditions, and previous purchase information.

- Staff information such as names, addresses, dates of birth, sex, education and qualifications, work experience, National Insurance numbers, tax codes, details of any known disabilities, emergency contact details, employment history, employment terms and conditions, any accidents connected with work, training taken and any disciplinary action.

- Finance information such as payroll, sales, purchases, stock, banking records, etc.

- Products/services information such as price lists, stock records, catalogues and specifications.

- Legal information such as the organisation's articles of association, shareholder register, etc.

- Operational information such as confidential records and legally required records.

Assessment criteria

This section covers assessment criteria 3.1, 3.2, 3.3 and 3.4

If you cannot find information on which the completion of a task depends, the task will be delayed with possible serious consequences. The purpose of storing information is to be able to retrieve it when it is needed. An effective information storage and retrieval system enables you to find complete, accurate and up-to-date information so that you can make decisions based on all the available information. Storing information is much more than simply keeping papers or saving electronic files. If there is no system for retrieving the information when it is required, the information is likely to be lost or difficult to find. This will inevitably lead to problems such as a waste of time and money and, possibly eventually, a loss of business.

Storage of information may be:

- on- or off-site
- on a desktop computer
- on an external hard drive
- on a network hard drive
- on a USB flash drive
- web-based
- in paper form.

Many organisations are moving towards a more general use of electronic information systems rather than the more traditional paper-based ones. To decide which is more appropriate in a given situation, you need to ask:

- What information needs to be stored? If the information is recorded currently on paper, it may be best to store it as paper. If the information is electronic, there is no point in printing it simply to store it as paper.
- Who is the information used by? If the people needing access to the information are situated in different locations, electronic records may be accessible to all of them via a shared server, whereas paper documents would have to be copied for each of them.
- How often is the information amended? Information which needs regular updating, such as customer names and addresses, may be best stored electronically as it is easier to amend than paper records which may need completely recreating to record the change.
- How is the information used? Some information, such as legal records including deeds, wills, contracts, etc may depend for its **validity** on signatures and witnesses' signatures. While these documents could be scanned into an electronic filing system, the original will need to be retained in case of any future dispute.

Validity

Having binding force in law

Once the decision has been taken whether to use paper-based or electronic information systems, you need to choose between the various different filing methods. There may be organisational policies or procedures already in place which will determine which are used.

FILING METHODS

ALPHABETICAL

Alphabetic filing systems group information together using the letters A–Z. Any type of information can be filed alphabetically and can be readily retrieved as long as certain rules are agreed and adhered to. If the information is to be filed under a person's name, it is usual to file it by reference to the surname followed by the forename. For instance if filing records for Ann Johnson, Anne Johnson and Amy Johnson, the sequence would be:

- Johnson, Amy
- Johnson, Ann
- Johnson, Anne.

Titles such as Mr, Mrs, Miss, Dr, Prof or Sir are ignored for this purpose. If, for instance, Amy Johnson were a doctor, her entry would be Johnson, Dr Amy, but she would still be filed before Johnson, Ann.

Alphabetical sequence needs to be strictly followed, so that records for McDougal, MacManus and Manning would be filed in the sequence:

- MacManus
- Manning
- McDougal.

Surnames that include 'St' as an abbreviation of 'Saint' should be filed as if the 'Saint' were spelt in full. Records for St John, Saint, Sampson and Sabberton would be filed in the sequence:

- Sabberton
- Saint
- St John
- Sampson.

Company names are filed under the full company name, so Amy Johnson Ltd, Amy Johnson Hairdressers and Amy Johnson & Co would be filed in the sequence:

- Amy Johnson & Co
- Amy Johnson Hairdressers
- Amy Johnson Ltd.

ACTIVITY

Sort the following into alphabetical order:

- Maroon 5
- Lianne La Havas
- The View
- Adele
- Linkin Park
- Lana Del Rey
- Train
- Jessie J
- J-Z & Kanye West
- Noel Gallagher's High Flying Birds
- One Direction
- Florence + The Machine
- Beady Eye
- Green Day.

COMMON MISTAKE

Filing names such as McTavish as if they were spelt MacTavish

Cross-referencing

A reference from one part of a file to another part containing related information

ACTIVITY

Sort the following into numerical order:

095673

0345

008485

123

45

99984754

ACTIVITY

Sort the following into alpha-numerical order:

PR9 9TY

PR9 6FA

PR9 9FA

CW5 5NA

CW2 5NA

CW6 1DE

Company names that consist solely of initials such as BBC, AA or RAC are filed at the beginning of the section for their first letter. Records for BBC, Barber & Co, BT and Burrows Ltd would be filed in the sequence:

- BBC
- BT
- Barber & Co
- Burrows Ltd.

The advantage of alphabetical storage of information is that, as long as the rules are agreed and understood by everyone involved, there is no difficulty in locating information. There is no need for any form of **cross-referencing.** The disadvantage is that names are not unique, so there may be two or more Michael Johnsons in the system. To retrieve the information on a particular Michael Johnson you would need to refer to another piece of information such as a middle name, date of birth or address.

NUMERICAL

Numerical filing is used for any information where the most important reference to it is its number, for example, invoices and purchase orders. The important thing to remember when creating a numerical filing system is that there must be sufficient digits in the system if electronic information systems are to be used. A computer will read numbers from left to right as if the digits were individual letters, so 111 will be read as starting with 1 while 27 will be read as starting with 2 and therefore stored after 111. To avoid this problem, if the numbers 000111 and 000027 are used, the computer will get it in the right order.

The advantage of a numerical system is that every number is unique and you can store and retrieve an infinite number of documents without ever duplicating their file name. The disadvantage is that if you don't know the number of the file you are looking for, there is no easy way to find it without a cross-referencing system.

ALPHA-NUMERICAL

Alpha-numerical filing is used where the file name consists of letters and numbers. The postal codes used in the United Kingdom are known as postcodes. A typical UK postcode may read as MK41 8LA. MK refers to the postcode area, as the letters at the beginning are based on letters from a city, town or district in the area. There are 120 postcode areas in the UK. MK41 refers to the district within the area. There are 2,900 districts within the country. The 8 in the second set of characters refers to the postcode sector. There are about 9,000 of these sectors. The final two characters are the postcode unit and define a group of about 15 properties within the sector, which could be a street, part of a street or even an individual large user. It is estimated that there are 1.6 million postcode units in the UK to cover 24 million delivery points.

Some special delivery points such as Buckingham Palace and the House of Commons have postcodes that may **differentiate** them from surrounding areas because of the large volume of mail that these sites receive from around the world.

GEOGRAPHICAL

Geographical filing is used where the information needs to be grouped with reference to its location within a country or region. For instance information will be divided into countries, sub-divided by region or county and then by town or city. So an address in Churchtown, Southport, Lancashire, England would be filed under:

- England
- Lancashire
- Southport
- Churchtown.

Within each division or sub-division information will be stored alphabetically.

The advantage of a geographical filing system is that information can be retrieved more easily covering a geographic area rather than having to extract specific information from an alphabetic system that covers the whole world or the whole country.

SUBJECT

Filing by subject is used where access to the information is needed by reference to its subject. Probably the most common example of filing by subject is the system used in reference libraries, where all the books about plumbing will be stored on one shelf and all the books about fishing will be on another. Similarly, information stored electronically may be stored in folders by subject.

The advantage of filing by subject is that all the information is in one place. If you want information on plumbing, you don't need to know the names of the authors to find it. The disadvantage is that a single piece of information may refer to more than one subject. The question then arises whether to make copies of the information to place in each subject file or to create a cross-referencing system.

CHRONOLOGICAL

Chronological filing simply means storing information in date order. It is mostly used within one of the other systems. For instance, correspondence with Amy Johnson will be placed in her file chronologically, with the most recent on top. This allows a record of events to be built up over a period of time in sequence. Often, people will reply to emails by using the 'reply' option which results in a sequence of emails each replying to the previous one. This creates a form of chronological information storage.

Differentiate

To establish a difference between two things or among several things

Filing by subject

It is important to remember when creating electronic records, that dates must be entered as YYYY/MM/DD if the record is to be stored chronologically. A computer will store 15/04/1971 before 25/12/1963, but will store 1963/12/25 before 1971/04/15.

The advantages of chronological filing are that information can be retrieved in chronological order, allowing you to see how one piece of information influences another and where information is to be deleted after a given period of time, and it is therefore much easier to recognise which information should be destroyed. The disadvantage is that a purely chronological filing system would make it very difficult to trace a particular piece of information if you didn't know the date it originated.

Paper files are stored in filing cabinets, usually in file folders. The two most common types of filing cabinets are vertical files and lateral files. A vertical file cabinet has drawers that extend from the short side of the cabinet. A lateral file cabinet has drawers that extend from the long side of the cabinet.

ACTIVITY

Make a list of the types of information that are stored in your organisation. Place the list in a table showing electronic and paper-based information and the sources of the information.

RETRIEVING INFORMATION

Some information will need to be kept secure and access to it controlled. Retrieval may require permission or the use of a password. This may be because the information is confidential or because it is commercially sensitive. The legal requirement to keep information confidential is covered by the Data Protection Act. The individual about whom data is held has rights which include being allowed to:

- know if data is held about them
- request a copy and description of the data
- inspect the data and have it changed if it is inaccurate
- seek compensation if the data is inaccurate
- know the purpose for which the data is being processed
- know who will have access to the data
- seek compensation if unauthorised access has been permitted
- prevent the processing of data likely to cause damage or distress
- ensure decisions against them are not made only on the basis of automatic processing.

Data subjects have to pay an administration fee to the data protection commissioner to prevent the processing of data or to correct or delete it.

As well as the legal requirement to protect personal information, there will be organisational requirements to keep information confidential. This may be because there is a duty of trust to your clients or customers or because the information would be useful to competitors.

HANDY HINT

Make sure there is a security system that protects confidential files, whether paper or electronic.

When storing or retrieving information it is important to confirm exactly what information is involved, as storing incorrect or unnecessary information is a waste of time and storage space. Retrieving incorrect information can, additionally, cause serious problems for the person you are providing the information to. For example, if someone is working on a contract with a customer whose name is Albert Smith and you provide them with information on Alfred Smith, this could create confusion and a possible loss of business. It is important, therefore, when asked to retrieve information, that you check the accuracy of the information carefully. If asked for a file on 'Albert Smith' you should check a separate piece of information such as the address or date of birth so that you can confirm that you have retrieved the correct file.

In many organisations, there is a system of signing out files so that you will always know where they are. This is extremely useful if someone else requests the file, as you will be able to direct them to the person who currently has it. It also allows you to trace the file should it not be returned when finished with.

It is also necessary to check when asked to retrieve information what format the information is required in and the timescales involved. Your information system will be capable of providing a whole range of information on any requested subject, but it will not be cost effective to produce a wide-ranging report if all that is required is the subject's contact details. For example, if you are asked for the purchase orders raised to a supplier in the last 12 months, it is more likely that what is wanted is a list containing information such as dates, values, etc than a pile of actual purchase orders. While checking this, you can also enquire whether the information should be supplied electronically or printed off. Similarly, if the information is required for an important meeting the following day, it will not be helpful to produce an in-depth dossier that will take three days to collate.

REQUIREMENTS FOR STORING BUSINESS INFORMATION

A frequent issue with the storage of information is the length of time for which it must be retained. The Data Protection Act (1998) says that personal information should not be kept for longer than is necessary, but this is not particularly helpful. There are a number of factors involved in deciding when records may be deleted including:

- legal requirements
- the cost of storage
- the need to refer to the information
- any historical value the information may have.

The last three of these factors will be decided at the organisation's discretion. Many documents that are available for academic research and public interest have survived only because an organisation has decided to retain their records far beyond the point at which they have a need to refer to them or a legal requirement to keep them. If organisations such as Cadbury, Lever Bros and the BBC hadn't kept archives of material from their early days, we would not have access to so much information today.

Outside of the organisation's authority are the legal requirements for retaining records. These apply to accounting records, personnel records, health and safety records, medical records, wills, military records, criminal records, academic records, contracts, etc. You need to know what the legal periods are for retention of any records that you are responsible for, as deleting information before the due date is a serious matter, possibly leading to criminal prosecution for the organisation.

Some examples of records that are kept by most organisations and their retention periods are in the table below.

Record type	Retention period
Income tax and salary records	6 years plus current year
Unsuccessful job applications	6 months after notification
Sickness and statutory maternity pay records	3 years after the end of the tax year
Purchase ledger, invoices and petty cash records	6 years from the end of financial year
Banking records	6 years from the end of financial year
VAT records	6 years
Employer's liability insurance certificate	40 years
Health and safety records	3 years; permanently for records relating to hazardous substances

Archive

A collection of documents such as documents or computer records, kept for future reference

Archiving records involves deciding which files are no longer required to be kept within the active storage system and organising their storage or destruction, depending on retention requirements. Files which are to be retained in a secondary, **archive** filing system should be kept in the same order and using the same system as is used in the live files. This makes them easier to find if necessary, and makes the activity of archiving quicker and simpler. Archiving files regularly:

- speeds up locating files by reducing the number of files in the active filing system
- makes disposal more efficient by reducing the backlog
- reduces the space required for current filing.

Many organisations will use an outside company to manage their archives. This is preferable to an in-house system where records are simply dumped in storerooms, which can lead to:

- vast backlogs of records no one knows about, some of which may be important
- poor storage conditions
- increased storage requirements.

The Freedom of Information Act (2000) applies to all public authorities within the United Kingdom including:

- government departments
- the Houses of Parliament
- the Northern Ireland Assembly
- the Welsh Assembly
- the Armed Forces
- local government bodies
- National Health Service bodies
- schools, colleges and universities
- police authorities
- companies wholly owned by the Crown, a public authority or a government department.

It is described in greater detail in Chapter 9 (Unit 205, B&A 17).

ACTIVITIES

- List the information which is stored in your organisation showing the length of time it must be retained.
- Explain how information is archived in your organisation.
- Explain how confidential information is disposed of when it is no longer required.

An example of a leaflet which was distributed without the content being properly checked caused the Advertising Standards Agency to uphold a complaint about a leaflet entitled 'Don't Run With The Pack', published as part of NHS West Sussex's 'Well Fit' campaign.

The leaflet was left at GP surgeries to advertise nicotine replacement therapy (NRT) to help people give up smoking. It read, 'Did you know that tobacco companies actively target young people to replace older smokers as they die off? Did you know that in some developing countries tobacco companies give out free cigarettes to children and young people to get them hooked? Did you know that you are twice as likely to succeed at stopping if you use NRT? Did you know that you are four times as likely to succeed if you use NRT and see a specialist advisor?' The leaflet also counted smokers who had given up for four weeks as being permanent quitters.

The ASA concluded the claims were 'likely to mislead' and asked the health service to withdraw the advert and that there was not enough evidence to demonstrate tobacco companies were targeting younger people in the UK.

The ASA decided the claim about people stopping smoking was misleading because 'stopping' meant going only four weeks without smoking. Its report said, 'We considered that readers were likely to expect that the references to stopping smoking were based on more permanent cessation and not merely the four-week period used under the NHS definition.'

UNIT 225 (B&A 37): TEST YOUR KNOWLEDGE

Learning outcome 1: Understand how to prepare business documents

1 Describe three different types of document that may be produced in a business environment.

2 Describe ways of integrating text and non-text.

3 Explain why it is important to agree and meet deadlines.

4 Explain why version control is important.

5 Explain what the Data Protection Act enforces.

6 Explain how to check a completed document for accuracy.

Learning outcome 2: Understand the distribution of business documents

1 Explain the importance of confidentiality.

2 State two distribution channels used in your organisation.

Learning outcome 3: Understand how information is managed in business organisations

1 State two reasons why it is important to agree objectives and deadlines before researching information.

2 State two reasons why files should be retained in archives using the same system as is used in the live filing system.

3 Complete the table showing what types of *confidential* information may be found in each type of record.

Types of record	Types of confidential information
Human Resource records	
Accounts records	
Telephone directories	
Register Office records	
Medical records	
Search engine information	

UNIT 226 (B&A 38) UNDERSTAND EMPLOYER ORGANISATIONS

Business is an economic activity for satisfying human wants. We all need food, clothing and shelter, and also have many other requirements to be satisfied. At the simplest level, we meet these requirements from shops, which get their supplies from wholesalers who in turn get them from manufacturers. The shopkeeper, the wholesaler and the manufacturer are doing business. Business means continuous production and distribution of goods and services with the aim of earning profits.

All business activities are directly or indirectly concerned with the exchange of goods or services for money. Business is carried on with the intention of earning a profit, which is a reward for the efforts of the businessman. Business is subject to risks and uncertainties. Some risks can be insured against, but others such as loss due to change in demand or fall in price must be accepted by the businessman.

Modern businesses are conscious of their social responsibility and are now service-oriented rather than profit-oriented. Public sector and voluntary organisations are run for reasons other than to make profit, but to be successful they must be run in a business-like way.

In this unit you will cover the following learning outcomes:

1 understand organisational structures
2 understand the organisational environment.

FRANCHISES

A franchise is created when firms which already have a successful product or service enter into a relationship with other businesses operating under the franchisor's trade name and usually with the franchisor's guidance, in exchange for a fee. Some of the most popular franchises include Subway and McDonalds. Again, the legal form of a franchise can be any of those described above.

A clothes shop is an example of a profit-making organisation

THE PUBLIC SECTOR

The public sector consists of:

- government departments such as the Home Office, the Foreign and Commonwealth Office and Her Majesty's Treasury
- non-ministerial government departments such as the Office for Standards in Education (Ofsted), Her Majesty's Revenue and Customs (HMRC) and the Charity Commission
- executive agencies such as the Food and Environment Research Agency, the Rural Payments Agency and the Maritime and Coastguard Agency
- non-departmental public bodies (NDPB) such as the Environment Agency, Sport England and the Royal Commission on Environmental Pollution
- local authorities such as county councils, district councils and unitary authorities
- public corporations such as the Audit Commission, the BBC and the Civil Aviation Authority
- trusts such as the BMA Medical Educational Trust and the many NHS Trusts.

The voluntary or not-for-profit sector

This comprises all organisations set up to achieve aims other than to make a profit, but not operated by the authorities, for instance charities and groups of people such as Neighbourhood watch.

These will differ in terms of purpose, size, budget, service provided, customers, governance, values and ethics. For instance, the stated purpose of the Home Office is the control of immigration and passports, drugs policy, counter-terrorism and the police; the Charity Commission regulates registered charities in England and Wales and is responsible for maintaining the register of charities and making charities accountable; the Rural Payments Agency provides rural payments, rural inspections and livestock tracing while enforcing the size and shape of vegetables and fruit sold in shops by warning and advising businesses; the Royal Commission on Environmental Pollution is set up to advise the government on environmental pollution; local authorities provide public services such as schools, social services, public transport, council housing, leisure facilities, planning, recycling and refuse collection.

THE VOLUNTARY OR NOT-FOR-PROFIT SECTOR

Organisations which are run for purposes other than to make a profit are often run in much the same way as profit-making organisations. The difference is that their purpose is to raise money to promote a cause. Often they are run by volunteers, although paid staff may be employed for their expertise in fund-raising or carrying on the business operations of the organisation. Among not-for-profit organisations are:

- Charities – these are often registered with the Charity Commission, or in Scotland the office of the Scottish Charity Regulator, and must conform with strict criteria in order to operate as registered charities.

A charity is an example of a non-profit making organisation

ACTIVITY

Research the organisation you are working in. What is its purpose? How did it start/evolve into the organisation it is today?

- Community Interest Companies (CIC) – these are social enterprises set up to tackle a wide range of social and environmental issues. Their surpluses are re-invested for the benefit of the community.
- Trusts – these are legal arrangements where one or more 'trustees' are made legally responsible for holding assets. The assets, such as land, money, buildings, shares or even antiques, are placed in trust for the benefit of one or more 'beneficiaries'. There are other types of trusts set up to operate as charities, or to provide means for employers to create pension schemes for their staff.
- Trade unions – these are organisations of workers who negotiate wages, working conditions and health and safety rules for their members. Their income is derived from members' subscriptions and used for the benefit of members.

ORGANISATIONAL STRUCTURES

Whatever the purpose of the organisation, there must be a structure in place if more than one person is involved. The structure is basically a plan that shows how the organisation will work. Each organisation will have evolved its structure as it has grown. Each organisation's structure is therefore unique, being the result of numerous decisions taken by managements over a period of years.

Organisational structures can be classified into six types. However, these have a certain amount of cross-over, and most organisations will have features of more than one type.

TALL ORGANISATIONS

Tall organisations have many levels of management, although seldom more than eight, and a long chain of command running from the Chief Executive down to the most junior member of staff.

Tall organisations – advantages and disadvantages

Advantages	Disadvantages
■ Staff can be closely supervised	■ Decision-making can be slow
■ Clear management structure	■ High costs of management
■ Clear lines of responsibility	■ Communication can be difficult
■ Clear progression routes	■ Staff have little scope to be innovative

FLAT ORGANISATIONS

Flat organisations have fewer levels of management, sometimes only one, with a short chain of command and a wide span of control.

Flat organisations – advantages and disadvantages

Advantages	Disadvantages
■ Easier decision-making	■ Staff may report to two or more managers
■ Lower costs of management	■ Less opportunity for organisational growth
■ Better communication	■ Strategic decision-making more difficult
■ Better team spirit	

Example of a flat structure

HIERARCHICAL ORGANISATIONS

Hierarchical organisations are a mix of tall and flat structures. The chain of command is typically pyramid shaped. At the top of the pyramid the span of control is narrow, but this gets wider towards the bottom.

Hierarchical organisations – advantages and disadvantages

Advantages	Disadvantages
■ Specialist managers bring expertise to the organisation	■ Can be slow to react to market forces
■ Clear progression routes	■ Communication can be poor
■ Clear lines of responsibility	■ Areas of the business may make decisions which benefit them but not the whole organisation
■ Staff loyalty to their area in the organisation	

Example of a hierarchical structure

CENTRALISED ORGANISATIONS

Centralised organisations have a head office, or a small group of senior managers, where the major decisions are made. In some organisations certain functions such as accounting and purchasing may be centralised to reduce costs and increase economies of scale. The advantages of centralisation are:

- cost savings from standardisation
- decisions taken for the benefit of the whole organisation
- strong leadership
- experienced management.

DE-CENTRALISED ORGANISATIONS

De-centralised organisations spread the responsibility for decision-making to the branches or regions away from head office. Branch managers are given the authority to take decisions that affect only their branch. Regional managers have the authority to make decisions affecting all branches within their region. The advantages of de-centralisation are:

- better motivated staff, producing greater output
- decisions taken in reaction to local factors
- empowered lower management
- senior manager able to concentrate on strategic decisions.

Few organisations will be wholly centralised or wholly de-centralised. It is really a matter of the degree of responsibility given to management in the field to make decisions.

MATRIX

The final type of structure is a matrix. This brings together people from different areas of the organisation to create teams for the purpose of carrying out a specific project. Once the project is complete the team will be dispersed, joining new teams for new projects.

Matrix structure – advantages and disadvantages

Advantages	Disadvantages
■ Problems are dealt with quickly	■ Management costs can be high
■ Team members are chosen for their specialist knowledge	■ More difficult to monitor teams working independently
■ Managers have specific responsibility to complete projects within deadlines and budget	■ Duplication of resources between different teams

There is no perfect structure for any organisation; most will contain a combination of types and will change and evolve this combination over time as the organisation grows.

THE ORGANISATIONAL ENVIRONMENT

It is important for a business to know and understand how it fits in and interacts with the surrounding environment. Researching the business environment will enable the business to develop a strategy for both the long and short term.

Internal influences on a business start from the structure of the organisation and teams within it, as these may delay decision-making. The right kind of leader, which can vary according to purpose and goals, can steer a business toward success or failure. A leader is often expected to be a visionary for a company, leading it toward increased productivity and profits. Leaders can also influence how business is conducted, within the company and with customers and clients. A poor leader can negatively affect a company's performance and operations and can be damaging to the business.

Other internal influences may include the organisation's policies, procedures and systems, its aims and objectives, and its culture. Different organisations have a distinctive culture, which simply means the way they see and do things. Organisations build up their own

ACTIVITIES

Find examples of organisations whose structures are:

- tall
- flat
- hierarchical
- centralised
- de-centralised
- matrix.

Select one and explain the reasons this is the most appropriate structure for this organisation.

Assessment criteria

This section covers assessment criteria 2.1, 2.2 and 2.3

Merger

The combining of two or more independent corporations under a single ownership

Acquisition

An action in which a company buys most, if not all, of another company's assets in order to assume control

culture through their tradition, history and structure. Culture gives the organisation a sense of identity, defining who they are, what they stand for and what they do.

Partnerships can have a major influence on businesses. They may include **mergers**, **acquisitions**, internal partnerships between departments or external partnerships with like-minded companies that decide to join together for a specific product or cause. Partnerships can be valuable in leading to a broader customer base.

MODELS OF ANALYSIS

PESTLE ANALYSIS

Businesses operate in an external environment in which, as well as competition from rivals, they have to take account of political, economic, social, technological, legal and environmental influences (PESTLE).

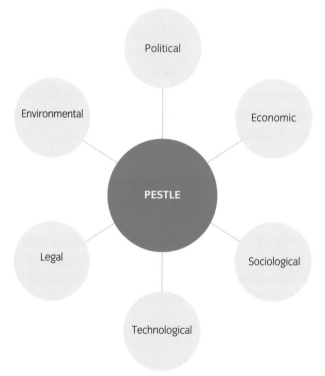

The components of a PESTLE analysis

A PESTLE analysis considers:

- Political – what is happening politically, eg with regards to tax policies and employment laws.
- Economic – what is happening within the economy, eg economic growth or decline, minimum wage, unemployment, cost of living.
- Sociological – what is happening socially, eg health consciousness, population growth rate.
- Technological – new technologies are continually being developed.

- Legal – changes to legislation which may affect employment, access to materials, resources, imports and exports, taxation etc.

- Environmental – what is happening with respect to ecological and environmental issues. Many of these factors will be economic or social in nature.

PORTER'S FIVE FORCES

Another framework for looking at external influences is Porter's Five Forces. The framework includes an analysis of five forces that affect a business's ability to compete. The five forces are:

- Threats of substitute products from competitors, including product differentiation, price performance of substitutes and a buyer's ability to switch to a substitute.

- Threat of the entry of new competitors, such as barriers to entry brand control, government regulation and capital requirements.

- Intensity of competitive rivalry, such as the number of competitors, economies of scale, diversity and depth among competitors and information complexity.

- Bargaining power of customers, such as concentration of marketing channels, buyer volumes, prohibitive switching costs to buyers and availability of competitive substitutes.

- Bargaining power of suppliers, such as prohibitive switching costs, availability of alternative suppliers, degree of labour solidarity and the sensitivity of selling price to supply costs.

SWOT ANALYSIS

To analyse the position of the business in its environment, one of the most common ways is to perform a strengths, weaknesses, opportunities and threats (SWOT) analysis of the business.

Strengths provide an awareness of business opportunities, while weaknesses in the business can cause immediate threats. The SWOT analysis is based on known information and is seen as the more basic approach of analysing the position of the business, but SWOT is a powerful tool to look for immediate benefits.

The best way to approach the analysis is to recognise the strengths and weaknesses before tackling the opportunities and threats. The most important rule is not to leave anything out no matter how small the issue may be. There is no one correct way to do a SWOT analysis, but it should be done in a way that you understand. The objective is to determine a strategy for the future to improve the company's overall performance.

Strengths can be considered as anything that is favourable towards the business for example:

ACTIVITY

Ask your tutor to help you carry out a PESTLE analysis of your organisation or department.

Use a SWOT analysis to analyse the position of the business

- the business has few debts, and is in a good financial position
- there is a skilled workforce, requiring little training
- the company's name is recognised by the public
- up-to-date machinery is installed
- the company owns its premises
- there are excellent transport links
- there is little competition.

When recognising weaknesses, be honest and realistic. Don't leave anything out, as it is important to realise what needs to be done. Examples of weaknesses are:

- the business is in a poor financial position with large debts
- there is an unskilled workforce requiring training
- the company's name is not recognised by the public
- machinery is not up to date and is inefficient
- premises are rented
- lack of transport links
- holding too much or too little stock
- too much waste being generated.

Bearing in mind the listed strengths, SWOT Analysis can now influence the opportunities for the business. These can be seen as targets to achieve in the future for example:

- good financial position creating a good reputation for future bank loans and borrowings
- skilled workforce means that they can be moved and trained into other areas of the business
- competitor going bankrupt may be an opportunity
- increased spending power in the local or national economy
- moving a product into a new market sector.

The final part of the analysis is identifying the threats. Taking into account your weaknesses, the threats will now be apparent, for example:

- large and increasing competition
- rising cost of wages, national minimum wage, etc
- relocation costs due to poor current location
- local authority refusing plans for future building expansion
- increased interest rates increasing borrowing repayments
- end of season approaching if the business is seasonal
- existing products becoming unfashionable or unpopular.

Once the SWOT analysis is complete put it all together and form a strategy. This will involve exploiting the opportunities and eliminating or dealing with the threats. This will depend on the company's original objectives, but the process will give an overall look at the current position.

SWOT analysis is used mainly to evaluate the current position of the business to determine a strategy for the future. Care needs to be taken when planning a strategy not to disturb the strengths, as they become weaknesses if not used.

ACTIVITY

Carry out a SWOT analysis of your organisation or department.

CHANGE IN THE BUSINESS ENVIRONMENT

The most effective organisations are constantly changing as a result of **innovations initiated** from within. These may be the introduction of new ideas or products, for instance:

Innovation

A new invention or way of doing something

Initiate

To cause something, especially an important event or process, to begin

- Creating value from ideas which save money or increase income. An example would be supermarkets expanding their range to include clothing or electrical items.

- New ways of satisfying customers, which increase sales. An example would be providing a computerised room design service in a furniture store.

- Improved product design as a result of carrying out a sales review. An example would be the iPhone 4 replacing the iPhone 3.

Other drivers of change include:

- Change in market share – increases in market share can improve profitability. Organisations try to expand their share of the market, as well as trying to grow the size of the total market by appealing to larger demographics, lowering prices, or through advertising.

- Globalisation – globalisation has increased the production of goods and services as the biggest organisations are no longer national firms but multinational corporations with subsidiaries in many countries. Globalisation has resulted in increased international trade, greater dependence on the global economy and freer movement of capital, goods and services.

- Sustainability – organisations should methodically analyse the environmental and social impact of the products they use and produce. Organisations that are sustainable attract and retain employees more easily and are more innovative and adaptive to their environments.

Another way in which organisations can change is by improving systems or processes that already exist, such as:

- New organisation structure or new strategies which improve efficiency and save money. An example would be re-organising from a centralised structure to a divisional structure.

- Making something in a different way which saves time or money. An example would be sewing products by machine rather than by hand.

- New ways of carrying out routine activities, perhaps through the introduction of new technology, which save time or money. An example would be computerising the accounts function.

- New approaches to work, which improve efficiency. An example would be introducing **flexi-time**.

The benefits of continually reviewing the existing ways of working are:

- increased efficiency
- increased profitability
- increased productivity
- greater competitiveness
- better use of resources
- reduced costs
- better response to customer requirements
- increased customer satisfaction
- reduction in waste
- more employee involvement.

Flexi-time

A variable work schedule, in contrast to traditional work arrangements, requiring employees to work a standard 9am to 5pm day

CASE STUDY
DRIVING CHANGE

Carey May, the office manager at Bullion Loading Ltd, has seen an advertisement for a photocopier which claims to be much more efficient than the model currently in use in the office. She thinks that by buying this new equipment she will be able to save enough on her stationery budget to justify the capital expense (the money spent on assets that have a useful life of more than one year) involved. She goes to see her director who asks her to put together a business case (justification for initiating a task or project) showing how the new equipment will save money in comparison to the existing model.

Carey decides to monitor the use of the existing photocopier for a month. This will allow her to put together comparative figures which will show where savings can be made by replacing the photocopier. At the end of the month she is surprised to find that a significant portion of the cost is actual wastage. This is caused by people not checking the quality setting or the quantity setting before starting a job and changing cartridges unnecessarily. She calculates that eliminating this will actually save more money than replacing the machine.

Carey decides to give a presentation at the next team meeting where she will demonstrate just how much this wastage is costing. She offers an incentive to the staff to reduce this wastage by 20%, calculating that the cost of the reward will be much less than the amount saved. After three months, the cost has been greatly reduced and the director gives Carey a bonus for saving on expenses without the need for capital expenditure.

UNIT 226 (B&A 38): TEST YOUR KNOWLEDGE

Learning outcome 1: Understand organisational structures

1 State two differences between organisations in the private sector and those in the public sector.

2 State the difference between a partnership and a corporation.

Learning outcome 2: Understand the organisational environment

1 State three external influences on your organisation.

2 Explain what is meant by a SWOT analysis.

3 Explain why change is important.

UNIT 239 (M&L 1) MANAGE PERSONAL PERFORMANCE AND DEVELOPMENT

Improving your performance in the way that you carry out your responsibilities will show your employers that you are capable of taking on further responsibility, leading to promotion, bonuses and increases in pay. As you gain experience of more responsible tasks you will be able to use this experience in future situations.

Taking greater responsibility will make your job more interesting, give you greater variety of tasks and make your work more satisfying. This will help to create a happier atmosphere in the team, which will have a motivational effect on your colleagues and help them to work better.

In this unit you will cover the following learning outcomes:

1   be able to manage personal performance
2   be able to manage own time and workload
3   be able to identify own development needs
4   be able to fulfil a personal development plan.

MANAGING YOUR PERSONAL PERFORMANCE

Producing work of a high standard is essential; your manager will provide an indication of the standards that are expected of you. This will include the time to complete the task and the style or format to be used as well as objectives that align with business needs, which you will need to agree with your line manager.

Objectives provide focus and clear direction, and should be SMART: specific, measurable, achievable, realistic and time-bound.

Specific	Clear, unambiguous, straightforward, understandable
Measurable	Related to quantified or qualitative performance measures
Achievable	With known resources
Realistic	Linked to business needs
Time-bound	Building-in completion date and review dates

Setting yourself always to complete work to a high standard can help you monitor your own performance and identify areas where you need to improve. Completing your work to a high standard will create a good impression of you and your work. It will also increase your confidence in your role.

You will be expected to produce a high standard of performance consistently. When being set a task to complete, ensure you are clear about what is required and when. Refer to previous examples to make sure you are using the correct **house style**. Concentrate on one task at a time, so you can complete it to the required standard, before moving on to the next.

It is important to measure progress towards objectives with your line manager because this will provide information on whether objectives are being achieved, allowing any adjustments or improvements to be carried out if required. Monitoring performance with your line manager will provide information for your appraisal or performance review. The criteria for measuring progress will depend upon the SMART objectives.

House style

A set of rules concerning spellings, typography, etc

ACTIVITY

List any issues that might prevent you completing tasks to a high standard. Take action to deal with the issue, or speak to your supervisor or line manager about how it can be dealt with.

COMPLETING TASKS

When accepting a new task, make sure the target for completing it is realistic when other tasks you already have are taken into account. An individual task may take three hours to complete, but you will only be able to agree to complete it in three hours' time if you have nothing else which must be done by that time.

Planning your work a day and a week ahead will help you make sure that you can agree realistic deadlines and meet them. Each day's plan should list the tasks to be completed that day, in order of their importance, together with an estimate of how long each will take and the deadline for its completion. This will alert you immediately to any task that you might not be able to complete on time.

Everyone will make mistakes occasionally. Mistakes should be looked upon as an opportunity to learn and improve. The important thing is to admit to your mistake as soon as you realise you have made it, and do whatever is necessary to rectify it. Denying your fault, or hoping nobody will notice, will only lead to more problems in the future when your mistake is discovered.

You may be given a deadline which at the time seems reasonable but is actually unrealistic; other things have come along and it has now become unlikely that you will meet the target deadline.

Telling your manager or colleague that you are struggling to meet a deadline is not an admission of incompetence. Your colleagues would much rather you tell them you are struggling than cover it up with excuses. They may be relying on your task to be completed on time and the earlier you ask for help the better. Explain what the problem is and you will get help in completing the work.

It is your responsibility to complete tasks to agreed timescales and **quality standards**. The quality standard used will depend on the organisation but the basis of all of them is that the features affecting quality are capable of being tested. It is up to you to recognise any problems that may arise which will put satisfactory completion at risk and take the necessary steps to overcome them.

RESOLVING AND REPORTING PROBLEMS

It is unlikely that you will go very long without encountering some kind of problem. These might involve:

- other staff being on holiday or sick leave, requiring you to cover their tasks as well as your own
- problems with equipment, for instance a jammed photocopier or a power cut
- a shortage of necessary stationery to complete the task
- an unusually high level of urgent tasks being required at the same time.

Problems with personal performance may arise for a variety of reasons, such as:

- unfair or unclear expectations as to the task or your role
- medical issues
- personal or family issues
- job dissatisfaction
- workplace conflict
- inadequate knowledge or skills.

Many of the problems that arise will be similar to those you have experienced before, and you will have developed strategies to deal with them. You may be able to take straightforward action to resolve the problem without involving your supervisor or line manager.

The best-laid plans sometime break down and progress may be affected by circumstances beyond your control. Keeping your line manager and colleagues informed about the progress of your work ensures they know what you have done and what you are able to complete. Your job role fits in with lots of others who may be depending on the completion of a particular task by you before they can proceed with their own.

Communicating how you are progressing through tasks will demonstrate that you are aware of the wider impact on the organisation. Delays could have a negative impact on the business as well as your personal performance if they are not flagged up early enough. Your organisation might lose sales, lose customers or in certain circumstances their reputation could be damaged. Letting other people know that work plans need to be changed provides an opportunity for them to discuss a solution such as extending the deadline or reassessing how the work can be completed.

Informing people of problems early on will help prevent delays further down the line

There are six stages to problem solving:

1 Identify the problem – you need to be able to recognise that there is a problem. It may have been pointed out to you that you or your team are not meeting targets or providing services to the standard expected.

2 Define the effects of the problem – if the problem has been pointed out to you, you will probably have been told the effect. If you have identified the problem yourself, you may need to investigate the effects.

3 Find the cause of the problem – you may need to investigate by asking other people in order to find out whether the problem has been a result of your failure or theirs.

4 Identify possible solutions – a one-off problem will require a short-term solution. A continuing problem will need a longer-term solution. Once you have analysed the cause of the problem you will be able to identify alternative ways of resolving it. These may include re-planning or re-prioritising your own work.

5 Choose between the solutions – look at the advantages and disadvantages of each solution, from the viewpoint of the whole organisation, not just yourself or your team. Select the solution with the most advantages and fewest disadvantages and set objectives that will deliver a solution that solves the problem.

6 Plan the way forward – make sure everyone involved agrees that the chosen solution is the best solution. This will help to obtain their commitment when planning the next steps.

It may be that the solution you have identified is beyond your **competence** or the limit of your authority to implement. This may be because the solution has financial or health, safety or security implications, impacts on the reputation of the organisation with external customers, may require a deadline to be met that is not in your power to achieve or may require the help of colleagues that are not within your authority to direct.

Competence

The ability of an individual to carry out a task properly to the required standard

Authority may be:

- line authority, which reflects the organisational hierarchy

- staff authority, the right to advise or assist those who possess line authority as well as other staff personnel

- functional authority, which is given to individuals who, in order to meet responsibilities in their own areas, must be able to exercise some control over organisation members in other areas.

Authority

The right to act in certain ways designated by the organisation and to directly influence the actions of others through instructions

Where solutions are beyond your authority you should refer the problem to your line manager or the department that has the authority to implement the solution. You will need to know who you should refer these kinds of problem to, and what the recognised procedure is for doing so.

MANAGING TIME AND WORKLOAD

Examples of time management tools and techniques include:

- Covey Time (Task) Management Matrix, which is explained in detail in Chapter 3 (Unit 225, B&A 37).
- 'to-do' list (monthly, weekly, daily)
- scheduling tasks and activities
- diary, paper-based or electronic
- bespoke time-management documentation or software.

One way to manage your time at work is to start your day the night before. Make a note of things you need to do. Think about the important things that you should work on for the day and reduce the things that are most likely to be time wasting. Wake up early and get an early start. Most people are more creative in the morning. It makes sense because after a good night's rest you should be feeling fresh and ready to go. If the house is quiet it creates a good environment to help you focus on things that are important to do.

When you are at work, take note of things that take up your time without you noticing. Distractions that are likely to limit the effective management of time and the achievement of objectives include:

- telephone interruptions
- colleagues dropping in without appointments
- meetings, both scheduled and unscheduled
- lack of objectives, priorities, and deadlines
- cluttered desk and personal disorganisation
- involvement in routine and detail that should be delegated to others
- unclear, or lack of, communication and instruction
- inability to say 'no'.

MINIMISING DISTRACTIONS

Take action to minimise disruptions. Make a note of these activities and try to eliminate them totally. Once you have done that, you find that you get more things done in a shorter time. Guard against over-promising. If you feel that you cannot do the work because of time constraints, politely ask for help. Keep your workplace and the things around you organised. Keep the things you need frequently near to you in order to reduce frustration and lost time.

Work on one thing at a time. It is better to focus and place all your energy at the task at hand, rather than spreading yourself and trying to

Your work area should be kept tidy and organised

work on several tasks at once. Time management is about getting the important things done and doing things efficiently so you can achieve more. If your head is full of confusion, you won't get as much done. Write down everything you need to do. If you're working on a task and something else pops into your head, write it down.

Write down the most important things you need to do tomorrow. Return phone calls during a certain time period and carry out all your computer work within a certain time period. It takes time to switch tasks so you'll save time by doing like activities together. Organise your surroundings. You'll save time if you don't have to step over and look through clutter. Try to find a quicker, more efficient way to do things. Talk to a friend or colleague to come up with ideas.

Your supervisor can also help you to manage your time at work by agreeing with you how long particular tasks should take and giving you training so that you can complete the tasks more quickly and with less help from your colleagues. Some tasks may be completed more quickly by using ICT instead of doing them by hand or on paper.

ACTIVITY

Keep a list of the interruptions to your work over a period of a week. Analyse them to identify those that you could actively prevent.

COMMON MISTAKE

Don't think that the people who are last to leave the office each day are the most productive – they may simply be unorganised.

WORK-LIFE BALANCE

Your work–life balance is very important to a healthy lifestyle. An important aspect of this is the amount of time you spend at work. Evidence suggests that long work hours may impair personal health, jeopardize safety and increase stress. Overall, men spend more hours in paid work and the percentage of male employees working very long hours is more than double the percentage of women.

There are benefits to the employer and to the employee from achieving an acceptable work–life balance.

Work-life balance does not necessarily mean an equal balance. Trying to schedule an equal number of hours for each of your various work and personal activities is unrewarding and unrealistic. Life is and should be more fluid than that. Your best individual work–life balance will vary over time, often on a daily basis. The right balance for you today will probably be different for you tomorrow. The correct balance for you when you are single will be different when you marry, or if you have children; when you start a new career versus when you are nearing retirement.

Benefits of a work–life balance

Employer benefits include:	Employee benefits include:
Reduced staff turnover	Reduction in the impact of work on home and family life and vice versa
Lower recruitment and training costs, due to decreased turnover	Reduced stress levels and higher levels of well-being
Reduced absenteeism due to higher levels of well-being	Control over time management in meeting work–life commitments
Gaining a reputation as a good employer or an employer of choice	Autonomy to make decisions regarding work–life balance
Better attraction and retention of staff	Increased focus, motivation and job satisfaction knowing that family and work commitments are being met
Reduced stress levels amongst staff	Increased job security from the knowledge that an organisation understands and supports workers with family responsibilities
Improved morale and job satisfaction amongst staff	
Greater staff loyalty and commitment	
Improved productivity	

A good work–life balance benefits both the employee and the employer

The more people work, the less time they have to spend on other activities, such as personal care or leisure. The amount and quality of leisure time is important for people's overall well-being, and can bring additional physical and mental health benefits. The average person devotes 62% of the day, or close to 15 hours, to personal care (eating, sleeping, etc) and leisure (socialising with friends and family, hobbies, games, computer and television use, etc). Fewer hours in paid work for women do not necessarily result in greater leisure time, as time devoted to leisure is roughly the same for men and women.

People spend one-tenth to one-fifth of their time on unpaid work. The distribution of tasks within the family is still influenced by gender roles: men are more likely to spend more hours in paid work, while women spend longer hours in unpaid domestic work. This trend, obviously, varies from family to family and is slowly changing.

IDENTIFYING YOUR PERSONAL DEVELOPMENT NEEDS

The purpose of continuously improving your own performance at work is, initially, to make sure that, as far as possible, you are secure in your current employment. In addition to this, from an organisational perspective, improving your own performance will have an effect on the performance of your team and, ultimately, the whole organisation. This will lead to greater efficiency, an improved service to your customers and cost savings. These, in turn, will further increase the security of your own employment and that of your colleagues.

An indirect benefit of being more efficient is that you will enjoy your work more, as it is always more motivating to feel that you are doing well than to feel that you are struggling to keep up with the demands of your job. Organisational policies relating to personal development will vary, depending upon the type and nature of the organisation, but may include:

- staff development policy
- training and development policy
- professional development policy
- organisational and professional development policy.

Analysing your own role and personal and team objectives identifies your future development needs for your career development and also for effective performance in your current role. In order to recognise where there is room for improvement, you will need to look at your current performance against internal documents such as job descriptions, person specifications, personal development plans, business plans, team plans and objectives, etc.

HANDY HINT

There is no perfect, one-size-fits-all balance you should be striving for. The best work–life balance is different for each of us because we all have different priorities and different lives.

ACTIVITY

Keep a record of the number of hours you spend working and the number of hours you spend on other activities.

Assessment criteria

This section covers assessment criteria 3.1, 3.2, 3.3, 3.4, 3.5 and 3.6

HANDY HINT

Be adaptable and willing to consider taking on anything that is asked of you.

Performance appraisals are a good opportunity to discuss your development needs

HANDY HINT

Keep a work diary to refer back to during your appraisal.

In most organisations there will be a system of formal one-to-one recorded reviews with the line manager, which will lead to a plan for future development. Performance appraisals are often annual events whose purposes include:

- clarification of job roles
- measurement of performance
- defining priorities and objectives
- resolving confusions and misunderstandings
- agreeing aims and targets
- identifying strengths and weaknesses
- identifying training needs
- delegation of additional responsibilities
- career planning.

The key is to prepare for the meeting well in advance. Keep notes between appraisals of your achievements as well as explanations for situations where things have not been carried out successfully despite your best intentions. Try to anticipate the topics that may be raised and prepare facts about them. Prepare some topics of your own that you want to raise. If an issue is raised that you don't have a ready-made plan to address, ask for time to think about it. Agree a future time when you will come back with the answer, and make sure you meet the deadline.

The performance appraisal should not be a one-way conversation. It is not intended to be an opportunity for your line manager to point out your faults. Ideally it is an opportunity for you and your line manager to measure your performance and ensure it remains in line with organisational goals and your own goals. If your performance fails to meet your manager's expectations, you have an opportunity to discuss this and set goals together to get your performance back on track. Hopefully, the appraisal will identify that you are meeting and, possibly, exceeding your existing targets and will enable you to look at opportunities to take on greater responsibilities.

The performance appraisal will generate a learning plan and formal feedback which should identify specific topics or issues. The feedback may be positive, detailing targets that have been met or exceeded or improvements that have been made since the previous appraisal, or negative, identifying areas of concern and the action needed to address them.

ENCOURAGING AND ACCEPTING FEEDBACK

Of course, it will be difficult to recognise where you need to improve unless you receive feedback. Feedback can come from your line manager, your colleagues or your customers. Feedback is important to keep you informed as to how well you are doing and to help you improve. Don't think that you have to wait for your annual appraisal in order to receive feedback. You are probably receiving informal feedback all of the time without realising it. This may be in the form of:

- Comments from customers. When a customer says 'thank you very much, you have been very helpful, that's exactly what I was looking for' they are giving you feedback.

- Approval from colleagues. When a colleague specifically asks for you to complete a task because you are recognised as the 'expert', they are giving you feedback.

- Daily encouragement from your line manager. If you are thanked for your contribution when you get ready to leave at the end of the day, you are being given feedback.

If you don't feel that you are receiving enough informal feedback, you may need to ask for more formal feedback. In this case, you need to be prepared in order to get the most out of the opportunity. Know what you want to achieve from the meeting. You may want feedback on your general performance, your job security or your future prospects, but you need to be specific if you are to get **constructive feedback**. Ask questions that will provoke useful answers; for instance, if you are looking for advancement, ask 'is there an opportunity for me to work towards perhaps a Level 3 unit within my apprenticeship?'

You may feel reluctant to seek feedback for a number of reasons:

- You may not want to bother your line manager. You may be working on the principle that no news is good news; if there were something wrong with your work you would have heard about it. The problem with this is that your manager may have concerns about your work but they haven't become a priority. If you ask for feedback, you may get the opportunity to improve before it becomes a major issue.

- You may be worried about the quality of your work. You may think that by not asking, you will be able to deflect criticism when it arrives by saying that you had not been told that there was a problem. This leads you to worry continuously about your work, always waiting for the day that you are told it is unacceptable. If you ask for feedback, if there is an issue you will be able to deal with it and, you may be pleasantly surprised to find that your line manager is perfectly satisfied with what you are doing. Either way, you will be able to stop worrying about it.

COMMON MISTAKE

Don't see negative feedback as personal criticism.

HANDY HINTS

- When asked for feedback, make sure it is constructive.
- View all feedback positively.

Constructive feedback

Feedback which involves telling the person what you think they can improve on and then providing an example or a suggestion

- The only feedback you ever get may be negative. Some people find it difficult to give feedback, which tends to mean that the only time they do is to point out areas of concern. If you ask for feedback you will force them into commenting on all of your work and, again, you may find that they are happy with far more of it than they are unhappy with.

- You may feel the feedback you get is worthless. A comment such as 'everything is fine' may be reassuring, but it isn't very helpful. If this is the kind of feedback you get, you need to ask specific questions so that you get the specific feedback you are looking for.

Whether you receive feedback informally or formally, the important thing is how you react to it. Constructive feedback may be positive or negative or, most often, a combination of the two. It is important that you take a balanced view of the feedback you receive. People who have high self-esteem will tend to hear the positive feedback and ignore the negative, while people who have lower self-esteem will react in the opposite manner.

Properly given, feedback should be about performance, not personality, so when receiving feedback you should not allow emotions to be part of your reaction. A positive attitude is required in order to listen carefully to what is being said, to take the time to consider the value of the feedback, and to ask the person giving the feedback on how you can improve.

It is fine to give yourself a pat on the back for the achievements that have been recognised as long as you also note the areas that need improvement. Dwelling on the negative feedback will be bad for your morale so use the feedback to plan improvements that you can achieve. It will be a boost to your morale when you are able to carry out the plan successfully.

PERSONAL DEVELOPMENT

The potential business benefits of personal development include:

- improved workplace performance
- linking training and development activities to business needs and career development
- identifying talent and potential in the organisation
- improved staff morale and motivation
- introducing fresh ideas in the organisation
- linking training and development to SMART objectives and performance management.

ANALYSE AREAS OF POTENTIAL IMPROVEMENT OR DEVELOPMENT

The first step to achieving the required improvements in your existing performance and any development opportunities identified in the performance appraisal is to analyse your training needs using a SWOT analysis. This analysis will have identified the areas for improvement or development.

A SWOT (strengths, weaknesses, opportunities and threats) analysis can help you uncover opportunities that you would not otherwise have spotted. Also, by understanding your weaknesses, you can manage and eliminate threats that might hinder your ability to move forward.

You need to identify your strengths by looking at:

- what advantages you have eg skills, qualifications, education or experience
- what you do better than your colleagues
- what other people see as your strengths
- whether you have any achievements that you are proud of.

Write down a list of your personal characteristics. Some of these will hopefully be strengths. Be as objective as you can.

Next, look at your weaknesses, which might include:

- tasks you usually avoid because you don't feel confident doing them
- what other people see as your weaknesses
- where you lack training, skills or experience
- your negative work habits eg poor timekeeping, lack of organisation, a short temper, poor at handling stress
- personality traits such as a fear of public speaking.

Consider your weaknesses from a personal point of view, but also consider whether other people see weaknesses that you don't. Be realistic – it's best to face any unpleasant truths as soon as possible.

Now look at the opportunities to contribute to team objectives that you have, for instance:

- whether new technology can help you
- where you can get help from others or via the internet
- whether your organisation is growing
- whether you have a network of contacts to offer good advice
- whether there are changes imminent in your organisation you can take advantage of

Carry out a SWOT analysis to identify areas for development

- whether competitors are failing to do something important you can take advantage of
- whether there is a need that no one is meeting
- whether your customers regularly complain about something that you could offer a solution to
- networking events, training courses or conferences you could attend
- a colleague leaving, meaning that you could take on some of their work.

Lastly, look at the threats that may exist, for instance:

- whether there are obstacles at work that prevent your development
- colleagues competing directly with you for projects or roles
- changes to your job role or the need for the things you do
- whether new technology may make your position redundant in the future.

Before completing the SWOT analysis, look at your strengths and ask yourself whether these open up any opportunities. Then look at your weaknesses, and ask yourself whether you could open up opportunities by eliminating them.

CREATE TRAINING NEEDS ANALYSIS

Having completed your SWOT analysis, you will be able to create a training needs analysis to address the weaknesses identified, to take advantage of the opportunities and to deal with the threats. It is important that while identifying these areas, the opportunities and resources needed to address them are also identified. The objectives must be realistic and the timescales achievable.

You will want to concentrate on the development opportunities identified in order to move on to the next stage of your career, but it is important that you deal with the required improvements to your current performance first. Until you are able to satisfy your line manager that you are fully competent to carry out your existing job role, you will not be in a position to be put forward for advancement to a more demanding job role.

LEARNING STYLES

The best way to identify which are the most appropriate opportunities for you is to recognise your learning style. The two most common learning styles models are the Fleming VARK learning model, and Honey and Mumford's adaptation of Kolb's experiential model. In the Fleming VARK model, learners are recognised as being inclined to one of four learning styles, unconsciously giving that style preference. The four learning styles are:

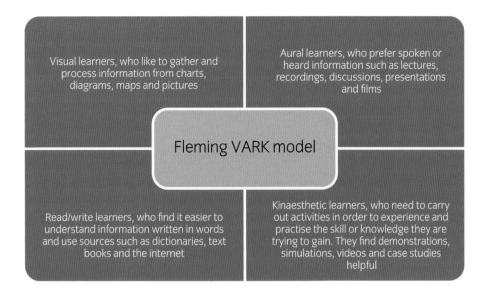

Fleming VARK model

- Visual learners, who like to gather and process information from charts, diagrams, maps and pictures
- Aural learners, who prefer spoken or heard information such as lectures, recordings, discussions, presentations and films
- Read/write learners, who find it easier to understand information written in words and use sources such as dictionaries, text books and the internet
- Kinaesthetic learners, who need to carry out activities in order to experience and practise the skill or knowledge they are trying to gain. They find demonstrations, simulations, videos and case studies helpful

In Kolb's model, learning styles are identified as:

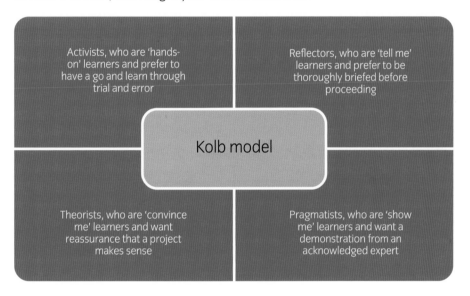

Kolb model

- Activists, who are 'hands-on' learners and prefer to have a go and learn through trial and error
- Reflectors, who are 'tell me' learners and prefer to be thoroughly briefed before proceeding
- Theorists, who are 'convince me' learners and want reassurance that a project makes sense
- Pragmatists, who are 'show me' learners and want a demonstration from an acknowledged expert

Although each of us will have a preferred learning style, in practice a mixture of two, three or even four styles will usually be the most effective.

FULFILLING YOUR PERSONAL DEVELOPMENT PLAN

Having identified your needs you will be able to agree a personal development plan which will list:

- Learning objectives – these will need to be SMART.

- Learning resources and requirements – these will state how the objectives will be achieved and may include in-house training, external training courses, coaching, mentoring, work-shadowing, e-learning and performance appraisals.

ACTIVITIES

- Prepare notes for your next performance appraisal.
- Describe an improvement you have made recently in your performance and the impact this has had on the organisation.
- Explain the benefits to your own job role from the improvement.
- Describe the objectives of your current learning plan.
- List the training you have received in the last 12 months.
- Explain how the training you have received has improved your own work and benefitted the organisation.

Assessment criteria

This section covers assessment criteria 3.7, 4.1, 4.2, 4.3, 4.4 and 4.5

- Responsibilities – who will be responsible for ensuring the learning objectives are met?
- Evaluation – how will the achievement of the objectives be measured?
- Cost – what budget is available to achieve the objective?
- Time – what is the target time for achievement of the objective?

Learning opportunities identified in your personal development plan may include formal and informal methods. Both have advantages and disadvantages.

Informal training results from daily activities related to work, family or leisure, and is not organised or structured in terms of learning outcomes and objectives. Typically, there are no specified training goals as such, nor are there ways to evaluate if the training actually accomplished these goals or not. This type of training and development occurs so naturally that many people probably aren't aware that they're in a training experience at all. Examples of informal training include:

- discussions among employees about a certain topic
- book discussion groups
- reading newspaper and journal articles about a topic
- sending employees to hear prominent speakers.

Working alongside a more experienced colleague is a good way to develop new skills

Informal training is less effective than formal training if you should intentionally be learning a specific area of knowledge or skill. Often little thought is put into what learning is to occur and whether that learning occurred or not. However, this form of training often provides the deepest and richest learning because this form is what occurs naturally in life.

HANDY HINT

Look for and take advantage of every opportunity for informal learning.

Formal training takes place in an organised and structured setting with explicit learning outcomes and objectives, and typically leads to certification or some other recognition that it has been completed to a certain standard. Formal training might include:

- declaring certain learning objectives or an extent of knowledge, skills or abilities that will be reached by learners at the end of the training

- using a variety of learning methods to reach the objectives

- applying some kind(s) of evaluation activities at the end of the training.

Formal training may include internal or external group training sessions

The timescales for different objectives may not be the same. Some objectives can be achieved in a matter of days while others may take weeks or even months. Where it is not possible to identify internal opportunities to develop your skills, you may need to look at resources such as attending your local college on a day release or evening class basis.

REVIEWING PROGRESS

You will need to review your learning plan regularly, in order to check that the objectives are being met within the planned timescales. If the plan has slipped, you will need to identify the reason. This may be that the required resources have not been made available, in which case you may have to discuss with your line manager how this can be addressed. It may be that you didn't allow enough time to continue carrying out your own job while meeting your development objectives. In this case, you will need to agree new timescales for the objectives. Whenever you change your learning plan, you will need to confirm the changes with everybody involved.

COMMON MISTAKE

Thinking that each person has only one preferred learning style.

ACTIVITY

Complete a VARK questionnaire to work out which is/are your preferred learning style(s).

If the objectives have been met, and achievement has been measured, you should be looking at how your new skills can be shared with others for the benefit of yourself and the organisation. Your new skills may improve your performance in your current job role and may allow you to identify further development opportunities which are now available as a result of gaining your new skills.

Reflecting on personal development provides an opportunity to ask such questions as:

- What went well?
- What didn't go well?
- What would I do differently next time?

Sharing lessons learned with others enables successes to be built upon and previous mistakes to be avoided, and may take place, for example, in a performance review or appraisal interview, a learning community, or as part of a review of a development activity.

CASE STUDY
TAKING THE INITIATIVE

Simon is not really very academic. When his results arrive, he has achieved average grades, and is not sure what to do next. The local authority is recruiting filing clerks. Simon applies and starts work at the town hall.

The job is quite dull and he decides to take evening classes to improve his ICT skills. Before his annual appraisal, Simon makes notes about how he feels his first year has gone. He's nervous but anxious to take on more responsibility. His manager's feedback is that Simon has performed well and he asks Simon what he thinks. Simon says he is happy with his own performance but would like the opportunity to take on more complex tasks.

Simon tells his manager he has enrolled in evening classes. He is impressed that Simon has taken this initiative and asks whether he is aware of the apprenticeship scheme which the local authority offers. Simon says he has seen the poster, but he didn't think it would apply to him. He is advised to fill in an application form.

Simon is accepted on the scheme and, two years later, has achieved an apprenticeship and his ICT qualifications. Simon now feels that he has chosen the correct career path and wants to continue to progress, as he can now see a future. When a team leader's position becomes available, Simon applies and is successful as his qualifications, supported by a recommendation from his line manager, who has been impressed by his commitment, make him the best candidate.

UNIT 239 (M&L 1): TEST YOUR KNOWLEDGE

Learning outcome 1: Be able to manage personal performance

1 State one purpose and two benefits of continuously improving performance at work.

2 Explain why it is important to accept responsibility for your own work.

3 Why is it important to report problems that are beyond your level of authority?

Learning outcome 2: Be able to manage own time and workload

1 What is meant by work–life balance?

2 What time management techniques do you use?

3 List two distractions that limit the achievement of your objectives.

Learning outcome 3: Be able to identify own development needs

1 Explain a benefit of:

    a Encouraging feedback from others

    b Accepting feedback from others.

2 Explain your organisation's policies on personal development.

3 What is your preferred learning style?

Learning outcome 4: Be able to fulfil a personal development plan

1 State one way in which learning and development can:

    a Improve your own work

    b Benefit your organisation

    c Identify career options.

2 List five purposes of a performance appraisal.

3 List four headings that would be found on a learning/personal development plan.

CHAPTER 6

UNIT 240 (M&L 2) DEVELOP WORKING RELATIONSHIPS WITH COLLEAGUES

Almost all jobs require some sort of interaction with others. This may include live face-to-face interactions, teleconferences, telephone calls, email, blogs, faxes etc. Tasks that involve working with others may be straightforward with clear rules and routines or they may be more complex where the interaction requires negotiating, dealing with unpredictable situations, goal setting and dealing with complicating factors. Working can involve having your work managed and co-ordinated by others or you may be required to oversee, manage and co-ordinate the work of others. Working as part of a team is much more interesting than working on your own, but it requires a level of co-operation and compromise.

In this unit you will cover the following learning outcomes:

1   understand the principles of effective team working
2   be able to maintain effective working relationships with colleagues
3   be able to collaborate with colleagues to resolve problems.

EFFECTIVE TEAM WORKING

All organisations are made up of a number of teams. During your career you will work in a number of teams, probably more than one team at a time. These teams will be not only within the organisation but may also include contacts such as suppliers, customers and contractors. A team is more than just a group of people working together. The main differences between groups and teams are:

Groups	Teams
Individual responsibility	Individual and shared responsibility
Share information	Share discussion, decision-making, problem-solving and planning
Focus on individual goals	Focus on team goals
Produce individual results	Produce collective results
Individual roles are kept separate	Individual roles are shared to help the team
Goals set by manager	Goals set by team leader with team members

HANDY HINT

Teams are groups, but not all groups are teams. Simply calling a group a team does not make them a team; hoping they will work as a team doesn't work either.

The benefits of working in a team include:

- teams offer support
- teams promote shared working and provide efficiency
- greater flexibility
- higher morale
- better ideas.

There are several characteristics of successful teams. One is diversity in team members. Diversity in culture, background, age and ethnicity are important for high-performing teams, but so too is personality diversity. All teams are made up of a diverse range of personalities.

The factors which help individuals understand themselves and their teammates are:

- The need for stability, which refers to the degree to which we respond to stress.

- **Extroversion**, which refers to the degree to which we can tolerate sensory stimulation from people and situations.

Extroversion

Interest in and involvement with people and things outside yourself

- Originality, which refers to the degree to which we are open to new experiences and new ways of doing things.

- Accommodation, which refers to the degree to which we defer to others.

- Consolidation, which refers to the degree to which we push toward goals at work.

There are many personality types that are constructive and help in producing a successful team. These include:

Personality type	Traits
The silent contributor	Gets the job done without saying much. They silently complete the tasks that are assigned to them, and very rarely create conflict.
The devil's advocate	Likes to challenge ideas and processes, acts as an internal check. Although this person can generate conflict, often it is healthy conflict that brings ideas to light or helps to challenge bias.
The facilitator	Likes structure in meetings and makes sure things run smoothly. These people make sure everything goes according to plan, on schedule and in order. They help to reduce the chaos that may ensue from random team members trying to accomplish their individual goals.
The leader	Is not afraid to take charge, delegate assignments, enforce accountability, encourage others and facilitate success. Some are natural born leaders, others simply learn by doing.
The follower	Is really good at following directions and assignments. They work hard to get their work done on time.

Some people contribute to team **cohesion** by their personalities, some don't and others are unwilling to. Some people have the gift of working with and leading a team and ensuring its success. These are hard-working people concerned with team cohesion and putting the success of the team above their own ego. This type of person will help others achieve their goals by working with them to resolve frustrations, remove impediments and create an atmosphere of mutual satisfaction. This type of team player encourages the rest of the team to work collaboratively towards the team goals.

Cohesion

The state or condition of joining or working together to form a united whole, or the tendency to do this

Others may not have **collaborative** personality traits. Although their intentions might be good, they may not see eye to eye with team members on processes, methods or goals. Often this type of person will be confrontational and impatient. While they would like the team to succeed, their own work ethic or personality gets in the way. This type of person can learn to work better within a team if they recognise their impact on others and are willing to make changes to their style.

Collaborative

Working together towards a common end

A successful team will work together to achieve their goals

Some people simply won't work with a team. This type of person thinks they can get the job done faster, easier or better than the team could, and therefore simply will not co-operate. This type of person must get past their own ego if they are to work successfully in a team, and this type of change must start from within.

Whether coming back from lunch, or after time off, some people find it hard to get themselves started. At some point, you may have to tell your colleague that they are not pulling their weight. Before you take this step, make sure you are not guilty yourself before approaching your colleague. People tend to pay more attention to what you do than you realise, so be careful not to be a **hypocrite**.

Take your colleague aside and don't put them in a defensive state. Confronting your colleague in front of everyone may trigger their **fight or flight** mechanism and they may react badly.

Give your colleague respect by considering who they are. Think about who you are talking to and what their personality is like before approaching. Take time to rehearse what you are going to say and how you are going to say it. Have facts and evidence to support your claim. Be objective when doing this so that it does not come off as a personal attack but rather something that will help the team. Using lots of adjectives is not wise as this may trigger a negative response. Remain as business-like as possible so they will know you are serious.

Let them respond and listen to what they have to say. There may be an assignment they have been given that you don't know about. Be prepared for the consequences. It is normal to have a counter-attack of some sort so stick to your guns when listening to their response. Remember that you are their colleague and not their line manager and this may have some bearing on their reaction.

Hypocrite

Somebody who pretends to have admirable principles, beliefs, or feelings but behaves otherwise

Fight or flight

A reaction that occurs in response to a perceived harmful event, attack, or threat to survival

Other characteristics of a successful team include:

- Honesty – it must be possible for team members to express their opinions openly.

- Trust – every team member must be able to rely on every other team member.

- Readiness to share the workload – each team member must be prepared to carry out any task allocated to them, not just the ones they like doing.

- Clarity of goals – every member of the team must know what the goals are and their part in achieving them.

- Motivation by achievement – the team must be focused on meeting their deadlines and targets, not the process of meeting them.

- Support – every member of the team must be willing to help other members who are having difficulties.

- Leadership – the team leader must ensure individual, group and team involvement through providing strong leadership by example.

- Communication – members of the team must be able to communicate effectively with each other and relevant other teams and individuals.

Teams will not work effectively unless their dynamics are correct. **Team dynamics** can be identified by observing the influences on team behaviour. These include:

Team dynamics

The unconscious, psychological forces that influence the direction of a team's behaviour and performance.

- Personality styles – for instance whether members of the team are introvert or extrovert.

- Workplace layout – this will influence team behaviour if it physically divides the team into two or more sub-teams.

- Tools and technology – these need to encourage communication between all members of the team.

- Organisational culture – where team members are on different pay grades this can be disruptive to the working of the team.

- Processes and procedures – rigid organisational processes or procedures can make effective team working difficult.

A major influence on team dynamics are the roles taken by members of the team. These roles include the following, according to **Belbin**:

Belbin

Meredith Belbin measured preference for team roles which he had identified

Role adopted	Role traits
Plant	The creative member of the team, solving problems in unconventional ways
Monitor evaluator	The logical team member who considers options dispassionately

Role adopted	Role traits
Co-ordinator	This team member concentrates on objectives and delegating work
Implementer	The team member who plans a strategy and ways of carrying it out
Completer finisher	The team member who checks for errors
Teamworker	The team member who helps the team to come together and is able to identify the work required to complete the task
Shaper	The team member who provides the drive to keep the team moving forward
Specialist	The team member with an in-depth knowledge of a particular area of the team's objectives

The most effective team has members taking all of the above roles. Each role contributes to the team as a whole, although in different teams the relative importance of each role will change. Where a role is not present in a team this can lead to a weakness in the team as a whole. The key is balance. A team with no 'plant' may struggle for inspiration but too many plants in a team can mean that too much time is spent discussing impractical ideas. On the other hand, a team with no 'shaper' lacks direction and misses deadlines, while a team with too many shapers will fight amongst themselves.

Productive working relationships don't exist when there's open conflict between team members

ACTIVITY

List the members of your team and identify which of the Belbin team roles you think each carries out. Remember to include yourself.

Organisations generally want their staff to work together amicably, because happy teams work harder and better. It is the responsibility of the team leader to develop productive working relationships with, and between, team members.

Productive working relationships exist when:	Productive working relationships don't exist when:
• Team members treat each other with courtesy	• There is an atmosphere of blame
• An atmosphere of loyalty is promoted	• Team members (or the team leader) don't listen to the views of others
• Decisions are explained so they can be seen to be fair and reasonable	• There are obvious favourites within the team
• Conflicting points of view can be discussed openly and rationally	• There is poor decision-making from the team leader
• Team members co-operate	• There is open conflict between team members
• People's feelings are considered	• Some team members are allowed to get away with contributing less than their share to the team effort
• Innovation is respected and supported	
• Praise is given for good work	

The work environment can also have an effect on the working relationships of the team. As people spend a large part of their day at work, their surroundings will affect their feeling of well-being, and the happier they are the more productive they will be. Organisations should strive to provide a work environment which has:

- effective heating and air conditioning
- enough natural light
- sufficient, comfortable and appropriate furniture and equipment
- the correct colour scheme for the purpose of the work area
- noise levels that allow for comfortable communication
- a separate area for eating/drinking away from the work area
- plants (or windows giving views of green areas) as these are a calming influence.

A pleasant working environment improves working relationships

FEEDBACK

One of the most effective ways of developing a team is by giving them regular feedback. Team members need to know what they are doing well and what not so well. For feedback to be effective the experience must be positive. While this doesn't mean that the feedback must always be positive, negativity should be used carefully as team members will react better to an approach focused on improvement rather than one that is critical or offensive.

Feedback should be given as soon as possible after the event. It is more productive to give feedback about a particular event than to wait for months to give feedback about regular failures. Avoid giving feedback, however, while feelings are running high.

Feedback should also be given regularly. Formal feedback may be given by the team leader annually or quarterly but informal feedback should be given as often as possible. Team members receiving frequent informal feedback will not be surprised during formal feedback as issues will already have been raised.

As a team member, you are more likely to be giving informal feedback, but even this needs to be prepared. Tell your colleague what in your view needs improvement. Don't tell them they have not met the required standard; tell them what they have done that you think is below requirements. Use only facts that you are personally sure of, do not rely on hearsay. Don't exaggerate – avoid saying they are always late, or never on time, as this is unlikely to be true.

Give feedback in private; public recognition is acceptable but public criticism is not. Feedback should be given from your perspective – 'I think you could improve your performance' rather than 'Do you think performance could improve?' Stick to one or two issues; don't run through a whole list of problems.

Use a 'praise sandwich'; start and finish with positive comments but don't overlook the point of the feedback by over-emphasising the positive, allowing them to ignore the opportunity for improvement that you wanted to identify.

When giving feedback to colleagues remember that the same criteria apply as when receiving feedback from others; it must be constructive and explain what they *should* have done as well as what they *should not* have done.

CONFLICT MANAGEMENT

One of the most difficult areas of working in a team may be handling **conflict**. Few of us actually enjoy getting into arguments with people and, despite the impression given on many TV programmes, it doesn't happen too often.

Conflict management is important in order to:

- maintain morale
- maintain performance standards
- minimise absenteeism
- promote a safe working environment
- maintain group cohesion.

Conflict within the team may arise from a number of causes, for instance:

- a difference of opinion over the way a task should be carried out or who it should be carried out by
- resentment over perceived favouritism or lack of effort
- ethnic or cultural differences
- character incompatibility
- personal issues from out-of-hours contact.

There are five ways people react to and manage conflict:

Conflict

The internal or external discord that occurs as a result of differences in ideas, values or beliefs of two or more people

AVOIDING

In this scenario people will not argue. They don't care if their point of view is accepted, nor if the other's point of view is, as they believe it is not worth the effort. When issues are unimportant, avoiding can be the best solution. The approach is to pick your battles. If tempers have flared, agree to get back together after a cooling off period; temporarily avoiding conflict can reduce tension and allow the parties to come back together and be more productive.

COMPETING

The second approach is competing. In this scenario people need to win at all costs. When tough, unpopular decisions need to be made this approach can be very useful. It means being willing to defend your point of view and not be swayed from it. People will argue for their point regardless of the other points presented and throw their weight around if their authority will get them what they want. Using this approach too often will result in no one wanting to present opposing views.

ACCOMMODATING

The third approach is accommodating. People using this approach will bend over backward to respect the views of other people, and do whatever it takes to keep the peace and create goodwill. This may be seen as **altruism** or as weakness without conviction. This approach can be appropriate when you are wrong or when the issue is unimportant to you and the social credit gained outweighs the need to win.

COMPROMISING

The fourth approach is compromising. People using this approach are looking to make a deal, finding the middle ground where no one is completely happy, but no one is completely unhappy. It makes sense to compromise when time is short and the issue is too complex for a simple right or wrong answer, but this can reduce trust between the parties, each believing the other is out to get as much as possible. It can also focus attention only on the aspects that the individuals involved care about, ignoring the big picture.

COLLABORATING

The final approach is collaborating. People using this approach look at the whole picture and try to incorporate solutions that are bigger than any individual views. It requires openness to possibility and a removal of the concept that any one view is the best view. Not every situation calls for collaboration. In situations that present a puzzle instead of a problem, collaborating could waste time.

Dealing with conflict is a skill which has tried the minds of some of the cleverest and most experienced people on Earth; there is no single method that works in every situation. It is important that the situation is dealt with promptly. The starting point should always be getting the people involved talking to each other. Many long-running conflicts start from misunderstanding. If the two sides talked honestly and openly to each other at the beginning, they might have realised they

---

HANDY HINTS

It is sometimes necessary to apologise, even when you think the argument may not be your fault.

Altruism

An attitude or way of behaving marked by unselfish concern for the welfare of others

had a good deal of common ground and were able to compromise over the areas of difference so that both sides can accept an agreement.

If they have tried talking it over and coming to a compromise and this hasn't resolved the situation, they will have to take the problem to a third person, which may be their line manager or the Human Resources department. They should allow both sides to put their cases, consider them both fairly and suggest a solution. Both parties should agree at the start of the process that they will accept the 'referee's decision', and should do so and get on with it. Life's too short to hold a grudge! If both parties cannot agree to resolve the conflict, disciplinary action may follow in order to prevent the situation detracting from the performance of the team.

Discussing work progress and any issues arising with team members provides an opportunity to:

- acknowledge team achievements and celebrate success
- discuss strengths and identify areas for improvement
- clarify and agree any steps required to improve performance
- identify how systems, procedures and work methods might be improved.

Providing support to colleagues might include the following:

ACTIVITY

Record an incident of conflict within a team you have been a member of. Describe the cause and the way it was resolved.

Assessment criteria

This section covers assessment criteria 1.5, 2.1, 2.2 and 2.3

WORKING WITH COLLEAGUES

Colleagues want to be appreciated, and recognising their contribution to the achievement of team objectives lets them know that their efforts are noticed and valued. Praise should be timely, direct, personal and specific, with colleagues being told exactly what they do well and why their contribution is appreciated.

There are numerous ways to recognise a colleague's contribution, and the praise must be given in a way that is meaningful to them. Some colleagues may prefer to be praised in public, for example, whilst others may be more comfortable with being praised in private, and some colleagues will find it more meaningful to have their contribution recognised by a higher-level manager. One of the most important factors in effective team working is recognising that each individual is unique with different experiences, points of view, knowledge and opinions to contribute.

Contrary

Not at all in agreement with something

Remember, the purpose of forming a team is to benefit from the various qualities of its members. If not, there would be no point in approaching projects, products or goals with a team. The more a team can bring out **contrary** points of view that are thoughtfully presented and supported with facts as well as opinions, the better. Creativity, innovation and different viewpoints should be encouraged. Comments such as 'we already tried that and it didn't work' and 'what a stupid idea' must not be allowed or supported.

> **HANDY HINT**
>
> Speak to every one of your colleagues when you arrive at work, if only to say 'Good morning', or the one you unintentionally ignore can feel upset, and their performance can be affected all day.

When developing productive working relationships it is important to treat colleagues with respect, fairness and courtesy at all times, and take account of diversity. A diverse team will include people with different skills, personality traits and attributes. Each individual member will bring the benefits of their own experience to the team. Each will have their own strengths, which may include:

- previous experience
- communication skills
- **empathy**
- listening skills
- tact
- presentation skills.

Empathy

The ability to identify and understand another's situation, feelings and viewpoints, and to put yourself in the other person's shoes

Complementary

Combining with something else in a way that enhances it or emphasises its qualities

Synergy

The working together of two or more people, organisations, or things, especially when the result is greater than the sum of their individual effects or capabilities

These strengths may be **complementary**, helping the **synergy** of the team. This way, the strengths of the team may add up to more than the strengths of the individuals:

$$1 + 1 + 1 = 4$$

Individual members' diversity needs to be respected; don't highlight the negatives, look for the plusses which diversity brings to the team. One way to treat colleagues with respect is always to fulfil any agreements you make with them. It is important that you are reliable and complete your work when promised. If you make a commitment and fail to fulfil it, the story is likely to follow you. If you make and keep promises, your satisfied colleagues will sing your praises and recommend you for other tasks. The number one rule for consistently doing what you say is to keep from over-committing. Think before you commit and consider other outstanding or upcoming projects. Avoid rushing into anything. Take your time before promising anything and everyone involved will be happier.

Fulfilling agreements is one way to ensure you develop working relationships with colleagues, within your own organisation and within other organisations, which are productive in terms of supporting and delivering your work and that of your organisation. Colleagues should be informed when agreements have been fulfilled, or advised promptly of any difficulties or where it will be impossible to fulfil agreements.

Your colleagues will also need to be kept informed of any imminent problems and changes that might affect them. Warning colleagues of problems and changes that may affect them allows issues to be addressed before they get out of hand and are still manageable, and allows possible solutions to be explored as opposed to merely reacting to a situation.

Failure to warn people might also threaten your relationships with colleagues, who will typically assume the worst if there is a failure to communicate. The impact of change can involve four stages.

ACTIVITY

Add to the list of team members you made in the previous section one strength each member brings to the team and one weakness you think you could help them to work on.

It's important to fulfil agreements made with colleagues

Stage	Expected behaviours
1. Shock and resistance	• Change generates resistance. • The status quo seems preferable, even if not ideal itself. • Fear of the unknown prevails. • Reluctance to lose familiar rituals, practices and colleagues. • Feelings of inadequacy emerge as people confront new roles and demands. • Feelings of resentment at loss of old relationships and practices in imposed change. • Status and authority seem under threat. • Perception of rewards and opportunities of advancement being under threat. • People may 'opt out' of trying to understand. • Evidence of resistance may show itself in the form of anger, sadness, anxiety, withdrawal, indifference, 'bloody-mindedness', excessive caution, apathy, 'yearning for the past', low effort and productivity, and grievances.

Stage	Expected behaviours
2. Confusion	<ul><li>Beginnings of acceptance having 'got it off their chests'.</li><li>Assumption of new roles and development of new relationships will begin.</li><li>Requests for information and clarification.</li><li>Negative behaviour still includes fear and confusion when others are seen to be coping better and doing well out of the change; when some aspects of change are still not going very well and when pace of change reinforces perceptions of loss of control and ability to cope.</li><li>Positive behaviour now includes seeking clarification of what is expected of the group and others; identification and expression of issues for discussion with managers and a preparedness to recognise new opportunities.</li></ul>
3. Integration	<ul><li>Optimism begins to replace depression.</li><li>Job satisfaction re-emerges.</li><li>Anxiety decreases.</li><li>New working relationships become established.</li><li>There is an awareness of behavioural expectations.</li><li>A sense of competence and self-worth returns.</li><li>More looking ahead than dwelling on the past.</li><li>Productivity is improving.</li></ul>
4. Acceptance	<ul><li>Contributions are being recognised.</li><li>Individuals no longer feel threatened.</li><li>Working relationships have been reconstructed and are largely harmonious.</li><li>New, effective channels of communication have been established.</li><li>Managers can once again distribute their attention between individuals, the team and the task.</li><li>Productivity is optimal.</li></ul>

There are different types of change including:

- Those done to us – as a rule nobody likes this type of change. People hate being told what to do. This is the type of change people are most likely to resist.

- Those we do to ourselves – we're in control. We're deciding for ourselves that doing something different is necessary. Because it's our decision, we don't 'resist' our decision to change. This does not mean this type of change is easy. Learning to play the bagpipes or speak Chinese, losing weight, moving to a new city, starting a new job are all difficult tasks, but we don't resist them in the same way we resist when someone else tells us we have to do these things.

- Those we do to others – this is the first type of change seen from the other side. Unless we take into account how we react to changes and accept that other people will see this as a change that is being done to them, the change will be unnecessarily difficult.

By giving your colleagues as much warning as you can of impending problems or changes, you will help them to start the process towards acceptance as soon as possible.

COMMON MISTAKE

Not all change is for the better.

Change can lead to confusion

RESOLVING PROBLEMS

Assessment criteria

This section covers assessment criteria 3.1, 3.2, 3.3 and 3.4

Successful leaders and managers work hard to understand others' viewpoints in a particular situation. They acknowledge others' viewpoints when making decisions and consider the impact of their choices on the well-being and interests of others. There are a number of problems which you will probably have to face at work, which might include:

- a fall in output
- an increase in complaints
- conflict between team members
- conflicts of interest
- lack of clear objectives
- lack of clear allocation of tasks
- lack of innovation
- lack of risk-taking
- ineffective meetings

- lack of communication
- lack of trust
- low morale
- lack of commitment to decisions.

To resolve a problem is to find an effective and satisfactory answer or solution, and a problem with working relationships with colleagues may be resolved formally or informally, depending upon the nature and extent of the problem. If the problem with a working relationship is a relatively minor issue, then an informal resolution may be possible. If, however, the problem is more serious, then it may be necessary to use the organisation's formal disciplinary or grievance procedures.

If the formal procedures are used, then each procedure should specify the level of authority appropriate to each stage. It is important to work with other members of the team when looking for solutions to problems that affect them rather than working in isolation and attempting to impose your solution. This will help to build their commitment and confidence, create opportunities for them to excel and create a vision which all members of the team can share.

Work with other team members to find solutions to problems

There are six stages to problem-solving:

1. Identify the problem
2. Define the effects of the problem
3. Find the cause of the problem
4. Identify possible solutions
5. Choose between the solutions
6. Plan the way forward

The more senior roles in an organisation will have greater authority to give instructions and make decisions and to ensure compliance with organisational policies and procedures, and problems that lie outside your own level of authority must be referred to a more senior manager at the appropriate level. You will need to know who you should refer these kinds of problem to, and what the recognised procedure is for doing so. Level of authority refers to the different hierarchical management levels in an organisation and the duties and responsibilities assigned to each of those levels.

The authority given to a role is usually formalised in a job description, which will generally include the roles and responsibilities of the job. It may be that the solution you have identified is beyond the limit of your authority to implement. This may be because the solution has financial or health, safety or security implications, will impact on the reputation of the organisation with external customers, requires a deadline to be met that is not in your power to achieve or the help of colleagues that are not within your authority to direct.

Involving your colleagues does not mean that you do not take ownership of problems. Where problems lie within your area of responsibility it is up to you to take the necessary decision to minimise disruption to business activities which provide a product or service that customers require. A disruption to business activities could have far-reaching consequences for the organisation, such as:

- loss of income
- loss of reputation
- loss of customers
- penalty payments for not meeting deadlines
- failure of the business.

Everyone in an organisation must take appropriate and effective action, within their own level of authority, to minimise disruption to business activities. Decision-making is all about choosing. When you come to a road junction, you can choose to go straight or to turn left or right. If you are new to the area, you may not be sure which way to go. Your goal is to reach a certain location, so you begin your decision-making by obtaining more information. You look at the map and discover that if you go straight ahead you can get to your objective, but going right gets you there too. Now you have to evaluate which direction is best. Going right is shorter, but the roads are all dirt. Going straight lets you drive on paved roads. Since it has just rained, you decide to go straight. Decision-making is the process of defining a problem, finding feasible solutions, choosing the best solution and implementing it. The process breaks down as follows:

Decision matrix

A matrix used by teams to evaluate possible solutions to problems. Each solution is listed. Criteria are selected and listed on the top row to rate the possible solutions. Each possible solution is rated on a scale from 1 to 5 for each criterion and the rating recorded in the corresponding grid. The ratings of all the criteria for each possible solution are added to determine each solution's score. The scores are then used to help decide which solution deserves the most attention.

SWOT analysis

SWOT analysis is a structured planning method used to evaluate the 'strengths', 'weaknesses', 'opportunities' and 'threats' involved in a project or business venture

Decision tree

A decision tree is a graph that uses a branching method to illustrate every possible outcome of a decision

COMMON MISTAKE

Many people forget that only very simple problems have a simple solution.

1 The first, and arguably the most important, step in decision-making is to identify the problem. Until you have a clear understanding of the problem or decision to be made, it is meaningless to proceed. If the problem is stated incorrectly or unclearly then your decisions will be wrong.

2 Sometimes your only alternatives are to do it or don't do it. Most of the time you will have several possible alternatives. It is worth doing research to ensure you have as many good alternatives as possible.

3 Rank the alternatives. Three logical approaches to this are to use a **decision matrix**, a **SWOT analysis** or a **decision tree**.

4 Eliminate all of the alternatives that do not make logical sense. It is time to review all the details of the remaining alternatives, so they are completely clear in your mind.

5 Carry out your decision. A decision has no value unless you carry it out. Part of this phase is follow-up, which ensures that the decision is implemented.

Test your decision by asking:

- Does the solution solve the problem?
- Does the solution solve the cause of the problem?
- Has everybody involved agreed to the solution?
- Is the solution practical in terms of cost, time, people and resources?
- Will the solution prevent the problem recurring?
- Have you considered all the disadvantages of the solution?
- Have you considered all the consequences of the solution?

If the answer to all of the above is 'yes', you may have found the best solution.

CASE STUDY
SUPPORTING A COLLEAGUE

Kevin had worked at Aspect Transport for three years, since leaving college. He was a pleasant young man, popular with his colleagues, and took an interest in other people. He was always willing to help out others whenever he was asked. He was eager to learn new skills and was the first to volunteer for tasks that no one else wanted to do. He started lending a hand in the administration department, supporting colleagues with tasks. After a period in the post room his manager saw his potential and he progressed to an administration assistant. A month ago he was made head of the administration department. Since starting at the company in a junior position he had been determined to achieve promotion to a department manager and he had now achieved his career aim.

Ishant had worked at the company for 10 years and was still working at the same job as a text processor in the administration department. He was generally sullen and fed up with his lack of progression. Kevin managed four people in the administration department including Ishant. Kevin had noticed that Ishant was always quiet, hardly spoke to others and never showed any enthusiasm for completing his work. While he always completed tasks on time and his work was of a very good quality, he clearly lacked confidence, had few communication skills and did not seem to have many friends.

Kevin decided to get to know Ishant a little better to find out a little more about him. After a few informal chats over coffee at lunchtime, Kevin began to understand that Ishant had never really been given any encouragement through regular feedback at work and had never been coached to help him reflect on goals. Ishant felt that no one really noticed how hard he worked and as a consequence did not bother to try very hard to communicate with others or get involved in their work.

Kevin aimed to resolve this situation and arranged a series of regular meetings with Ishant to help him set professional and personal goals. He gradually gave him extra responsibilities for tasks and Ishant started to take a renewed interest in his work and colleagues around him. Over the next six months Ishant became a more active team member and looked much happier at work. Kevin was very pleased and started to consider the next steps he could discuss with Ishant and how he could help him achieve them.

UNIT 240 (M&L 2): TEST YOUR KNOWLEDGE

Learning outcome 1: Understand the principles of effective team working

1 Describe two benefits of effective team working.

2 Describe the features of two of the team roles identified by Belbin.

3 Explain what is meant by constructive feedback.

4 Describe situations where the compromise approach to conflict management is useful.

Learning outcome 2: Be able to maintain effective working relationships with colleagues

1 Explain why it is important to acknowledge the contribution of individuals to the achievement of team objectives.

2 Explain why it is important to treat colleagues with respect.

3 State two benefits of fulfilling agreements made with colleagues.

4 Explain why change that is done to us is most likely to meet resistance.

Learning outcome 3: Be able to collaborate with colleagues to resolve problems

1 Explain how taking others' viewpoints into account helps in decision-making.

2 Describe how to take ownership of a problem.

3 Explain why it is important to minimise disruption to business activities.

4 Explain why you should resolve only problems within your level of authority.

OPTIONAL UNITS

UNIT 203 (B&A 15) COLLATE AND REPORT DATA

When you are asked to collate and report information, you will often be given a format that the data is required in and a timescale to complete the data. The way that you have organised the information will determine how you will best be able to report it.

There are two basic ways of reporting information, either in the form of a written report or in the form of statistical information presented as charts or tables. If you are not given instructions on the format to supply the information in, you should consider whether you are presenting factual information, with the need to make recommendations based on the facts, or numerical data leaving the reader to draw conclusions for themselves.

Charts and tables may, of course, form part of a written report, providing the facts from which the recommendations are drawn.

In this unit you will cover the following learning outcomes:

1 understand how to collate and report data
2 be able to collate data
3 be able to report data.

Parameter

A fact or circumstance that restricts how something is done or what can be done

Qualitative

Relating to or based on the quality or character of something, often as opposed to its size or quantity

Quantitative

Relating to, concerning, or based on the amount or number of something

COMMON MISTAKE

Collecting too much information can be as unhelpful as collecting too little.

Database

An organised collection of data.

COLLATING DATA

When collating information you will need **parameters** to work to, as information is effectively infinite. In order to produce the information required, you will need to know:

- what level of detail is needed
- what the information is to be used for
- how much time is available for research
- what resources are available
- whether **qualitative** or **quantitative** information is needed.

Once you have agreed the objectives and deadlines, you will be able to start. In order to choose the most efficient sources of information you will need to decide what information:

- you already have
- is available from previous research
- is available from within the organisation
- is available from the internet
- will need research from other sources.

Other sources may be paper-based, electronic or the experience of other people. Start with the information you already have; if that covers the information required, you won't need to look elsewhere. If not, check whether the information has been researched previously; it may just need updating.

The next step is to check whether the information is available elsewhere in the organisation. This will require liaison with other departments, unless there is a central repository of information in the organisation. If all of these fail, the internet is often the quickest source of information; the downside of internet information is that you need to be able to check that it is accurate, reliable, credible, current, factual and not over-biased.

If you are unable to find reliable information on the internet, you could consider other sources such as:

- telephone directories
- trade directories
- libraries
- reference books
- magazines.

Information can be organised and stored either in paper form or as data stored on a computer. Either way, the storage of information will create a **database**.

STORING INFORMATION IN A DATABASE

There are a number of advantages to storing information in a computerised database, including the flexibility and speed in organising, displaying and printing the information. Data in a computerised database is structured as follows:

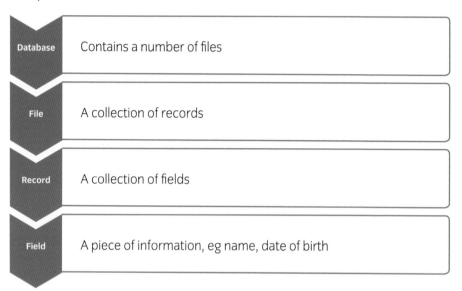

Database	Contains a number of files
File	A collection of records
Record	A collection of fields
Field	A piece of information, eg name, date of birth

There are two types of computerised database, flat-file and relational. Flat-file databases are suitable only for simple applications as only one file of records can be stored. Relational databases store several files and allow the data in one file to be combined with data from other files. Files in relational databases are known as tables.

When you have found the information, remember to keep a list of the sources in order to be able to find it again easily. Information found on the internet can be bookmarked for this purpose.

ORGANISING DATA

Statistical information may be collated in a straightforward table or in any of a number of different types of graph or chart.

These include scatter graphs, pie charts, bar or column charts, line graphs, and radar or spider charts.

SCATTER GRAPHS

These are used to show trends. Data points from two variables are entered and a 'best fit' line drawn. The closer the data points are to the line the stronger the effect one variable has on the other. If the best fit line increases from left to right, the scatter plot shows a positive **correlation**. If the line decreases from left to right, there is a negative correlation.

Correlation

A relationship in which two or more things are mutual or complementary, or one is caused by another

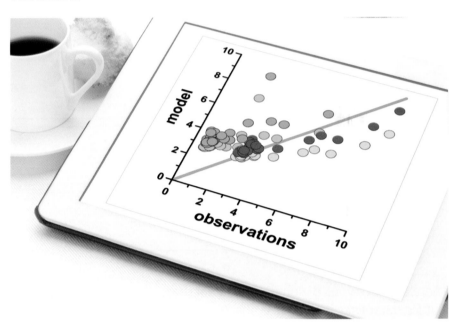

PIE CHARTS

Pie charts are used to show percentages. The whole circle represents 100% and is subdivided into slices which represent data values. The size of each slice shows what part of 100% is represented.

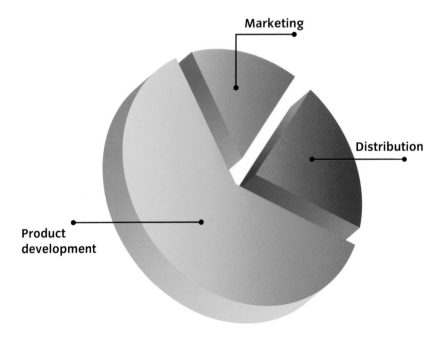

BAR OR COLUMN CHARTS

Bar or column charts make it easy to see the differences in the data being compared, as the height (or length) of the bar or column indicates the number represented.

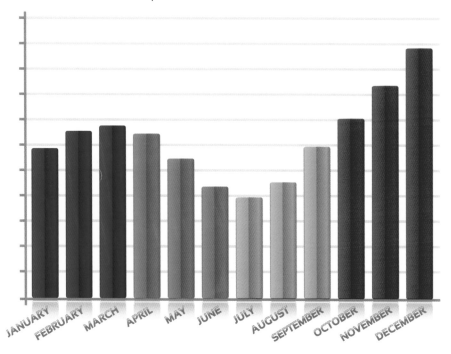

LINE GRAPHS

These have a vertical axis and a horizontal axis on which individual data points are plotted and then connected with a line which clearly indicates changes in data values over a period of time.

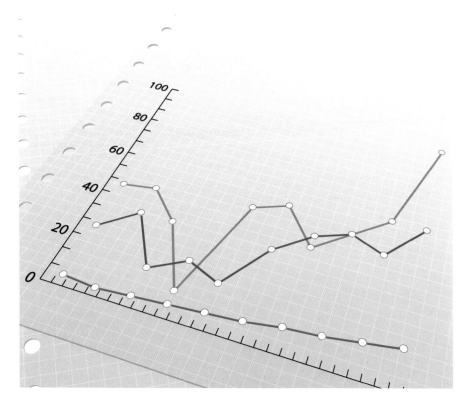

Comprehensive

Including everything, so as to be complete

RADAR OR SPIDER CHARTS

These plot data values along axes that start in the centre of the chart and end on the outer ring.

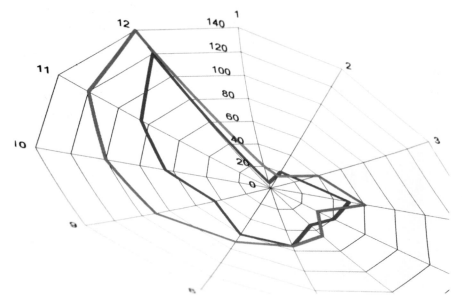

Information is only useful if it is accurate and up to date. It is important, therefore, that regular checks are made to ensure that information is **comprehensive** and current. This may involve asking for feedback on the accuracy and relevance of information provided. Where necessary information needs to be updated or amended.

ACTIVITY

Using the information in the table below, create:

- A scatter graph
- A pie chart
- A bar chart
- A line graph
- A spider chart.

	Population 1950	Population 2014	Population 2050 estimated
China	562,579,779	1,390,113,852	1,385,000,000
India	369,880,000	1,260,528,245	1,620,000,000
USA	152,271,000	321,453,538	400,000,000
Russia	101,936,816	142,668,652	121,000,000
Japan	83,805,000	127,085,641	108,000,000
Indonesia	82,978,392	251,508,419	321,000,000
Germany	68,374,572	82,775,116	73,000,000
Brazil	53,443,075	201,282,525	231,000,000
UK	50,127,000	63,328,796	73,000,000
World	2,555,948,654	7,204,701,275	9,551,000,000

Adapted from www.geohive.com

REPORTING DATA

Assessment criteria

This section covers assessment criteria 1.4, 2.4, 3.1, 3.2 and 3.3

The purpose of collating information is to be able to retrieve it when required. When asked to present information, you must first check the format required. The information may be required as a written report or as a statistical report, displaying the information as a table or chart.

Having collected the information, you will need to organise it in order to meet the requirements of the person who asked for it in the first place. The way in which you do this will depend on the purpose the information is to be put to.

Data should be presented in the agreed format

The purpose of the information will decide whether the most appropriate way to report it is:

- Verbally – this is probably only appropriate if there is only a small amount of information and it is relatively simple.
- By an oral presentation – this will allow you to explain the information, possibly through the use of slides or handouts.
- With the use of charts, diagrams, graphs and tables – this enables more complex information to be reported pictorially.
- On a notice or display board – this enables you to make the information available to everybody involved.
- Through brochures or leaflets – this will usually be used to make the information available outside of the organisation.
- In a report – a formal report will be used for complex information or where decisions are to be taken based on the data.

HANDY HINT

Agree the format data is to be presented in before you start producing a report.

The information will need to be presented in line with your organisation's house style.

The finished article needs to be evaluated to ensure that the information contained:

- is a true representation of the facts
- is reliable and credible
- is current or dated
- is not biased
- is not simply the opinion of the writer
- comes from a valid source.

A written report should provide information and facts as **succinctly** as possible, and will usually contain a conclusion and often an appendix containing material which is referred to in the report which requires greater detail.

Research information can be validated by checking the sources of the information and the credibility of its author.

Succinct

Expressed with brevity and clarity, with no wasted words

A written report should include a conclusion and often an appendix

LEGISLATION

It is important to remember when reporting information that all organisations who handle personal information are bound by the Data Protection Act. This act says that:

- Organisations must process only as much information as they need. They must identify the minimum amount of information needed for a specific purpose, which must be lawful. There are extra restrictions on the use of particularly sensitive data.

- When information about an individual, whether they are an employee or a customer, is used they must be properly informed of what is going to be done with their information. You should ensure that they are aware of who you are, what information you hold and why, and any other information, such as third parties you intend to pass the information to, which may make your use of personal information fair.

- The information held must be accurate and up to date. You need to be able to prove you have taken 'reasonable steps' to ensure the accuracy of the information you hold. If anyone complains about the accuracy of the information you hold on them, you must be prepared to investigate and to amend it or at least note their complaint on file.

- The information must be kept securely. Information must not be passed on to third parties without just cause. You can use external data processors (for example, payroll bureaux), but you must have a written guarantee they will keep your information secure. You must ensure that any information you keep on the premises is safe.

- There must be an arrangement for deleting information on old disks, tapes and any back-up or iCloud storage and for securely disposing of paper records about people.

- If information is sent abroad, the country must have adequate data protection laws. You must get consent from the individual in question or ensure the organisation you are sending the data to has acceptable security arrangements.

- The information must be deleted as soon as you have no reason to keep it. You need a very good reason to hold on to information beyond its immediate use. For example, you might want to hold information on potential recruits in case one of the unsuccessful ones tries to sue you for discrimination.

- You must observe the subject's rights. These include the right to see all the information you hold on them. They have to ask in writing, provide evidence of identity, and pay any fee requested up to £10. You need not comply if their name is only mentioned unimportantly. The courts have pointed out that the act exists to allow individuals to check whether their privacy is being infringed. It is not an 'automatic key' to any information on matters in which he or she might be involved. You can sometimes withhold the information if a third party in involved. Individuals can ask for corrections; you must investigate and at least make sure the request is on file.

ACTIVITY

Produce a set of data, using either data from your workplace or from your tutor/assessor. Report it in a variety of formats such as bar charts and pie charts.

Other legislation to bear in mind is the Copyright, Designs and Patents Act 1988, which is the main legislation covering intellectual property rights in the United Kingdom and the work to which it applies. This act gives the creators of literary, dramatic, musical, artistic works, sound recordings, broadcasts, films and typographical arrangement of published editions, rights to control the ways in which their material may be used. The rights cover:

- broadcast and public performance
- copying
- adapting
- issuing, renting and lending copies to the public.

In many cases, the creator will also have the right to be identified as the author and to object to distortions of his work. International conventions give protection in most countries, subject to national laws. There is a wide range of types of work protected including:

- Literary – song lyrics, manuscripts, manuals, computer programs, commercial documents, leaflets, newsletters and articles etc.
- Dramatic – plays, dance, etc.
- Musical recordings and scores.

- Artistic – photography, painting, sculptures, architecture, technical drawings/ diagrams, maps, logos.

- Typographical arrangement of published editions – magazines, periodicals, etc.

- Sound recording – this may be recordings of other copyright works, eg musical and literary.

- Film – video footage, films, broadcasts and cable programmes.

The Copyright (Computer Programs) Regulations 1992 extended the rules covering literary works to include computer programs. Copyright is an automatic right and arises whenever an individual or company creates a work. A piece of work needs to be regarded as original, and show a degree of labour, skill or judgement. Interpretation is related to the independent creation rather than the idea behind the creation. For example, an idea for a book would not itself be protected, but the actual content of a book would be.

DELIVERING THE DATA REPORT

The information must be delivered within agreed timescales. It is important to be realistic when agreeing timescales. Build in enough time so that you can get the work done comfortably. If you know it will be difficult to get something ready by Wednesday, for example, say you will have it first thing Friday morning. Don't set an extended deadline just so you can waste time. Work just as hard on the task before Wednesday, but just knowing that you don't have to get it fully completed by Wednesday will reduce your stress levels significantly.

Your colleagues waiting for the information will be much happier if you meet the deadline that you set rather than be late. It certainly does not make a good impression to have Wednesday come and go, and have to tell them, 'I'm sorry; this won't be ready as planned'. If you complete it on Thursday, you will be a day early, rather than a day late.

Before distributing the report, check that it meets its purpose, is factually accurate, logical and contains all relevant information. Distribute the report to the people on the distribution list – this may be a regular list to which all similar reports are distributed, or a specific list created by the person requesting the report. Regular distribution lists must be checked and updated regularly so that information is not distributed to people who do not need it, or people who should not be in receipt of it, and information is received by all those who need it.

COMMON MISTAKE

It can be tempting to manipulate information so that it supports your opinion, ignoring information that tends to lead to a different conclusion.

ACTIVITY

Produce a report on a subject agreed with your supervisor or your tutor/assessor.

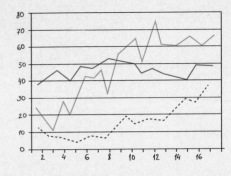

Penny York works as a research assistant. She was asked to write a report on the changes in the housing market over the previous 12 months. She has access to information on a variety of databases as well as statistics published online. Her research revealed that there were at least seven organisations publishing house price indices (scales expressing the price, value or level of something in relation to something else or to a base number) each month. Sometimes their findings agreed, at other times they conflicted. Penny decided that she needed to investigate how each index was compiled in order to consider which one gave her the information she was really looking for.

Her findings were as follows:

- Halifax used the average price agreed on a property using a Halifax mortgage.

- Hometrack used a survey completed by estate agents gathering their opinions on selling prices.

- Land Registry used the asking price of properties bought.

- Nationwide used the average price agreed on a property bought using a Nationwide mortgage.

- The Office for National Statistics used the average price on completion for a property.

- Rightmove used the average asking price for properties put on the market.

- The Royal Institution of Chartered Surveyors used a survey of surveyors gathering their opinions on changes in prices, sales and interest.

Penny decided the most reliable sets of figures were those produced by Halifax, Nationwide and Land Registry and compiled a graph showing their monthly statistics over the previous 12 months. Using a line graph she was able to show that while all three sets of figures differed each month, the trends on all three were the same.

Penny presented these findings and was congratulated on the way she had organised and reported the data.

UNIT 203 (B&A 15): TEST YOUR KNOWLEDGE

Learning outcome 1: Understand how to collate and report data

1 Describe two different ways of organising information.

2 Describe two different ways of reporting information.

3 Explain why it is important to present information to the agreed format.

4 Explain the purpose of reports.

5 Name the main legislation relating to copyright.

Learning outcome 2: Be able to collate data

1 Why is it important that information is complete, accurate and up to date?

2 How would you validate research information?

3 Describe a method of organising information to enable meaningful analysis.

4 Explain why it is important to present information within the agreed timescale.

Learning outcome 3: Be able to report data

1 What is meant by 'house style'?

2 Why is it important that reports are distributed only to authorised readers?

UNIT 204 (B&A 16) STORE AND RETRIEVE INFORMATION

In recent years, there has been a theory that it is possible to operate a paperless office. The development of the computer was expected to reduce the need for hard copies of documents to nil. What has happened in practice is that producing documents has become so much easier and their number has greatly increased. We are all guilty of printing off an email so that we can consider our response. We then send a reply email to the original sender, who prints off both our reply and their original email! This is environmentally unfriendly, as well as being an expensive waste of resources such as paper and ink. Storing and retrieving information has never been more important.

In this unit you will cover the following learning outcomes:

1 understand information storage and retrieval
2 be able to gather and store information
3 be able to retrieve information.

Assessment criteria

This section covers assessment criteria
1.1, 1.2, 1.3, 1.4, 2.1, 2.2, 2.3 and 2.4

STORING INFORMATION

If you cannot find information on which the completion of a task depends, the task will be delayed with possible serious consequences. The purpose of storing information is to be able to retrieve it when it is needed. An effective information storage and retrieval system enables you to find complete, accurate and up-to-date information so that you can make decisions based on all the available information. Storing information is much more than simply keeping papers or saving electronic files. If there is no system for retrieving the information when it is required, the information is likely to be lost or difficult to find. This will inevitably lead to problems such as a waste of time and money and, possibly eventually, a loss of business.

Many organisations are moving towards a more general use of electronic information systems rather than the more traditional paper-based ones. To decide which is more appropriate in a given situation, you need to ask:

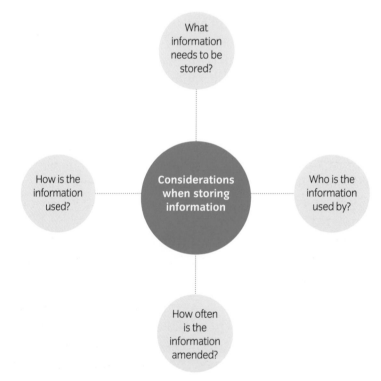

- What information needs to be stored? If the information is recorded currently on paper, it may be best to store it as paper. If the information is electronic, there is no point in printing it simply to store it as paper.

- Who is the information used by? If the people needing access to the information are situated in different locations, electronic records may be accessible to all of them via a shared server, whereas paper documents would have to be copied for each of them.

- How often is the information amended? Information which needs regular updating, such as customer names and addresses, may be best stored electronically as it is easier to amend than paper records which may need completely recreating to record the change.

- How is the information used? Some information, such as legal records including deeds, wills, contracts etc, may depend for its validity on signatures and witnesses' signatures. While these documents could be scanned into an electronic filing system, the original will need to be retained in case of any future dispute.

LEGAL AND ORGANISATIONAL REQUIREMENTS

A recurring issue with the storage of information is the length of time for which it must be retained. The Data Protection Act says that personal information should not be kept for longer than is necessary, but this is not particularly helpful. There are a number of factors involved in deciding when records may be deleted including:

- legal requirements
- the cost of storage
- the need to refer to the information
- any historical value the information may have.

The last three of these factors will be decided at the organisation's **discretion**. Many documents that are available for academic research and public interest have only survived because an organisation has decided to retain their records far beyond the point at which they have a need to refer to them or a legal requirement to keep them. If organisations such as Cadbury, Lever Bros and the BBC hadn't kept **archives** of material from their early days, we would not have access to so much information today.

Discretion

The power to make decisions sensitively on the basis of one's knowledge and the ability to keep sensitive information secret

Archive

A collection of documents or computer records, kept for future reference

Outside of the organisation's authority are the legal requirements for retaining records. These apply to accounting records, personnel records, health and safety records, medical records, wills, military records, criminal records, academic records, contracts, etc. You need to know what the legal periods are for retention of any records that you are responsible for, as deleting information before the due date is a serious matter, possibly leading to criminal prosecution for the organisation.

Some examples of the types of records that are kept by most organisations and their retention periods are shown in the following table.

Record type	Retention period
Income tax and salary records	6 years plus current year
Unsuccessful job applications	6 months after notification
Sickness and statutory maternity pay records	3 years after the end of the tax year
Purchase ledger, invoices and petty cash records	6 years from the end of financial year
Banking records	6 years from the end of financial year
VAT records	6 years
Employer's liability insurance certificate	40 years
Health and safety records	3 years; permanently for records relating to hazardous substances

Archiving records involves deciding which files are no longer required to be kept within the active storage system and organising their storage or destruction, depending on retention requirements.

Archiving files regularly:

- speeds up locating files by reducing the number of files in the active filing system
- makes disposal more efficient by reducing the backlog
- reduces the space required for current filing.

Many organisations will use an outside company to manage their archives. This is preferable to an in-house system where records are simply dumped in storerooms, which can lead to:

- vast backlogs of records no-one knows about, some of which may be important
- poor storage conditions
- increased storage requirements.

Some information will need to be kept secure and access to it controlled. This may be because the information is confidential or because it is **commercially sensitive**. The legal requirement to keep information confidential is covered by the Data Protection Act. This act covers personal data which relates to a living individual who can be identified from the data or from the data and other information in the possession of the **data controller**. There are eight principles of information handling outlined in the act. These say that data must:

Commercially sensitive

Information that an organisation would not like to be in the public domain as it may give an advantage to a competitor

Data controller

The person who decides the purpose for which personal data is to be processed

- be fairly and lawfully processed
- be processed for limited purposes
- be adequate, relevant and not excessive
- be accurate and up to date
- not be kept for longer than is necessary
- be processed in line with the rights of the data subject
- be secure
- not be transferred to other countries without adequate protection.

The data subject is the individual about whom data is held. Data subjects have rights which include being allowed to:

- know if data is held about them
- request a copy and description of the data
- inspect the data and have it changed if it is inaccurate
- seek compensation if the data is inaccurate
- know the purpose for which the data is being processed
- know who will have access to the data
- seek compensation if unauthorised access has been permitted
- prevent the processing of data likely to cause damage or distress
- ensure decisions against them are not made only on the basis of automatic processing.

Information must be stored in accordance with the Data Protection Act

Data subjects have to pay an administration fee to the data protection commissioner to prevent the processing of data or to correct or delete it.

As well as the legal requirement to protect personal information, there will be organisational requirements to keep information confidential. This may be because there is a duty of trust to your clients or customers or because the information would be useful to competitors.

One of the principles of the Data Protection Act that causes organisations some difficulty is the requirement that information must be accurate and up to date. The Information Commissioner's Office (ICO) provides some useful information on this which can be applied to all stored information.

The ICO says that the Data Protection Act does not define the word 'accurate', but it does say that personal data is inaccurate if it is incorrect or misleading as to any matter of fact. It will usually be obvious whether information is accurate or not. For example, if an individual has moved house from Chester to Wilmslow, a record showing that he currently lives in Chester is obviously inaccurate. However, a record showing that he once lived in Chester remains accurate, even though he no longer lives there. You must always be clear about what a record is intended to show.

There is often confusion about whether it is appropriate to keep records of things that happened which should not have happened. Individuals understandably don't want their records to be tarnished by, for example, a penalty or other charge that was later cancelled or refunded. However, the organisation may legitimately wish its records to accurately reflect what actually happened – in this example, that a charge was imposed, and later cancelled or refunded. Keeping a record of a mistake and its correction might also be in the individual's interests.

It is acceptable to keep records of events that happened in error, provided those records are not misleading about the facts. You may need to add a note to a record to clarify that a mistake happened. This depends on what the information is used for. If the information is used for a purpose that relies on it remaining current, it should be kept up to date. For example, your employee payroll records should be updated when there is a pay rise. Similarly, records should be updated for customers' changes of address so that goods are delivered to the correct location. In other circumstances, it will be equally obvious when information does not need to be updated.

Also, where information is held only for statistical, historical or other research reasons, updating the information might even defeat the purpose of holding it. Where you use your own resources to compile personal data about an individual, then you must make sure the information is correct. You should take particular care if the information could have serious implications for the individual. If, for example, you give an employee a pay increase on the basis of an annual increment and a performance bonus, then there is no excuse for getting the new salary figure wrong in your payroll records. It may be impractical to check the accuracy of personal data someone else provides. In recognition of this, the act says that even if you are holding inaccurate personal data, you will not be considered to have breached the fourth data protection principle as long as:

- you have accurately recorded information provided by the individual concerned, or by another individual or organisation
- you have taken reasonable steps in the circumstances to ensure the accuracy of the information
- it is made clear to the individuals accessing the data if the individual has challenged the accuracy of the information.

The definition of taking reasonable steps will depend on the circumstances and, in particular, the nature of the personal data and what it will be used for. The more important it is that the personal data is accurate, the greater the effort you should put into ensuring its accuracy. So if you will be using the data in making decisions that may significantly affect the individual concerned or others, you will need to put more effort into ensuring accuracy. This may mean you have to get independent confirmation that the data is accurate. For example, most employers will only need to check the precise details of job applicants' education, qualifications and work experience if it is essential for that particular role, when they would need to obtain authoritative verification. If your information source is someone you know to be reliable, or is a well-known organisation, it will usually be reasonable to assume that they have given you accurate information. However, in some circumstances you will need to double check – for example if inaccurate information could have serious consequences, or if common sense suggests there may be a mistake.

Some information may also be subject to the Freedom of Information Act (2000) that makes information in relation to certain organisations accessible to members of the public. Refer to Chapter 9 (Unit 205, B&A 17) for more information on the act.

As well as your legal responsibilities, if you have access to information systems you must act **ethically** when using the technology. The law considers some computer activities illegal. Accessing, using or destroying hardware, software or the information contained in information systems can be a form of theft. It is also illegal to use an information system to release unauthorised information. The theft of copyrighted material is also illegal. You must not use computer networks for piracy or to obtain protected information.

Ethical

Consistent with agreed principles of correct moral conduct

Information systems have transformed the way organisations such as banks and hospitals keep records and organise their customers' or patients' personal information. On the other hand, information storage brings risks to the privacy of the individuals with personal information filed in the system. Sometimes databases are broken into and people's personal information such as names, addresses and national insurance numbers are stolen. Identity thieves use stolen personal information to steal from their victims' bank accounts or take out credit cards or loans in the victims' names.

Some employers closely monitor their employees' computer use, sometimes going as far as logging websites or looking at email. Other employees think computer monitoring is an unethical form of privacy invasion. Privacy is one of the chief concerns when it comes to ethics in information technology, especially in a work environment. Computer users expect privacy when it comes to their passwords, personal information and emails, while employers want to determine if the employee's time is being used inappropriately. Many organisations have installed programs to track the websites that employees visit. While this may seem unethical to some computer users, the fact that the organisation owns the computers means it has rights regarding what can be done with them. If you don't want your employer to know which sites you visit, limit personal use to your home computer.

Hospitals use information systems to store patients' personal information

INFORMATION STORAGE SYSTEMS

There are different information systems available with different features to meet the organisation's business needs. Three main information systems are:

- transaction processing systems
- management information systems
- decision support systems.

Transaction processing systems (TPSes) process business transactions. Transactions can be any activity, for example, in a hotel reservation system, booking, cancelling, etc are all transactions. Any query made is a transaction. Some transactions are common to almost all organisations, such as employees' holiday entitlement, purchase ledger systems, etc. TPSes provide high speed and accurate processing of record keeping of basic operational processes including calculation, storage and retrieval.

Management information systems (MISes) help in problem-solving and making decisions. They use the results of transaction processing and other information. They handle queries as quickly as they arrive. An important element of an MIS is the database. A database is a collection of interrelated data that can be processed through application programs and is available to many users.

Decision support systems assist management to make long-term decisions. They handle unstructured or semi-structured decisions. Some decisions have to be made infrequently or even only once, so a decision support system must be very flexible. The user should be able to produce customised reports by giving particular data and format specific to particular situations.

Features of different information systems are summarised in the following table.

Information systems and their features	
Transaction processing system (TPS)	Substitutes computer-based processing for manual procedures. Deals with well-structured processes. Includes record-keeping applications.
Management information system (MIS)	Provides input to be used in the decision process. Deals with supporting well-structured decision situations. Typical information requirements can be anticipated.
Decision support system	Provides information to make judgements about particular situations. Supports decision-makers in situations that are not well structured.

Once the decision has been taken whether to use paper-based or electronic information systems, you need to choose between the various different filing methods. There may be organisational policies or procedures already in place which will determine which are used.

Paper-based information can be stored in either vertical or lateral filing cabinets

FILING METHODS

ALPHABETICAL

Alphabetic filing systems group information together using the letters A–Z. Any type of information can be filed alphabetically and can be readily retrieved as long as certain rules are agreed and adhered to. If the information is to be filed under a person's name, it is usual to file it by reference to the surname followed by the forename. For instance if filing records for Ann Johnson, Anne Johnson and Amy Johnson, the sequence would be:

- Johnson, Amy
- Johnson, Ann
- Johnson, Anne.

Titles such as Mr, Mrs, Miss, Dr, Prof or Sir are ignored for this purpose. If, for instance, Amy Johnson were a doctor, her entry would be Johnson, Dr Amy, but she would still be filed before Johnson, Ann.

Alphabetical sequence needs to be strictly followed, so that records for McDougal, MacManus and Manning would be filed in the sequence:

- MacManus
- Manning
- McDougal.

Surnames that include 'St' as an abbreviation of 'Saint' should be filed as if the 'Saint' were spelt in full. Records for St John, Saint, Sampson and Sabberton would be filed in the sequence:

- Sabberton
- Saint
- St John
- Sampson.

Company names are filed under the full company name, so Amy Johnson Ltd, Amy Johnson Hairdressers and Amy Johnson & Co would be filed in the sequence:

- Amy Johnson & Co
- Amy Johnson Hairdressers
- Amy Johnson Ltd.

Company names that consist solely of initials such as BBC, AA or RAC are filed at the beginning of the section for their first letter. Records for BBC, Barber & Co, BT and Burrows Ltd would be filed in the sequence:

- BBC
- BT
- Barber & Co
- Burrows Ltd.

The definite article ('the') is ignored when filing. For example The Bathroom Company is filed under 'B'.

The advantage of alphabetical storage of information is that, as long as the rules are agreed and understood by everyone involved, there is no difficulty in locating information. There is no need for any form of **cross-referencing**. The disadvantage is that names are not unique, so there may be two or more Michael Johnsons in the system. To retrieve the information on a particular Michael Johnson you would need to refer to another piece of information such as a middle name, date of birth or address.

NUMERICAL

Numerical filing is used for any information where the most important reference to it is its number. For example, invoices and purchase orders. The important thing to remember when creating a numerical filing system is that there must be sufficient digits in the system if electronic information systems are to be used. A computer will read numbers from left to right as if the digits were individual letters, so 111 will be read as starting with 1 while 27 will be read as starting with 2 and therefore stored after 111. To avoid this problem, if the numbers 000111 and 000027 are used, the computer will get it in the right order.

COMMON MISTAKE

Filing names such as McTavish as if they were spelt MacTavish.

Cross-referencing

A reference from one part of a file to another part containing related information

The advantage of a numerical system is that every number is unique and you can store and retrieve an infinite number of documents without ever duplicating their file name. The disadvantage is that if you don't know the number of the file you are looking for, there is no easy way to find it without a cross-referencing system.

ALPHA-NUMERICAL

Alpha-numerical filing is used where the file name consists of letters and numbers. The postal codes used in the United Kingdom are known as postcodes. An example is the postcode. A typical UK postcode may read as MK41 8LA. MK refers to the postcode area, as the letters at the beginning are based on letters from a city, town or district in the area. There are 120 postcode areas in the UK. MK41 refers to the district within the area. There are 2,900 districts within the country. The 8 in the second set of characters refers to the postcode sector. There are about 9,000 of these sectors. The final two characters are the postcode unit and define a group of about 15 properties within the sector, which could be a street, part of a street, or even an individual large user. It is estimated that there are 1.6 million postcode units in the UK to cover 24 million delivery points. Some special delivery points such as Buckingham Palace and the House of Commons have postcodes that may **differentiate** them from surrounding areas because of the large volume of mail that these sites receive from around the world.

Differentiate
To establish a difference between two things or among several things

GEOGRAPHICAL

Geographical filing is used where the information needs to be grouped with reference to its location within a country or region. For instance information will be divided into countries, sub-divided by region or county and then by town or city. So an address in Churchtown, Southport, Lancashire, England would be filed under:

- England
- Lancashire
- Southport
- Churchtown.

Within each division or sub-division information will be stored alphabetically.

The advantage of a geographical filing system is that information can be retrieved more easily covering a geographic area rather than having to extract specific information from an alphabetic system that covers the whole world or the whole country.

Information can be filed geographically

SUBJECT

Filing by subject is used where access to the information is needed by reference to its subject. Probably the most common example of filing by subject is the system used in reference libraries, where all the books about plumbing will be stored on one shelf and all the books about fishing will be on another. Similarly, information stored electronically may be stored in folders by subject.

The advantage of filing by subject is that all the information is in one place. If you want information on plumbing, you don't need to know the names of the authors to find it. The disadvantage is that a single piece of information may refer to more than one subject. The question then arises whether to make copies of the information to place in each subject file or to create a cross-referencing system.

CHRONOLOGICAL

Chronological filing simply means storing information in date order. It is mostly used within one of the other systems. For instance, correspondence with Amy Johnson will be placed in her file chronologically, with the most recent on top. This allows a record of events to be built up over a period of time in sequence. Often, people will reply to emails by using the 'reply' option which results in a sequence of e-mails each replying to the previous one. This creates a form of chronological information storage.

It is important, when creating electronic records, that dates are entered as YYYY/MM/DD if the record is to be stored chronologically, although we use DD/MM/YYYY when we date a letter, for example. A computer will store 15/04/1971 before 25/12/1963, but will store 1963/12/25 before 1971/04/15.

The advantages of chronological filing are that information can be retrieved in chronological order, allowing you to see how one piece of information influences another and where information is to be deleted after a given period of time, it is much easier to recognise which information should be destroyed. The disadvantage is that a purely chronological filing system would make it very difficult to trace a particular piece of information if you didn't know the date it originated.

Electronic information systems will carry out these functions automatically; manual systems will require the skill and knowledge to handle these categories. To help electronic information systems to **classify** information, it is important to name electronic files in a consistent and coherent way. A number of file-naming **conventions** have been established to facilitate this. These include:

- making names short and clear
- avoiding repetition
- using capital letters to delimit words

Classify

To assign things or people to categories

Conventions

The customary way in which things are done within a group or organisation

- using at least two digits when including numbers; 09 will appear before 10, but 9 will appear after it
- when using dates in file names, always stating the date YYYYMMDD as this maintains a chronological order
- when using names, putting the surname first
- avoid words like 'draft', 'letter' or 'memo' at the start of file names.

Where large numbers of files are involved, they are often grouped into folders and directories to enable them to be retrieved more easily.

RETRIEVING INFORMATION

When retrieving information it is important to confirm exactly what information is involved as retrieving incorrect information can cause serious problems for the person you are providing the information to. For example, if someone is working on a contract with a customer whose name is Albert Smith and you provide them with information on Alfred Smith, this could create confusion and a possible loss of business. It is important, therefore, when asked to retrieve information, that you check the accuracy of the information carefully. If asked for a file on 'Albert Smith' you should check a separate piece of information such as the address or date of birth so that you can confirm that you have retrieved the correct file.

SEARCHING DATABASES

Information can be retrieved from a database using search functions. As you become more experienced in using different databases you will find this easier. It is important to take care when typing terms into the search box. If you enter too many terms, you may retrieve no references or very few references because the database is trying to find references that contain all the words entered. If you type too few words, you may retrieve too many references. If you don't enter terms commonly used to describe the subject you are searching for, you may retrieve irrelevant references.

Some databases search the full text of the references that they contain. Other databases only search a brief description, or summary, of the references. If you are searching a full-text database, you will be able to search on very specific terms. If you are searching a database that only has summaries of the references, you may have to use fewer terms and less specific terms.

Connectors, sometimes called Boolean operators, are used to combine search terms. There are three connectors:

- 'AND' placed between words means both words must appear in each reference. This will narrow your search. For example, 'audio AND video' will retrieve all references which contain both 'audio' and 'video'.

- 'OR' placed between words means that either word or all words may appear in each reference. This will broaden your search. For example, 'audio OR video' will retrieve all references with 'audio' or 'video' as well as references which contain both 'audio' and 'video'.

- 'NOT' placed between words means that the second word must not appear in any reference. This will narrow your search. For example, 'audio NOT video' will retrieve all references with 'audio' except references which include 'video'. Take care when you use this connector as you may exclude useful references.

If you use more than one type of connector in a search statement, eg AND as well as OR, you need to use parentheses to keep the groups of terms together. This procedure is sometimes called nesting. For example '(women OR woman OR female) AND (smoking OR tobacco)'. This is a technique for experienced searchers. The less sophisticated alternative is to do several searches with different combinations of the search terms.

Truncation, or the use of wildcards, involves abbreviating words to retrieve all the alternative terms. For example, using the term 'comput*' will retrieve 'computer', 'computers', 'computate' and 'computation'. Some databases also provide internal truncation to facilitate searching on alternative spellings. For example, 'p?ediatric' will retrieve 'paediatric' and 'pediatric'. Wildcards vary from database to database. Some databases will automatically include plurals or variant spellings in the search. Familiarise yourself with each database's requirements by consulting the help screens or searching tips.

Some databases will assume that a string of words should be searched for as a phrase and will only retrieve references in which the words occur side by side or in very close proximity. This works well if you have entered the phrase 'information technology', but it will be a problem if you have entered 'depression teenagers' instead of 'depression in teenagers'. In some databases, there will be a separate search box for phrase searching.

Many databases will give you the option to limit your results. For example, you may be able to specify that you want to retrieve only articles with full text, or articles from peer-reviewed journals. Or you may be able to limit your results to articles published in certain years or in a particular journal. Field searching is another way of limiting your results. The references on the database are normally split up into fields, such as author, title, journal title or subject descriptor. If the database has an advanced search option, you will probably be able to restrict your search to a particular field. If your search terms appear in the title or subject descriptors of the reference, the reference is likely to be more relevant. Field searching can also be used to distinguish between, for example, Dickens as an author and Dickens as a subject. You may also be able to search electronically by reference number or by storage end date.

Some databases keep a record of all the searches that you have done during the current session. Use this search history to retrieve an earlier search. You can also use it to combine two or more searches that you have already done, using the normal Boolean operators (AND, OR, NOT).

SUPPLYING INFORMATION TO A THIRD PARTY

Having collected the information, you will need to organise it in order to meet the requirements of the person who asked for it in the first place. The way in which you do this will depend on the purpose the information is to be put to. It is also necessary to check when asked to retrieve information what format the information is required in and the timescales involved. Your information system will be capable of providing a whole range of information on any requested subject, but it will not be cost effective to produce a wide-ranging report if all that is required is the subject's contact details. For example, if you are asked for the purchase orders raised to a supplier in the last 12 months, it is more likely that what is wanted is a list containing information such as dates, values, etc than a pile of actual purchase orders. While checking this, you can also enquire whether the information should be supplied electronically or printed off. Similarly, if the information is required for an important meeting the following day, it will not be helpful to produce an in-depth dossier that will take three days to collate.

In many organisations, there is a system of signing out files so that you will always know where they are. This is extremely useful if someone else requests the file, as you will be able to direct them to the person who currently has it. It also allows you to trace the file should it not be returned when finished with.

You need to be able to search through large volumes of information to find what you need

DEALING WITH PROBLEMS

The worst problem that could possibly occur with the storage of information would be if it were permanently lost or destroyed. For this reason, most organisations will have some form of back-up system. This may involve keeping the most important information from paper documents on an electronic record so that, if the paper records are destroyed, the information can be recreated. Electronic records are usually backed up onto **peripheral** storage media such as external hard drives, pen drives or CD-ROMs which are either removed from the premises or stored in fire-proof cabinets. It is likely that CD-ROMs will be phased out in the near future as technology progresses.

Peripheral

Externally related or connected, for example, a device linked to a computer to provide communication (as input and output) or auxiliary functions (such as additional storage)

Filing needs to be done frequently so that records are up to date, otherwise you may not be able to find the information you need.

Day-to-day problems that you may experience with electronic information systems include a system crash. This is where a computer or a program ceases to function properly. The computer may freeze, so that there is no reaction to input from the keyboard or mouse. Depending on the type of program you are working on, you may be able to close down your computer and start it again to solve the problem or you may have to call for technical support. When inputting new data or editing existing data, frequent saving of the information should be carried out to prevent any loss through a system crash.

Other problems with electronic information systems include accidental deletion of records or infection with a computer virus. You may be able to recreate deleted records if you still have the source information. Where source information is not available or a virus is detected you may require a restore by your technical support.

HANDY HINT

Make sure there is a security system that protects confidential files, whether paper or electronic.

Computer viruses are a risk when storing information electronically

ACTIVITIES

- Create a form which can be used in your organisation by people requesting information. The form should be sufficiently detailed to ensure that the correct information is retrieved.
- Keep a work diary recording when you have stored and retrieved information.

Paper records are really only subject to two types of problem. They may be damaged by mishandling, fire or flood or they can be lost through misfiling or poor description. Misfiling is a potential nightmare as it is very difficult to guess where the file might have been put by mistake. The only advice we can give is to use educated guesswork. The file might be one letter away from where it should be, under 'N' instead of 'M' or it could be filed under the forename instead of the surname. The person responsible for filing it away may remember that they filed it under a different system.

CASE STUDY
ARCHIVING INFORMATION

Janice was appointed Office Manager at a company providing financial services. They had amassed a large volume of highly confidential files. It was vital that the files be secure and accessible over the long term to support the company's day-to-day operations, and for use in the event of customer default. The files were also needed to respond to regular internal and external audits requiring occasional retrieval and delivery of up to 300 files at short notice.

The company had for several years been using the services of a storage company. Whilst resolving a storage problem, archiving remained time-consuming and retrieval was becoming increasingly difficult. The list of archived files was often found to be inaccurate, the storage company would deliver boxes rather than just the required files and a request for a single file required delivery of up to 10 boxes for the company to search.

Janice designed a solution which involved identifying errors in the existing boxes, such as absence of department or destroy dates, or inadequate contents description; collection of boxes from the storage company; and destruction of obsolete records. In future, the system enabled the company to have access to all files via a tracking system. The company's files were now securely stored, precisely tracked and available upon demand.

Accuracy of file-tracking was greatly improved, and labour costs and overall cost of archiving were reduced.

UNIT 204 (B&A 16): TEST YOUR KNOWLEDGE

Learning outcome 1: Understand information storage and retrieval

1 For how long must unsuccessful job applications be retained?

2 Give two reasons why files should be retained in archives using the same system as is used in the live filing system.

3 Complete the table showing what types of confidential information may be found in each type of record.

Types of record	Types of confidential information
Human Resource records	
Accounts records	
Telephone directories	
Register Office records	
Medical records	
Search engine information	

4 True or false?

   a It is an offence under the Data Protection Act to transfer information on an individual to a country outside of the European Union.

   b The employer's liability insurance certificate must be retained for 40 years.

5 State the most effective way of storing each of the following, explaining your reasons:

   a Purchase invoice

   b National insurance numbers

   c Vehicle registrations.

Learning outcome 2: Be able to gather and store information

1 Explain how confidential information is disposed of when it is no longer required.

2 List the legislation which affects the storing and retention of information in your organisation.

3 List the types of confidential information dealt with in your organisation and how it is stored.

Learning outcome 3: Be able to retrieve information

1 List the information which is stored in your organisation showing the length of time it must be retained.

2 Explain how information is archived in your organisation.

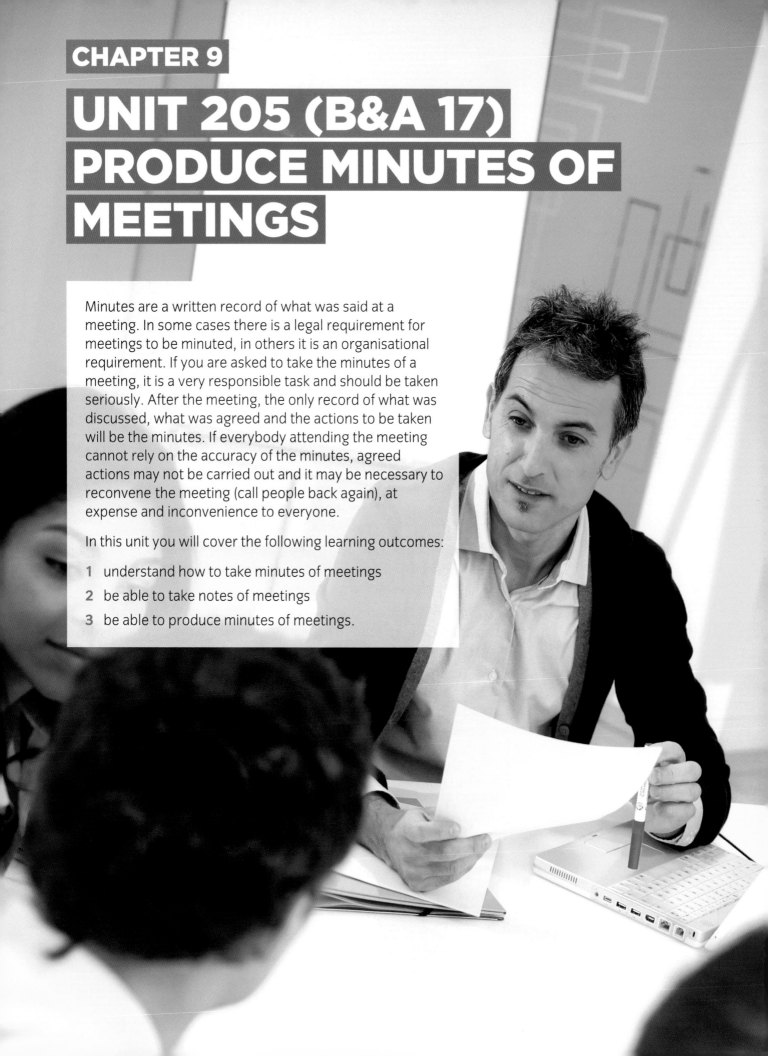

CHAPTER 9

UNIT 205 (B&A 17) PRODUCE MINUTES OF MEETINGS

Minutes are a written record of what was said at a meeting. In some cases there is a legal requirement for meetings to be minuted, in others it is an organisational requirement. If you are asked to take the minutes of a meeting, it is a very responsible task and should be taken seriously. After the meeting, the only record of what was discussed, what was agreed and the actions to be taken will be the minutes. If everybody attending the meeting cannot rely on the accuracy of the minutes, agreed actions may not be carried out and it may be necessary to reconvene the meeting (call people back again), at expense and inconvenience to everyone.

In this unit you will cover the following learning outcomes:

1 understand how to take minutes of meetings
2 be able to take notes of meetings
3 be able to produce minutes of meetings.

TAKING MINUTES OF MEETINGS

THE PURPOSE OF MEETINGS

Meetings are held in organisations for a wide variety of purposes, some formal and many more informal. At informal meetings one or more of the attendees may take notes of what has been agreed, but at formal meetings there is usually an appointed minute-taker.

Informal meetings include occasions where two or more members of the team get together to discuss an immediate problem or where an unplanned discussion takes place. Formal meetings usually fall into one of a number of categories:

- Shareholder meetings – all public companies with shareholders are required to hold an annual general meeting (AGM). These give shareholders an opportunity to question directors and raise any concerns. If urgent issues arise between AGMs an additional meeting can be called if the holders of 10% of the shares agree. The additional meeting is known as an Extraordinary General Meeting.

- Board meetings – these are regular meetings between the directors at which decisions are taken on the strategy to be followed by the organisation.

- Management meetings – these are regular meetings held by senior managers to decide how the strategy of the organisation is to be put into action on a practical level.

- Team meetings – at these, decisions made at management meetings are **cascaded** by team leaders to members of staff who will be directly involved in putting them into practice.

- Committee meetings – there may be committees formed within the organisation to oversee particular areas of activity. In a commercial organisation their responsibilities will be confined to areas such as health and safety or staff welfare, but in a public organisation such as a local authority, committees are powerful groups responsible for areas of policy such as planning or transport.

Minutes and other meeting records are used to share information, which can help people make decisions, resolve problems and develop new ways of working.

Cascade

Pass information on in a downward flow or direction within an organisation

THE CITY & GUILDS TEXTBOOK

LEGAL AND ORGANISATIONAL REQUIREMENTS FOR MINUTE-TAKING

Organisational requirements will probably dictate that minutes are taken at formal meetings; at some meetings there is a legal requirement under the Freedom of Information Act (2000) that makes information in relation to certain organisations accessible to members of the public.

A meeting room

The Freedom of Information Act (2000) applies to all public authorities within the United Kingdom including:

- government departments
- the Houses of Parliament
- the Northern Ireland Assembly
- the Welsh Assembly
- the Armed Forces
- local government bodies
- National Health Service bodies
- schools, colleges and universities
- police authorities
- companies wholly owned by the Crown, a public authority or a government department.

There are some **exemptions** to the above including the **Intelligence Services** and any information which could compromise security and defence forces.

Exemption

Permission or entitlement not to do something that others are obliged to do

Intelligence Services

An organisation that gathers information about the secret plans or activities of an adversary or potential adversary

In effect, public authorities have 20 working days to respond to an information request. To reduce the number of requests for similar information, public authorities also have a duty to release important information such as annual reports and accounts as a matter of routine.

Obviously, in order to be able to meet requests for information it is important that accurate records are made of meetings at which decisions are made which may affect members of the public. Minutes meet the organisational and legal requirements for accurate recording of decisions and the discussions that led to them.

TYPES OF MINUTES

In order to correctly record the discussions at a meeting, you will need to understand some terms which are commonly used in meetings. A list of these can be found at the end of this chapter.

Chairperson

The person nominated to run a meeting

Documents for the meeting could include working documents, background papers, general information documents and any briefing notes. There are different types of minutes which can be taken – if you are taking minutes of a particular meeting for the first time, look back at previous meetings or ask the **chairperson** of the meeting which type is required:

- Verbatim minutes, like transcripts, are a record of every single word said at a meeting. They are often long and can be difficult to search quickly for a particular piece of information. With the exception of parliamentary and courtroom proceedings, a verbatim record of a meeting is rarely necessary. Verbatim minutes will not always follow the agenda.

- Action minutes record the decisions reached and the actions to be taken, without recording the discussion that led to the decisions. These are the most common form of minutes used. They include a report of actions taken since the last meeting as well as planned actions. It is important to note who is responsible for upcoming actions.

- Discussion minutes are lengthy and may include information which is not essential to the focus of the meeting. It may be necessary to keep discussion minutes in a situation where the process behind the decisions may be in question later. Discussion minutes contain everything that is included in action minutes as well as the discussion which led to the actions decided upon. Do not include any discussion which is not relevant to the topic.

There may be a question of security and confidentiality when recording information discussed at meetings. Care should be taken not to leave minutes of meetings where they may be read by people not involved in the meeting. As the minute-taker, you should record the meeting in the agreed organisational format; it is usually the chairperson's responsibility to deal with any issues before the minutes are circulated.

THE ROLE OF THE CHAIRPERSON AND OTHER OFFICIALS IN MEETINGS

Every formal meeting has a person nominated to run the meeting. In different organisations this person may be known as the chairman, chairwoman, chair or chairperson. Their responsibilities during the meeting are to:

In formal meetings a chairperson will be responsible for running the meeting

- start the meeting on time
- clarify roles and responsibilities
- establish ground rules and guidelines
- participate as an attendee
- follow the agenda and keep the meeting focused on agenda items
- retain the power to stop what's happening and change the format
- encourage accountability
- summarise key decisions and actions
- record recommendations and allocate responsibilities for specific tasks
- make the most of the experience present – ask questions to draw out people with experience
- allow time to hear experts' points of view but allocate time with clear directions
- for important issues when time is limited set up a sub-committee to collect facts, review the situation, and prepare recommendations to be considered at the next meeting
- close the meeting on time.

They also have responsibilities to help the minute-taker by:

- agreeing the items to be included on the agenda
- following agenda items in sequence and informing the minute-taker of any departures from the agreed agenda
- summarising specific points, decisions or courses of action agreed for each specific agenda item before moving on to the next item
- providing specific guidance to the minute-taker on what to record for a particular agenda item where lengthy discussion has occurred or a complex issue has been discussed
- taking time to review the minutes when they are drafted.

Other formal responsibilities within meetings are held by the treasurer and secretary. The treasurer will be responsible for reporting on financial matters while the secretary will often be the minute-taker, although sometimes this function will have been **delegated**. The secretary may be responsible for ensuring the required documentation and any correspondence to be discussed or referred to at the meeting is available.

Whether you are an experienced minute-taker or taking minutes for the first time, it is important to prepare each time. Decide whether you are going to use pen and paper, a laptop, tablet or a digital recorder and check that your chosen equipment is in working order. Always take a spare pen with you: if all other equipment fails you will still be able to keep up. Familiarise yourself with the agenda so that you know what is coming next.

Delegate

Give authority to somebody else to act, make decisions or allocate resources on one's behalf

HANDY HINT

Always have a spare pen with you – even if using a recorder, a pen will be useful to make notes.

If you are responsible for taking minutes make sure you have everything you need

The agenda will follow a formula agreed by the chairperson and usually following the format of all previous similar meetings within the organisation. An example would be:

- apologies for absence
- approval of minutes of last meeting
- matters arising
- items to be discussed
- any other business (aob)
- date of next meeting.

In addition to the agenda itself, there may be documentation and correspondence that needs to be available so that it can be referred to during the meeting. It is important that the minute-taker works in partnership with the chairperson in order to ensure that the meeting is as effective as possible.

TAKING MINUTES AT MEETINGS

When taking minutes it is important that you hear everything that is said, so you must listen carefully and remain focused. If you allow yourself to become distracted, even momentarily, you may miss something that proves to be vital.

For more information on active listening, refer back to Chapter 1 (Unit 222, B&A 34) page 15.

If you are taking verbatim minutes, you will probably be recording the discussion on audio equipment or using shorthand, as it will not be possible otherwise to write out every word that is said. You will need to have a method of noting who is speaking when, if recording the meeting, as you may not be able to recognise the individual voices when **transcribing** the recording. Using the speaker's initials is a useful way, unless of course you have two people with the same initials, in which case you might use an alternative style eg Sue Smith and Sharon Stone might become SS and Shaz.

Shorthand is a system used to transcribe quickly

Transcribe

To write out an exact copy of something heard such as a discussion or audio recording

TAKING NOTES

If you are taking resolution or **narrative** minutes, your notes should record the discussion in such a way that your minutes give a precise account of the points made for and against a proposal and the reasons given in support of those points. Remember, you are not trying to record every word spoken, only a summary of what was said.

It is a good idea to leave a line between each line of notes taken. This will allow you to add in further comments if the chairperson decides to go back to an item after the meeting has moved on.

Narrative

Narrative minutes are a summary of the meeting including discussions and conclusions

Motion

A proposal put forward for discussion at a meeting

Amendment

An addition or alteration to a motion

Resolution

A firm decision to do something

ACTIVITIES

- Study the terms listed at the end of the chapter. Find out which are used in meetings at your organisation and learn their meanings.
- Attend a meeting and take notes – this could be at work or outside work. Produce a set of minutes from your notes and check against the official minutes, if available, or with the chairperson, that your minutes have recorded the meeting accurately.

Assessment criteria

This section covers assessment criteria 2.1, 2.2, 3.1, 3.2, 3.3 and 3.4

House style

A set of rules concerning spellings, typography, etc

HANDY HINT

You do not need to record any irrelevant comments made, only those that refer directly to the agenda item.

Objective

Based on facts rather than thoughts or opinions, free of any bias or prejudice caused by personal feelings

Motions, **amendments** and **resolutions** must be recorded word for word to prevent any dispute later. Record the name of the person who proposed the motion, who seconded it and the result of the vote. Where a decision leads to an action point, record who has been made responsible for carrying out the action and any timescale agreed.

Minutes should enable anybody who was not at the meeting to understand what decisions were made, what alternatives were considered and the reasoning behind the decision.

Although minute-takers are, usually, not participating in the meeting, it is essential that you understand what is taking place sufficiently to accurately record the discussion. If you do not understand something that is said, and you feel that this will affect the accuracy of the minutes, ask the chairperson for clarification. Address all requests for clarification directly to the chairperson: do not get drawn into discussion with the other attendees.

WRITING UP MINUTES AND RECORDS OF MEETINGS

Type up your notes as soon as possible after the meeting. The longer you wait, the more difficult you will find remembering what your notes mean. The structure, style, tone and language used in the completed minutes will probably be set by the organisation's **house style**, but should always be written using professional language. The important points are that minutes should be:

- Consistent in the way they are written
- Written in plain English
- Accurate
- Concise
- Grammatically correct.

For more information on using correct grammar, punctuation and sentence structure refer back to Chapter 1 (Unit 222, B&A 34) pages 7 to 12.

It is important that the minutes are **objective**, record the facts rather than your view of them, and focus on action points rather than the discussion that led to them. They must include the:

- Names of the people who attended and any apologies for absence
- Proceedings
- Agreed actions
- Allocated responsibilities for agreed actions
- Agreed attachments and/or appendices.

Write minutes in the past tense – for instance 'Mrs Christian said that…' and indicate where any action is required, and who by. Many organisations will use a column to the right of the text for this. Check the accuracy of the minutes using a spellcheck but also proofreading them to look for common errors not picked up by a spellcheck such as 'right' and 'write'. Number the pages and remember to create an appendix for any additional documents.

When you have drafted the minutes, ask the chairperson to check them before circulating them. This will avoid the need to send out a new set of minutes if the chairperson spots an error. Send copies of the approved minutes to everyone who attended the meeting, those who sent their apologies and anyone else who is expected to take any action as a result.

Occasionally, someone will request a change to the wording of the minutes. This should be made a note of so that it can be discussed at the next meeting during the agenda item 'approval of the minutes of last meeting'. If it is agreed that an alteration should be made, this will be done before the chairperson signs off the minutes as correct.

Signed-off copies of the minutes should be filed together with a copy of the actual notes taken and final versions of any documents and reports which have been considered at the meeting.

HANDY HINTS

- Make a seating plan at the start of the meeting, noting the names of attendees, or send round a register asking attendees to sign. This will help you to record who said what.
- Record those who arrive late or leave early.

HANDY HINT

Develop your own abbreviations for common phrases, names and places. The less you have to write the better you will be able to pay attention.

COMMON MISTAKE

If you get too interested in what is being said, you can forget to record it.

Trying to use language which is more formal than necessary can make the minutes unintelligible to people reading them.

ACTIVITY

Minutes must be written in the past tense. Write up these notes as minutes:

- Imran Tahir says that Tuesday will be acceptable as a deadline.
- The production figures will be produced tomorrow.
- Everybody present agrees that the deadline is achievable.
- Brian James said 'my assistant will stand in at the next meeting as I am on holiday'.
- Point 4 on the agenda is carried forward to the next meeting.

USEFUL TERMS

Ad hoc Meaning literally 'for this' or 'for this situation' so for a particular purpose, for example, when a sub-committee is set up especially to organise a works outing

Adjourn To hold a meeting over until a later date

Adopt minutes Minutes are 'adopted' when accepted by members and signed by the chairperson

Advisory Providing advice or suggestion, not taking action

Agenda A schedule of items drawn up for discussion at a meeting

Apologies Excuses given in advance for inability to attend a meeting

Articles of association Rules required by company law which govern a company's activities

Attendance list In some meetings a list is passed round to be signed as a record of attendance

Bye-laws Rules regulating an organisation's activities

Casting vote An extra vote that a chairperson may use to reach a decision if votes are equally divided

Chairperson Leader or person given authority to conduct a meeting

Chairperson's agenda Based upon the meeting agenda but containing explanatory notes

Collective responsibility A convention by which all meeting members agree to abide by a majority decision

Committee A group of people usually elected or appointed who meet to conduct agreed business and report to a senior body

Consensus Agreement by general consent, no formal vote being taken

Constitution Set of rules governing activities of voluntary bodies

Convene To call a meeting

Decision minutes Resolution minutes are sometimes called 'decision minutes'

Eject Remove someone (by force if necessary) from a meeting

Ex officio Given powers or rights by reason of office

Executive Having the power to act upon taken decisions

Guillotine Cut short a debate – usually in parliament

Honorary post A duty performed without payment, eg Honorary Secretary

Intra vires Within the power of the committee or meeting to discuss and carry out

Lie on the table Leave item to be considered instead at the next meeting (see 'table')

Lobbying A practice of seeking members' support before a meeting

Motion The name given to a 'proposal' when it is being discussed at a meeting

Mover One who speaks on behalf of a motion

Nem con From the Latin 'nemine contradicente', literally 'no one speaking against' so with no one dissenting, unanimous

Opposer One who speaks against a motion

Other business Either items left over from a previous meeting, or items discussed after the main business of a meeting

Point of information The drawing of attention in a meeting to a relevant item of fact

Point of order Querying or drawing attention to a breach of rules or procedures – proceedings may be interrupted on a 'point of order' if procedures or rules are not being kept to in a meeting

Proposal The name given to a submitted item for discussion (usually written) before a meeting takes place

Proxy This means 'on behalf of another person' – a proxy vote signifies that one person is authorised to vote on behalf of another person who may be absent

Quorum The minimum number of people needed to be in attendance for a meeting to be legitimate and so commence

Refer back To pass an item back for further consideration

Resolution The name given to a 'motion' which has been passed or carried, used after the decision has been reached

Seconder One who supports the 'proposer' of a motion or proposal by 'seconding' it

Secret ballot A system of voting in secret

Secretary Committee official responsible for the internal and external administration of a committee

Shelve To drop a motion which has no support

Sine die From Latin, literally, 'without a day', that is to say indefinitely, eg 'adjourned sine die'

Standing committee A committee which has an indefinite term of office

Standing orders Rules of procedure governing public sector meetings

Table To introduce a paper or schedule for noting

Taken as read To save time, it is assumed the members have already read the minutes

Treasurer Committee official responsible for its financial records and transactions

Ultra vires Beyond the authority of the meeting to consider

Unanimous All being in favour

CASE STUDY
DEVELOPING A NEW SKILL

Helen Wiggins had worked for a firm of solicitors for two years, answering the telephone, entering data into clients' files and typing letters. She found the most interesting aspect of her job typing up the minutes of meetings from notes taken by the senior clerk, Bill Townsend.

Helen asked Bill whether he would help her to learn how to take the minutes herself. Bill said that he didn't think the solicitors, or their clients, would want an extra person attending meetings as they were sometimes stressful for the clients, but he would think about how Helen could learn.

Bill brought her a list of abbreviations that he used to make his notes and suggested that if Helen could learn them, he would ask if she could attend some of the less important meetings with clients as minute-taker. Helen worked hard on learning the phrases and a week later showed Bill that she had learnt them all. Bill had spoken to the solicitors and they were willing to give her a chance. He reminded her that she must not try to take part in the meeting, however interesting she found it. Helen promised, and the next day she attended her first meeting as minute-taker.

Although she was nervous, Helen took notes, using the abbreviations she had learnt, typed them up and took them to the solicitor who had been in the meeting to check. The solicitor read them carefully and told Helen that they were completely accurate and could be sent out to the client.

Helen now regularly attends meetings as minute-taker and finds her job much more interesting. Bill has been able to reduce the hours that he works, to prepare for his retirement and is very proud of the way Helen took on the opportunity.

UNIT 205 (B&A 17): TEST YOUR KNOWLEDGE

Learning outcome 1: Understand how to take minutes of meetings

1 Explain why it is important that minutes are accurate and grammatical.

2 Describe the legal requirements that apply to minute-taking.

3 Explain terms that are commonly used in meetings.

4 Describe the role of the chairperson in a meeting.

5 Explain the importance of working in partnership with the chairperson when taking minutes.

Learning outcome 2: Be able to take notes of meetings

1 Give an example of a meeting at which you would need to record verbatim minutes.

2 Explain why it is important to record allocated responsibilities for agreed actions.

Learning outcome 3: Be able to produce minutes of meetings

1 Describe how you would make notes at a meeting to ensure that all relevant points had been recorded.

2 Explain what you would do if you required clarification of a point during discussion of an agenda item.

3 Explain what is meant by 'active listening'.

4 Explain why professional language is used in minute-taking.

UNIT 207 (B&A 19) PROVIDE RECEPTION SERVICES

The receptionist is usually the first person that a visitor sees on arrival at the premises. The impression given by the receptionist is the impression the visitor will take of the organisation. The receptionist must put forward a positive image by being well-presented, well-spoken and having a good working knowledge of the organisation and the surrounding area. They must be able to help visitors by answering their questions or directing them to the person or department they have come to visit. Receptionists are also in the front line when it comes to ensuring the security of the premises, people and property, so they must fully understand the procedures in place and follow them at all times.

In this unit you will cover the following learning outcomes:

1 understand reception services
2 be able to provide a reception service.

Ambassador

An official representative of an organisation

PRESENTATION, GREETING VISITORS AND FIRST IMPRESSIONS

A particular type of personality is required to carry out the varying duties of a receptionist in a business environment. You need to be friendly, upbeat and keen to please people. You have to make a good impression and represent the organisation in a positive way. You must be able to act as an **ambassador** for the organisation so that the visitor feels they have come to a professional office where their needs will be dealt with.

The way you dress and the way you behave sets the tone for the whole organisation. Dress should be smart and professional and, most importantly, clean and fresh. Your organisation may have a uniform or dress code that you will need to adhere to. Your behaviour should, equally, be professional. Visitors will get an impression about you before you even speak to them, so make sure you look as if you are there to work.

Wear a smile, and remember in this role you have to look good no matter what you may be feeling inside. Your visitors may not be as polite or patient as you would like, but this may be because of the business they have come to the organisation to carry out. They may be feeling nervous, anxious or just downright angry. Remember this is not directed at you personally; treat them professionally and with kindness.

The receptionist represents the organisation

One of the most important skills for a receptionist to master is the ability to listen. Your visitor may be fully aware of the procedures to follow, and how to reach the person they have come to see. Some, however, will not understand the correct procedures or the precise lines of communication within the organisation. It is your job to listen to what they say carefully so that you can direct them to the best solution to their problem. When a visitor approaches reception, if you already know them, use their name and ask how you can help. If you don't know them, ask their name and use it in further conversation. Some visitors will know who they want to see and may have an appointment. In this case, ask them politely to wait while you contact the person they are visiting. It is much better if the visitor is collected from the reception area and taken to the area they are visiting. Follow the organisation's procedures, which might state that visitors must be escorted to the area they are visiting, for security reasons. Even if this is not the case, while to you it will seem straightforward to find a particular office or meeting room, to a visitor it can be a very **daunting** experience trying to find their way through unfamiliar corridors.

You will usually have tasks to carry out between greeting visitors but, if at any time you have nothing to do, use the time to learn by watching or helping your colleagues. Greet colleagues by name, if you know it. Making small talk about how their holidays went or whether they had a good weekend is fine. Say 'good morning', 'good night' or 'have a good weekend' but don't encourage people who work in the building to look on the reception area as somewhere they can come for a chat when they have nothing better to do. This will give a poor impression to visitors, especially if they are able to overhear office gossip while they are waiting to be collected. If you make it clear that you are busy, people will move on.

Remember, however, that you are there to help your colleagues, as well as visitors, so if they have genuine reasons to come and speak to you, don't give the impression that you are too busy to help them. No reasonable request should be too much trouble – be polite, pleasant and considerate at all times.

PRINCIPAL RECEPTION TASKS OVERVIEW

There will be a number of procedures to follow when working in reception. These will cover entry and departure of visitors, health and safety, security and dealing with any emergencies that might arise. It is important that you understand the structure of the organisation that you are working in and how this affects the lines of communication. There are many different types of organisational structures. Traditional structures are based on functional division and departments. These have precise authority lines for all levels in the management. Traditional types of structures include:

HANDY HINT

Smile, even if you don't feel like it. Visitors will react well to a pleasant greeting.

Daunting

Likely to discourage, intimidate, or frighten somebody

ACTIVITY

Keep a work diary, recording situations in which you feel that you have successfully made a positive impression on visitors.

ACTIVITIES

- Produce a list of activities you should carry out while on reception and those you shouldn't.
- Make a list of additional tasks you carry out, explaining how you fit them within your receptionist duties.

- Line structure – this has a very specific line of command and is suitable for smaller organisations. It allows for easy decision-making and is also very informal in nature.
- Functional structure – this classifies people according to the function they perform. The organisation chart may consist of Chief Executive, sales department, customer service department, production department, accounting department and administrative department.

Other types of organisational structures include:

- Bureaucratic structure – tasks, processes and procedures are all standardised. Suitable for huge enterprises that involve complex operations and require smooth administration of them.
- Team structure – different tasks and processes are allotted to specialised teams of personnel.

When you have received all the necessary training to carry out your responsibilities in the reception area and have had the opportunity to practise for a while, you will want to develop your role further. An important area of development is to fully understand the structure of the organisation and the lines of communication that are established. Visitors will ask you questions and it is important that you give them accurate information, where you have it, or know who to contact for the information. It is also important to understand how much information you can give without breaching confidentiality, and when it is time to pass the visitor on to someone else. There will also be occasions when you will be in possession of information which is confidential to the visitor, such as those attending medical appointments or interviews. It is important that you respect this information and do not pass it on unnecessarily.

You will also be in a position to protect your colleagues from unnecessary interruptions. When possible, you can give visitors information about products and events without them needing to speak to your colleagues. If you have access to a **communal** calendar you can see where and when events or promotions are taking place. If you are kept informed of your colleagues' appointments and any times they will be out of the building, you will be able to help visitors more efficiently.

COMMON MISTAKE

Failing to record the departure of visitors – this could be fatal in the event of an evacuation.

ACTIVITY

If there is an organisation chart available for the organisation, obtain a copy and show the lines of communication, indicating where your role fits in. If there is no organisation chart available, create one.

Communal

Used or owned by all members of a group or organisation

A reception area

You may be able to make suggestions for improving the layout or design of the reception area from your unique viewpoint of working in the environment and observing visitors. You may, for instance, feel that the colour, materials, layout and branding displayed give a poor impression or that visitors experience difficulty in finding their way to the reception desk or the lift without asking. There may be improvements you can suggest for the manning of reception, so that more staff are available at busy times or when other duties have to be carried out. Make your suggestions politely and positively – don't present them as a problem, present them as an improvement to the existing situation.

ACTIVITY

Make a suggestion in writing to your supervisor on an improvement you feel could be made to the reception area. Explain how this will improve the situation for visitors and staff.

Receptionists may have other duties, such as dealing with incoming and outgoing post

ADDITIONAL DUTIES

In all but the busiest reception areas you will be expected to carry out additional duties, rather than standing idly waiting for the next visitor. Among the duties many receptionists are asked to carry out are:

- answering the telephone
- dealing with incoming and outgoing post
- photocopying
- data entry.

Many receptionists answer the telephone as well as greeting visitors. Your organisation will have procedures that must be followed when receiving telephone calls. These will include:

- Answering within a set number of rings – even though you may see answering the telephone as a minor part of your role it is important not to keep the customer waiting.

- Greetings/introductions – answering a business telephone with 'hello' would not be very helpful to the caller, who wants to know that they have got through to the right person or department. Your organisation will have an approved style which may be, 'Good morning, Aspect Training. How can I help you?' or something similar.

- Actions to take when colleagues are unavailable – this may be to take a message or to ask the caller to call again later.

- How to take messages – you may have a message pad or an electronic system for taking messages or you may just scribble it down on a scrap of paper, but the important thing is to get the caller's name, telephone number and the information recorded accurately and to make sure the message gets to the person it is intended for.

- Transferring or passing on calls – you may need to transfer or pass on the call. If the caller has explained the reason for their call to you, pass on this information to your colleague so that the caller does not have to repeat themselves.

- Giving out information – depending on the organisation that you work in, there will be confidential information which you should not give out over the telephone. This will include any personal information on customers or colleagues, which you should not pass on unless you have their specific permission to do so.

UNDERSTANDING RECEPTION TASKS

RECORDING ARRIVALS AND DEPARTURES

In all except the smallest organisations there will be procedures to record the names of people on the premises at any time. It is one of the receptionist's responsibilities to prevent visitors without an appointment or a legitimate reason to be in the building from entering. This is mainly so that, in the event of an emergency, checks can be made that everybody is accounted for. These procedures may involve requiring all visitors to record their arrival and departure in a visitors' book, or alternatively you might have a computer system whereby you enter the details of the visitor, who they have come to see etc. Ask visitors to complete information including their name, their organisation's name and the time of their arrival so that you will be able to see at a glance who is in the building. Ask them to record who they are visiting, so that you can contact them if necessary, and, if they have parked in the car park, record their registration number in case of any problems.

Make sure the visitor is made aware of any security and emergency procedures that apply to the building. Many organisations print these on the reverse of the visitor's badge, but in this case point them out to the visitor and encourage them to read them. Remind the visitor that it is important that they report to Reception when they leave and return their visitor's badge so that you know they are no longer in the building. Many visitors do not appreciate the problems they may cause if they do not let you know when they leave, but in the event of an emergency, time could be lost or even people's lives put at risk searching for someone who has already left.

SECURITY

Another major area of responsibility for the receptionist is security of the premises, the people and property. Security of the premises is covered by the procedures for allowing entry. Some organisations will have **swipe cards** which allow access to the building to employees. These provide an up-to-the-minute record of who is in the building, but only if they are used properly. It is important that colleagues who arrive without their swipe cards because they have forgotten or lost them follow company procedures and are not simply allowed through because you know who they are. It is also important that, as the receptionist, you are made aware of starters and leavers so that you can check that starters have the necessary card and information about entry and departure procedures and that leavers have handed in their cards before leaving.

Assessment criteria

This section covers assessment criteria 1.4, 1.5, 2.3 and 2.7

ACTIVITY

Draw a plan of the reception area, showing emergency exits and security equipment.

Swipe cards

A card inserted into a reader to allow access

If followed correctly, these procedures should prevent any unauthorised access. People and property can be protected by putting procedures in place to limit the risks such as ensuring only minimal amounts of cash are kept in the reception area, and in a lockable container. Where cash is kept, alarms should be available so that the reception staff can call for assistance if needed. Reception staff, in some types of organisation, are sometimes vulnerable to abuse or, possibly, physical assault from visitors. In organisations where there is a real risk of this occurring, the design of reception areas should take this into account, providing higher and deeper reception desks or even security screens, although it is equally worth being aware of the fact that high-security design can provoke the very response from visitors that it is designed to prevent. Providing staff with a separate entry/exit to a safe area may be a better solution.

HEALTH AND SAFETY

One of the most important areas of responsibility when working in reception is health and safety as required by the Health and Safety at Work Act 1974. Because the reception area is used by both staff and visitors, it is important that it is kept tidy and free from potential hazards. Floor surfaces which are highly polished can be slippery, while steps or ramps can cause visitors to trip. Where carpets meet tiled areas or where rugs are placed on a hard floor there is another risk of tripping, as there is if the floor is damaged, with cracked or broken tiles or holes in carpets. Wet floors can also be slippery, so make sure 'wet floor' warning signs are used if liquid has been spilt or if it is raining outside and water is being brought in on people's clothes, shoes or umbrellas.

A less obvious hazard is patterned floors. These can cause vertigo and alter depth perception, particularly in people wearing **varifocal** lenses. Visitors with additional needs such as wheelchair users or those who have guide dogs will need to be given particular attention. Make sure you know the organisation's policy on providing access to visitors with particular needs and follow the procedures closely.

Electrical hazards in a reception area can include cables trailing across areas where people could trip over them or damage the cables by walking on them, leaving live wires exposed. Appliances often found in reception areas, such as coffee machines or water coolers, can also cause hazards if they become damaged or faulty, as well as providing the potential for burns and scalds from hot liquids and spillages making the floor slippery. Where children may be in a reception area it is important that electrical sockets which are not in use are covered as children may insert objects such as toys or spoons into the outlet.

Varifocal

Spectacles with composite lenses for distant, intermediate, and near vision

Be aware of potential hazards in the reception area

Deliveries left in the reception area can cause an obstruction which may be a tripping hazard or injure visitors who bump into them. Where possible deliveries should be made to a separate entrance, but where the reception has to be used, they should be removed as soon as possible. Where visitors use the reception area as a waiting area, a rubbish bin should be provided so that any waste can be disposed of. Check the area regularly and tidy up any rubbish as it will create a poor impression of the organisation as well as being a safety hazard if left to accumulate. Check the contents of notice boards for out-of-date material and remove or replace this where necessary.

While some health and safety issues will only apply when you are working in specific types of organisation, the need to understand emergency procedures and your part in carrying them out will be important in whatever context you are working. You may have a situation where a colleague or a visitor is in need of first aid. You will need to know how to contact a qualified first aider and what to do (or perhaps more importantly, what not to do) until they arrive.

You will also need to know what to do in case of an evacuation of the building because of fire or any other type of threat to the premises. Your responsibilities in the event of evacuating the building will probably include:

- making sure that visitors understand the procedures
- confirming visitors have left the building with the person they had come to meet
- contacting colleagues to ensure visitors are evacuated safely
- closing the entry door when you leave the building
- taking the visitors' book and any staff signing-in records from reception and passing them to the person responsible for checking everybody is accounted for.

You will also need to be trained in how to deal with possible bomb threats which may be received or any suspicious packages delivered or found in the reception area. Make sure you know, and follow, your organisation's procedures and everything will be safe and secure.

DEALING WITH CHALLENGING PEOPLE

As the first point of contact for visitors, receptions may occasionally have to deal with challenging people. This could include confused or upset visitors, rude and demanding people and even violent or aggressive behaviour.

ACTIVITY

Carry out a risk assessment of the reception area, highlighting any areas where health and safety may be a problem.

HANDY HINT

Always have a list of first aiders and their contact numbers handy, and make sure it is always up to date

You may be faced with challenging visitors and will need to know how to deal with difficult situations

If you are faced with aggressive visitors, being able to call for assistance from staff trained in dealing with these situations will be helpful, but being trained in dealing with them yourself may help to prevent them escalating. When a visitor becomes aggressive, he or she may shout, swear, or threaten you and the people around you. Sometimes, verbal aggression can be a prelude to physical violence. It's important to try and soothe the visitor through calm discussion that will address his or her concerns. However, your first priority should always be a back-up system that allows you to call for help when things spiral out of control.

Vocations where aggressive visitors are common include the healthcare field, education, government services and police work. Schools, hospitals and government offices see their fair share of angry and agitated visitors. Understanding how to defuse anger with a calm response can be helpful. Explaining the reality of rules, waiting times, regulations and service restrictions may also help. It's important to avoid angry emotions of your own while dealing with an agitated visitor. Sometimes mental illnesses or substance abuse problems may trigger violent outbursts from visitors.

Being informed of visitors with a history of aggressive behaviour will also help you to be prepared. The design of the reception area can help to reduce the risk of aggression from visitors. Where there is adequate spacing between seats and eye contact between visitors is minimised, access to refreshments such as water or tea or coffee is provided and heating and ventilation are maintained, visitors will be much less likely to become aggressive.

CASE STUDY
WORKING ON RECEPTION

Rebecca works as a receptionist in a hotel. She gets to know a lot of people and generally has a good time. Working in the hotel industry brings a lot of benefits such as cheap weekend stays and the opportunity to work abroad.

When on early shift Rebecca has to get up at 6.00am to arrive at work at 6.45am and she has breakfast at 10.30am. After the morning rush she goes through the reports. Rebecca knows it is important to know her customers, who they are and when they are arriving so she can be fully prepared and welcome them to the hotel.

Lunch is served in the staff restaurant free of charge. After lunch Rebecca counts the takings before the next shift starts. She hands over to a colleague and makes sure messages are passed on and customer requirements are noted so they can have an enjoyable stay.

Originally Rebecca did a placement year working in a hotel in Spain where she got her first experience of the hospitality industry and has never looked back. She enjoys dealing with people and working in a team. There are times when she finds it stressful but when she has helped a customer and they leave happy, it is very rewarding.

Rebecca also says there are great training opportunities. She has just completed a first aid course and is now a first aider. She would like one day to be a front-of-house manager and, as there are always transfer opportunities in this country and abroad, there is no telling where that might be.

UNIT 207 (B&A 19): TEST YOUR KNOWLEDGE

Learning outcome 1: Understanding reception services

1 Describe how the role of the receptionist is important in creating a positive impression of the organisation.

2 Explain how to present a positive image of yourself and why this is important.

3 Explain the purpose of suggesting improvements to a reception area.

4 Describe the structure of your organisation.

5 Describe the procedures for answering the telephone in your organisation.

Learning outcome 2: Be able to provide a reception service

1 Describe the role of the receptionist in the event of an emergency evacuation.

2 Explain the purpose of entry and departure procedures.

3 Describe the health and safety hazards typically found in a reception area.

4 Describe the types of problem that may be encountered with visitors.

5 Describe additional duties a receptionist might carry out.

UNIT 211 (B&A 23) UNDERSTAND THE USE OF RESEARCH IN BUSINESS

One of the most interesting aspects of working in administration is being asked to research information. The topic to be researched will, of course, depend on the organisation you work for and the department you work in, but the process for researching information generally remains the same.

You will need to agree the objectives and deadlines for researching the information, to identify and agree the best sources of information and the methods of recording and storing the information once you have found it. You will also need to understand whether you are being asked for quantitative or qualitative information and whether you should be carrying out primary or secondary research, but all research is fascinating – you never know when you start what you will discover.

In this unit you will cover the following learning outcomes:

1 understand the research process
2 understand how to use research in business.

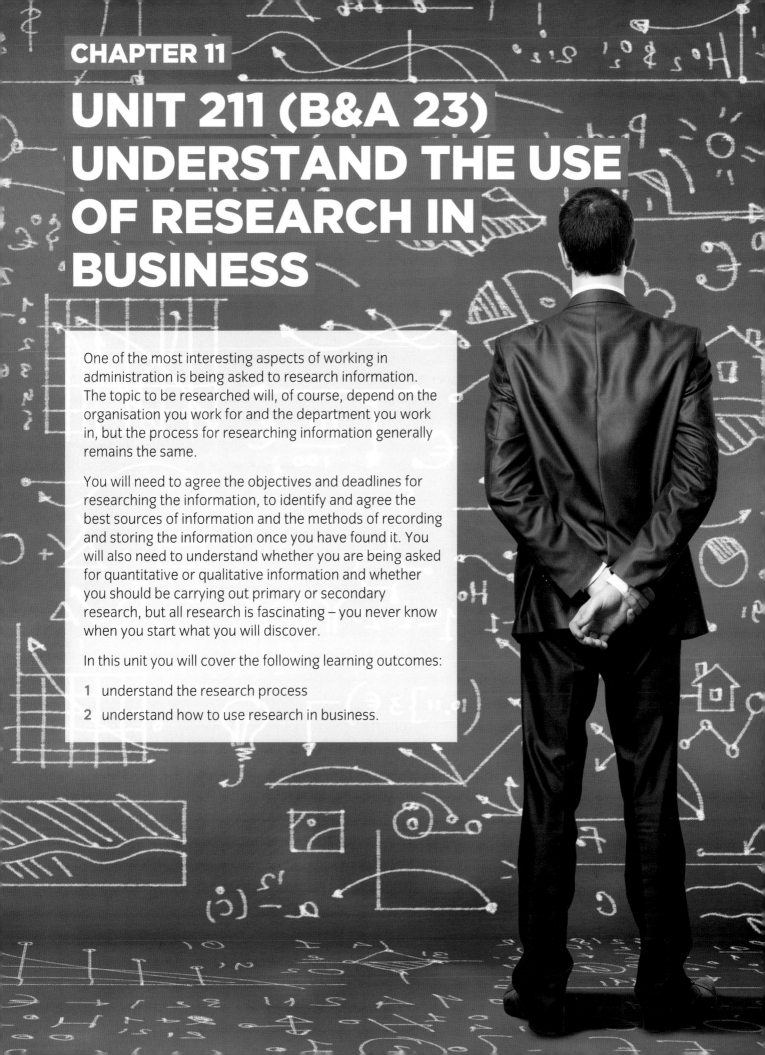

Assessment criteria

This section covers assessment criteria 1.1, 1.2, 1.3, 1.4, 1.5, 1.6, 1.7, 1.8, 2.2 and 2.3

Interviewing members of the public is an example of primary research

HANDY HINT

The research you have been asked for may already have been carried out by someone else in the organisation. Ask around before you start.

Quantitative

Capable of being measured or expressed in numerical terms

Qualitative

Relating to or based on the quality or character of something, often as opposed to its size or quantity

THE RESEARCH PROCESS

When you are asked to research information, the person making the request will have an objective in mind and a deadline for receiving the information. It is important that you understand the research brief. It will not be helpful to supply a list of cast members for every film directed by Tim Burton three weeks after being asked to find out who played The Penguin in *Batman Returns* if the answer was needed the next day.

Once you understand the objective and the deadline involved, you will be able to identify which method of research you will use and whether you will be carrying out primary or secondary research. Primary research uses first-hand data such as interviewing members of the public or an original source such as a company's annual report. Secondary research uses information compiled by other researchers or commentators, such as the results of surveys or a magazine article commenting on the company's annual report.

The advantages of primary research are that it allows you to examine both qualitative and quantitative issues, it addresses specific research issues and it allows you to focus on specific subjects. It also gives you greater control over how the information is collected.

The advantages of secondary research are that there is a wider variety of opinions and resources available. However, the information may be inaccurate.

Primary research may be very expensive. Costs can be incurred in producing the paper for questionnaires or the equipment for an experiment of some sort. Primary data collection requires the development of a research plan and takes longer than secondary research.

Having considered primary or secondary research, the next step is to clarify whether you are being asked to supply quantitative or qualitative information. **Quantitative information** can be analysed to produce hard facts and statistics, for example 37% of people in Eastbourne live in bungalows. **Qualitative information** will provide an understanding of why 37% of people in Eastbourne live in bungalows. Quantitative research and qualitative research differ in the following ways.

Quantitative	Qualitative
Larger samples	Smaller samples
Produces statistics	Produces understanding
Analyses numbers	Analyses opinions
Uses closed questions	Uses open questions
Measures	Explains
Analyses	Produces **anecdotal** evidence

Anecdotal

Consisting of or based on second-hand accounts rather than first-hand knowledge, experience or scientific investigation

DATA COLLECTION

You now need to consider the most reliable sources of information. These can basically be divided into electronic or paper-based sources. In many organisations, there will be a wealth of information available internally, either in a library or on the organisation's intranet. In most cases, the first source will be the internet, but remember that because there is little or no regulation of content posted on the internet: information may not be accurate, comprehensive or unbiased.

Not all the information you find is necessarily valid and reliable. It is important to validate information, wherever it comes from. This may take a little extra time but is worth the effort. Whether the information is found online or offline, the publication date will affect its validity. Some subjects will remain unchanged over time. Information on historical events or the arts will remain factual even if it is found in older books or websites. On the other hand, information in areas that are evolving, such as science, requires a careful check on the date the source material was published.

Very little information is written from first-hand experience; the author will have acquired it from another source. When reviewing information look for its sources. If sources are not listed, that might be a cause for concern. When they are listed, take the opportunity to validate them, as questionable sources are a different problem.

Information can be produced by anyone, so always take the time to check the credentials of the author. If the person writing about a subject has the education and life experience to make them an expert in the field, this increases the validity of their information.

COMMON MISTAKE

Relying on a source such as Wikipedia where there is no control over the accuracy of the information

When researching online try to find at least three sources of information

Search engine

A website designed to search for information on the World Wide Web

Domain names

The name of the website as it appears in the address bar (followed by a suffix such as .com, .edu etc and often preceded by www.)

If time allows, always try to find at least three sources of information. This will reduce the risk of it being unreliable. If you are searching on the internet, convert your topic into a question. This will give you a list of keywords which you can enter into a **search engine**. When the search engine provides you with a number of websites which might contain the information you are looking for, try to judge which will be the most reputable sources. Websites with **domain names** ending with .edu or .gov will be educational or government websites.

When you have found information, evaluate whether it is good information. You need to ask whether the information:

- comes from a credible source
- is up to date
- is not biased
- is free of mistakes
- quotes an original source
- is easy to find.

Much of the above is equally relevant when using more traditional sources of information such as the library. One advantage of the library is that many librarians are specially trained in researching information. Asking them for advice could save many hours of pointless searching; treat them as a kind of human search engine. Even in a small branch library, they will usually have access to the resources of the whole city or county.

Libraries are a traditional source of information

Often the best way to research on paper is to start by looking up your keywords in an encyclopaedia or textbook. The library may have specialised dictionaries for particular topics which give better information than a general dictionary. When you have found references to your keywords, look at the **bibliography** listed at the end of the article – this will direct you towards further sources of information. Don't forget that many professions and trades have specialist magazines or periodicals which may contain useful information.

If you find you are getting too much information, or not specific enough information, narrow your search by combining some of your keywords. If you are getting too little information, you need to simplify your keywords to widen your search.

Use library databases as well as indexes and periodicals. There will be reference books that house factual information and may be designed specifically for the area of expertise you are researching.

Once you have gathered all of the information which you think is relevant, you need to go back to the original objective of the person requesting the research. This will help you to check that the data is suitable for the purpose of the research and to decide how you should record and store the information.

Once the data has been collected it can be analysed and the results presented. Having analysed the data you will be in a position to draw conclusions and present the information. The most common methods of analysing numerical data are visual representations such as charts, graphs and tables.

Bibliography

A list of referenced books and articles which appears at the end of a book or other text

COMMON MISTAKE

Finding too much information. This can be as unhelpful as not finding enough.

ACTIVITY

Keep a work diary of research you are asked to carry out. Record how you went about it, the sources of the information and how you met objectives and deadlines.

HANDY HINT

Try to find three independent sources for any information – this will give a fair chance of it being reliable.

USING RESEARCH IN BUSINESS

Present the information in a format which will allow the objective to be most readily met and make sure you meet the original deadline. Present the information using the correct house style if your organisation uses one. Store the information in a way that allows it to be retrieved easily if needed again – your research, whether primary or secondary, could become secondary research for someone else in the future and save them a lot of time in searching for the information again. Make sure you refer to the sources of the information, in case it is necessary to go back to the original source for confirmation or clarification, or in case any copyright issues arise. It is also important that you understand the information you have researched, as you may be asked to expand on it at a later date.

TYPES OF RESEARCH

The range and purpose of research will differ from organisation to organisation. In commercial businesses, the majority of research will be carried out in order to increase sales and profits. Examples include:

- Marketing research – this is the gathering, recording and analysing of data that relates to a specific problem in marketing products or services, often carried out as a reaction to a problem that occurs.

- Market analysis – this involves analysing market segment factors to decide the potential market for a product or service. Data is gathered and analysed to identify factors that affect possible sales. The analysis is also used to determine how much money should be invested in marketing and how much has to be produced to fulfil the needs of the market.

- Product research – this is conducted to measure the potential acceptance of new products, find improvements or additions for existing products, make changes or improvements in product packaging or determine acceptability of a product over a competitor's product.

- Pricing research – this can be used to assess the correct level of prices for products or services. While prices must be high enough to cover production and operating costs, often the formula used for achieving a given profit margin causes prices to be set above or below acceptable market levels.

- Advertising research – this can determine the potential effect advertising might have on a target audience. Businesses often conduct research into the content, the media and the effectiveness of advertisements before they invest heavily in an advertising campaign. Content research measures how the desired content comes across to an audience sample.

- Sales research – this is used to study customer records and other available data to uncover marketing opportunities. Selling research, on the other hand, analyses whether the sales presentation effectively holds the interest of customers and allows them to understand the product.

While research is practical for organisations that make products that do not have high production costs, its application may be limited for other organisations by the research cost itself. Test marketing, for instance, may not be a viable method of research for businesses producing large, expensive goods. Chocolate is easily test-marketed at a relatively low cost; the cost of test-marketing submarines, on the other hand, is prohibitive.

LEGISLATION RELATING TO SOURCE MATERIAL

Remember that most published information is subject to the Copyright, Designs and Patents Act. The law gives the creators of literary, dramatic, musical, artistic works, sound recordings, broadcasts, films and typographical arrangement of published editions, rights to control the ways in which their material may be used and acknowledged.

Types of work protected by the act include song lyrics, manuscripts, manuals, computer programs, commercial documents, leaflets, newsletters and articles, plays, dance, musical recordings and scores, photography, painting, sculptures, architecture, technical drawings/diagrams, maps, logos, video footage, films, broadcasts and cable programmes.

The Copyright (Computer Programs) Regulations 1992 extended the rules covering literary works to include computer programs. Copyright is an automatic right and arises whenever an individual or company creates a work.

Personal information is also covered by the Data Protection Act, so it is important to ensure that you are complying with its requirements when including this kind of information in your research.

Ethics can affect the conduct and use of research

ETHICS

As well as legislation, research is affected by ethics. Many professional associations, government agencies and universities have adopted specific codes, rules and policies relating to research ethics. Ethical principles that these address include:

- Honesty – it is important to report data, results, methods and procedures, and publication status honestly. You should not fabricate, falsify or misrepresent data or deceive your colleagues or the public.

- Objectivity – try to avoid bias in research where objectivity is expected or required.

- Carefulness – avoid careless errors and negligence; examine your own work and the work of your colleagues carefully and critically. Keep accurate records of data collection.

- Openness – share data, results, ideas, tools and resources. Be open to criticism and new ideas.

- Respect for intellectual property – respect patents, copyrights and other forms of intellectual property. Do not use unpublished data, methods or results without permission. Give credit where credit is due. Give proper acknowledgement or credit for all contributions to research.

- Confidentiality – protect confidential communications, such as personnel records, trade or military secrets and patient records.

ACTIVITIES

- Go to your local library and research information on a topic of your choice. Produce a report on the topic, using your research without reference to the internet.
- Look at a research paper or report that has been produced in your organisation. Identify whether primary or secondary research has been used and whether quantitative or qualitative data has been produced.

CASE STUDY
MARKET RESEARCH

One of the Food Standards Agency's main aims is to identify what customers want, need or expect to see on food labelling. The FSA's objective is to help consumers make informed choices about which foods they buy; for instance, if they had a nut allergy or were on a low calorie diet.

To meet their aims and objectives the FSA devised a market research campaign with a series of questions. These included:

- What sort of information would you like to see on packaging?
- How could the information be set out for ease of communication?

Each year the FSA carries out face-to-face interviews with consumers to produce its 'Consumer Attitudes to Food' survey. This research method means that people get a chance to say exactly what they think.

For example, over 3,500 people gave their views for the 2007 survey. The 2007 survey showed that:

- Many people had an increasing awareness of the 'five-a-day' fruit and vegetables message.
- About 30% more consumers were aware that they should eat five portions of fruit and vegetables a day compared with the year 2000.
- Increasing numbers of consumers were worried about the amount of fat, salt and sugar in food because they understood how these might damage their health.
- A growing number of consumers said that they looked at nutritional information on the labels to check the fat and salt content.

However, the survey showed that there was still room for improvement. It showed that whilst 40% of people snacked on fresh fruit in between meals, almost 35% snacked on biscuits or cakes and a further 20% on crisps or savoury snacks.

UNIT 211 (B&A 23): TEST YOUR KNOWLEDGE

Learning outcome 1: Understand the research process

1 State two reasons why it is important to agree objectives and deadlines before researching information.

2 Explain how to record and store information researched.

3 Explain why it is necessary to make a record of and acknowledge the information sources used.

4 Explain why it is important to check the reliability of sources of information.

5 Compare internet and paper-based sources of information in terms of reliability and ease of access.

Learning outcome 2: Understand how to use research in business

1 Explain the limitations on application of research in your organisation.

2 Describe how research information can be validated.

3 List the legislation which affects the publication of research findings.

4 Explain the role of ethics in relation to research.

UNIT 215 (B&A 27) CONTRIBUTE TO THE ORGANISATION OF AN EVENT

Events are different from meetings. They will be larger, last longer, involve more people and sometimes even be open to the public. They don't just happen, they have to be planned and organised in great detail. The event organiser will need a wide range of skills including communication, negotiation, project management, budget management, staff management, public relations and interpersonal skills. The measure of successful event organisation is that people attending the event are completely unaware of the amount of planning that has gone into it.

Co-ordinating an event involves making sure that everything runs smoothly on the day. You may be a full-time event co-ordinator or this may be a part of your job which happens only occasionally. You may be co-ordinating an event that you have organised yourself or you may be liaising with the organiser. Organising the event ends on the day the event takes place. Co-ordinating the event takes over at this point.

In this unit you will cover the following learning outcomes:

1 understand event organisation
2 be able to carry out pre-event actions
3 be able to set up an event
4 be able to carry out post-event actions.

Assessment criteria

This section covers assessment criteria 1.1, 1.2, 1.3, 1.4, 1.5, 1.6, 2.1, 2.2, 2.3, 2.4 and 2.5

PRE-EVENT ACTIONS

The organisation of events may be a full-time occupation or an occasional task added to a long list of other responsibilities. In either case, it is a complex and demanding role requiring the ability to take a hands-on attitude to the task while working as part of a team. When organising events you will need to be able to communicate clearly, organise effectively and pay close attention to detail. The event will have a client who has required the event to be organised. The client may be internal or external to the organisation, but will have objectives to be met and a budget to be kept to.

You will need to liaise with the client to find out exactly what their requirements are and what their overall budget is. You will then be able to look at the possible venues that can stage the event. You will need to know what type of event the client wants. There are a large range of different types of event, each of which has different features which you'll need to consider when at the planning stage.

POSSIBLE EVENT TYPES

EXHIBITIONS OR TRADE SHOWS

Exhibitions, or trade shows, are occasions when manufacturers and producers can exhibit their products and talk to potential customers. These can range from small, chamber of commerce-sponsored events, to national conferences held in convention centres. They are an opportunity to introduce your organisation's products or services to their targeted audience.

Unless the event has some history, it will be difficult for the people selling space to give you a good idea on the number of attendees, and they definitely won't be able to give you any idea of the number of **qualified buyers** that will come through the event.

Qualified buyer

An individual or company who is in the market and displays some evidence of being financially able to buy

Whether the event is new or tested, ask some questions before you commit your organisation to exhibit at the event. Find out how they are marketing the event and whether the exhibit area is free or only available to paid conference attendees. There will be many more attendees if the exhibit area is free, but they might not be qualified buyers. These people are more likely to be unqualified prospects looking to see what is new, what their competition is doing, or people attempting to sell things to exhibitors.

If the event appeals to you but you are unsure of attendance, you will be taking a risk that qualified prospects won't be there, and it might just be a learning experience for you. If you aren't sure whether you should be an exhibitor or not, consider going to the event as an attendee first. You can network among other attendees to see if there is interest in what you offer, and decide whether or not you want to participate in the future.

Before you book space at the exhibition or trade show, find out exactly what you're paying for. An exhibit space may just be a six-foot table, a booth made of pipe and curtaining, with a draped table and a couple of chairs. It might be a space that can accommodate, or might even require, a freestanding booth that you buy or rent. Find out exactly what you get and whether electricity and telecommunications are included if you need them in your exhibit. Ask how many staff members are allowed in your booth and if you get free passes to the event. Find out if any marketing, sponsorship or advertising is included. Don't forget to factor in the cost of travel and staff time.

In most cases, sponsors or hosts of the event, past exhibitors and people buying the largest booth spaces get to select their location first. If you're a new exhibitor, ask what the layout of the space will look like. Remember that areas with the most traffic will be at the front, near the entrances. If you are stuck in the back or far corners of the room, you can still make the show work for you, if you have the budget. Have entertainment in your booth or offer a fabulous promotional item that everyone will want. Make sure it's something that is very visible when carried or worn so other attendees can see it and ask where they got it. Also make sure you have people work for this item by watching a presentation or completing a questionnaire or survey and get their contact information, don't just give things away free.

Trade shows are an opportunity to exhibit products and meet potential customers

Some shows don't allow you to actually sell things in your exhibit area. If this is the case, you will only be allowed to gather contact information so you can follow up later. This type of event may not be for you if you rely heavily on people buying your products on impulse.

If, however, you establish relationships before selling and expect a longer sales cycle, you could do well in this environment.

Consider the staff you'll need to keep someone at your booth at all times during exhibit hours. If the event doesn't have scheduled free time, or if there isn't time dedicated for attendees to visit exhibits, you'll be fighting with speakers to get the attention of the audience, and the speakers usually win. If you decide to become an exhibitor, you'll want to make sure attendees have plenty of time to visit the exhibit area to learn about you.

It doesn't do any good to get qualified prospects if the organisation doesn't have the time to follow up after the show. There should be a timeline and strategy in place for contacting prospects and potential business partners for follow-up before the organisation gets involved in an event.

CONFERENCES

Conferences are among the most important events for event organisers to be involved in. They may be held in venues ranging from meeting rooms in hotels to large conference centres.

Considerations when selecting venues include:

Conferences may be held in a variety of venues, such as hotels or conference centres

- Cost – during difficult economic times, many organisations are reducing the size of their conferences. Many companies are relocating conferences to smaller cities that offer cheaper rates. Some are hosting conferences on their own premises rather than hosting them at conference centres. Smaller organisations are taking advantage of the facilities at the universities in their area to save on cost.

- Convenience – a gathering of sales people from a northern organisation is more likely to be held relatively locally, for example in Manchester rather than in London. This reduces the cost for the attendees and planners. Equally, even if a venue has an excellent conference room, if there are not enough hotels in town for all of the attendees, it does not make sense to hold it there. While many attendees would be willing to drive from miles away to attend, many would not.

- The conference room at the venue – if you need to make a presentation on a large screen, having the screen and a means to project those images already available in the room is hugely important. You may have to pay extra for the convenience of not having to provide your own screen and projector. The acoustics and seating arrangements also factor in the room set-up.

There are many different types of conferences. While all share some similarities, there are some differences:

- Business conferences may be annual general meetings, held for shareholders to announce the company's results for the past year and to plan the company's future. If an organisation has many sites around the country, the management teams will get together to talk about the organisation's future and to share best practice. This may be the only time the management teams are in the same location. Often these conferences are held in the company's headquarters.

An annual general meeting in progress

- Training conferences – large organisations will hold these several times a year. This gives everyone the opportunity to learn new information and share best practice with their colleagues. Some training conferences will be presented by a training organisation and will be open to people from different organisations. These conferences require a classroom type of setting and easy access to restaurants if lunch and dinner are not included in the session.

Conferences may involve a large number of delegates

Delegate

Give authority to somebody else to act, make decisions or allocate resources on one's behalf

Marketing kiosks can be used to launch a product, such as a new soft drink at a sporting event

- Academic conferences can be held for two main reasons. University scientists may hold them either to announce research results or to present newly published information to a group. Many of these conferences are held on the campus of a large university.

- Internet conferences have grown in popularity as travel costs have increased while budgets have not. Even though they may seem as simple as just getting online, these conferences require planning – particularly if the participants are in different time zones.

Conference-planning involves every little detail from making sure there are enough water glasses on each table to making sure the sound system works. These tasks may be **delegated** to several people but are overseen by the event organiser, who carries a huge responsibility.

PRODUCT LAUNCHES

Product launches are an essential component of the marketing mix of large companies. They give the public and the media a chance to hear everything about the product. Product launch events introduce the product to investors and other partners. Often new products are launched at the annual shareholder meetings. This gives the shareholders a chance to see and perhaps even test the product before it is introduced to the general public. However, if the product is a major new addition to the organisation's range the company may want to create a huge event and the shareholders may find out at the same time as the media and the company's customers.

Product launches to introduce the product to old and new customers may not be formal events. For example, a company announcing a new soft drink may set up a kiosk at a major sporting event or large fair. These events require just as much planning as setting up a major event. Space has to be reserved, displays have to be set up and staff have to be hired.

Product launches to introduce the product to the media could be in the form of a press conference. If you are planning a product launch where the media is invited you must make sure there is room for photographers – both still photographers and film cameras. They must have an excellent view so that they can capture the action. Prepare a 'press kit' that contains information about the product and the company.

If you are given the task of handling the market introduction of a new product, you have a huge responsibility. Some things to consider are:

- Venue – most product launch events happen in big cities or in cities where the company is located. Sometimes these launches are held in big conference centres so that there is room for the shareholders and the media. However, some product launches are held in the boardroom of the organisation. The venue depends on how big the company is, how big the product is and how much money the company wants to invest in the market introduction.

- Timing – usually the introduction of a new product, such as a new toy or game console, coincides with the Christmas season. New soft drinks may be launched during a big sporting event like Wimbledon or the World Cup. Millions of people watch these events and announcing the new product and airing commercials during these events will create interest.

If the client wants food at the event, you have a lot of decisions to make. Will it be a buffet or a full-course meal? What time of day will the new product launch event be held? What kind of food will be best for the attendees? How much food should be ordered? Will waiting staff be needed?

The small details may not seem important, but they could make or break an event. Can you imagine launching a new product and half the attendees having to stand because there are not enough chairs? Most product launches include an information pack that is given to the guests. These packages need to be ready and there need to be enough for all the attendees. The organiser is responsible for making sure the small details are handled. Product launches are some of the most exciting events for any organiser, but these events are also the most stressful. The key, as it is for any event, is in proper planning.

ACTIVITY

Your organisation has decided to hold a product launch to which the media are to be invited. Research suitable venues and obtain estimates of the cost. Write a note to your line manager suggesting the most appropriate venue, with reasons.

TEAM-BUILDING EVENTS OR AWAY DAYS

Team-building events or away days can increase overall employee performance, promote co-operation among team members and across teams, improve job satisfaction and help to broaden the understanding of organisational goals and objectives. If they are improperly designed or administered, on the other hand, they can be completely pointless.

The events should serve as small-scale versions of the problems and solutions that staff face at work and the challenges of the events should relate to the struggles they are challenged with daily. If an important current team challenge is, for example, adapting to a new organisational structure, matching exercises involving small, specialised teams working together to achieve a common goal would be a good idea.

Remember that physical endurance, strength and dexterity are not likely to be the major attributes of team members. Fitness and physical ability should, therefore, not play a major role in team-building events. Consider the members of the team and set the level of physical assertion necessary low enough so that each team member can participate satisfactorily. Physical activities, especially outdoors, can be memorable and successful as long as everyone can be included.

Often, team-building exercises are administered as stand-alone events, while they should be the opening episode in a continuing drive towards success. Don't create events that are too taxing or too mindless. In an effort to ensure that employees have fun while completing team-building exercises, some organisers make them too light and silly, while some create events that are unduly draining, emotionally or otherwise. Try to strike a balance so that events aren't too funny or too difficult, as either of these extremes will undermine the main messages of the event.

Consider hiring professionals to create and administer the exercises. Depending on your cost and time constraints, and the complexity of the exercises, professional consultants can help to identify the message, facilitate the event and implement the feedback and measurement components afterward.

Team-building events can help improve employee performance

WEDDINGS

Wedding planning will normally be carried out by full-time wedding planners or the staff of wedding venues. The basic principles are the same as planning for any other event, but as this is the most important day in the life of the client, it is useful to have a checklist to plan all the necessary stages.

Ten to twelve months before the wedding:

- Agree with the bride and groom whether the wedding is to be formal or casual, religious or civil.

- Agree the budget and who will pay for the wedding.

- Agree a date and time. Have back-up dates in mind, in case a key element is unavailable on the chosen date.
- Agree the ceremony and reception venues.
- Sign a contract with the wedding caterer.
- Book the wedding florist and choose arrangements.
- Book the musicians and/or DJ for both the ceremony and the reception.
- Select and confirm the wedding photographer and videographer, if you're using one.

Four to six months before the wedding:

- Reserve any rental equipment you'll need, including dishes, tables, chairs, linens, tents.
- Select the wedding cake designer, and order the wedding cake.
- Arrange transport.
- Order stationery.
- Book accommodation for out-of-town guests.

Planning for a wedding will usually begin months in advance

Two to three months before the wedding:

- Agree a list of 'must-take' photographs and give it to the photographer.
- Discuss menus with the caterer.
- Check that wedding invitations have been sent.
- Send wedding announcements to local newspapers.

The month of the wedding:

- Check that the marriage licence has been applied for.
- Contact the caterer, cake baker, photographer, videographer, florist, musicians, transportation, hotels, etc to confirm arrival and delivery times.
- Arrange printing of the wedding programme.

AWARDS CEREMONIES

Awards ceremonies may be organised to recognise people's performance and make people aware that good work will be rewarded. They show the general public and other staff that the organisation is aware of outstanding accomplishments. Recognition motivates others to strive for excellence. Being rewarded for doing well is one of the biggest incentives anyone can receive.

If you are asked to organise an awards ceremony, agree the budget. This will determine the menu, the number of guests, the venue of the event and other details that involve spending money. Decide where to hold the ceremony. Think about what kind of event you're going to hold and then find a venue to match. Your organisation may have a recreation centre or a presentations room. If not, you will need to rent a room somewhere else. Consider whether you are going to serve food and what you need in the room. Think about how big the venue needs to be. A big hall will look empty if there are only a few people in it, and a small one will limit how many people you can have.

The venue selected for an event such as an awards ceremony will depend on the budget that has been agreed

Awards should fit the action being recognised, the person and the occasion. Possible types of award include:

- pins
- statuettes
- certificates
- plaques
- framed recognition citations
- gifts.

Bear in mind the surprise element. Is the recipient going to be told in advance that they are going to receive an award? Surprises can be fun, but you don't want the recipient to have a heart attack from shock before reaching the podium to accept the award.

When considering the number of guests include the immediate guests and their guests, family and friends. You'll want to serve refreshments. The size of the event and the resources the venue offers will help decide what kind of food you'll serve. You will not be able to serve a sit-down dinner at a venue with no kitchen.

When considering refreshments, you can either plan it yourself or get help from a caterer. Doing it yourself can save money, but remember, you have to plan, buy, prepare and serve the food and clean up, all of which the caterers will do. On the other hand, you're paying the caterer for a pre-established number of people, whether they show up or not.

You may need people to set the place up, serve the food, put the water glass close to the speakers, serve the guests and clean up afterwards. You may need to hire support staff to help or leave this to the caterers.

No matter how small the ceremony, you don't want people tripping over tables or sitting with their backs to the podium. If the ceremony is large, then you need to consider who will sit where and with whom. Also consider who needs to be close to the podium.

Decorating the venue will depend to a large extent on the tone you want the ceremony to take. Silly balloons and festive noise-makers would be inappropriate for a sober, dignified ceremony. Consider the following decorations for a formal awards ceremony:

- flowers
- balloons
- bows
- tablecloths
- centre pieces
- pictures on the wall

- banners
- posters
- plants
- candles.

Finally you will need to consider:

- Who is going to actually present the awards. A choice could be made depending upon the recipient's job or accomplishment. It could be a colleague, the recipient's spouse, parent, or child. Whoever it may be, you need to contact that person in advance and to allow time for preparation. If necessary, arrange a rehearsal to fine-tune length and tone of speeches
- Who is going to speak first.
- How you are going to start the ceremony.
- When it will end.
- At what time the award will be presented.

The presentation schedule doesn't have to be followed to the minute, but you want to know who speaks after whom, so you can print a programme for the guests. Also, people should know how much time they have to present their speeches and comments. If you expect everyone to take about three minutes, and someone takes thirty, it can not only be boring for the audience, but it can throw off the timing of the whole event and change the feeling of it. The clearer you can be about timing, the more likely you are to get close to what you want.

WORKSHOPS

Workshops are a flexible and effective method of training, learning, development, change management, team building and problem solving. If you are organising a workshop, consider and agree the aims. It might be useful to invite suggestions from delegates beforehand for workshop subjects and aims that will make the most of commitment and **empowerment**.

Adapt the content and structure of workshops to the particular situation. Consider what you or the delegates are seeking to achieve. Establish and agree a measurable output or result that represents the aims and then think how to structure the workshop.

Empowerment

Giving somebody a greater sense of confidence or self-esteem

You will need to think about what equipment is required for the event, such as flipchart and marker pens for a workshop

It is often a good idea to have the delegates use flipchart paper and coloured marker pens and hang the sheets around the walls. This enables delegates to be far more dynamic and creative than modern technology media. Encourage people to use creative methods that are appropriate for their personal styles and learning styles:

- Visual, spatial, creative people enjoy working with flipcharts, colours, 'post-it' notes, etc.

- People-centred individuals and teams enjoy human interaction, such as role-plays, discussions, mutual interviews, etc.

- Logical, numerate, process-oriented people are happier with more structured planning tools and computers.

Think about the sort of people in the workshop groups and provide tools, materials and methods that they will be comfortable using.

CONSULTATION

Consultation is a process by which the public's input on matters affecting them is sought. Its main goals are in improving the efficiency, transparency and public involvement in large-scale projects or laws and policies. It usually involves:

- notification to publicise the matter to be consulted on

- consultation, a two-way flow of information and opinion exchange

- participation, involving interest groups in the drafting of policy or legislation.

Public consultation is typical of countries such as the United Kingdom, Canada, New Zealand or Australia, though most democratic countries have similar systems. Ineffective consultations are considered to be cosmetic consultations that were carried out for show and not true participatory decision-making. If, as part of a consultation, you are asked to organise a consultation event, you need to consider:

- ensuring the consultation method is appropriate for your target audiences
- taking advice from members of the target audience, to ensure the consultation method is appropriate
- ensuring the consultation exercise is well publicised in a variety of media to attract your target audience
- explaining clearly from the outset what you are consulting on and what the options are
- ensuring information is available in the right format, for example other languages
- ensuring venues are fully accessible for the target audience
- ensuring the venue is appropriate, for example community buildings such as schools, day centres, council offices
- ensuring the layout is appropriate, for example chairs 'in the round' rather than with an audience and top table
- the need to provide translators or interpreters or sign language interpreters
- whether the timing is appropriate for your audience
- the need to provide crèche facilities
- providing transport for those who need it or offering to pay transport costs
- providing refreshments
- providing any other incentives for attendance
- who the key stakeholders are in this exercise
- ensuring that all groups, internal and external, that are likely to be affected are involved.

At the end of the meeting, remember to thank the participants and tell them how and when you will be feeding back the results. Ensure the results of the consultation exercise are widely communicated in a variety of media.

SEMINARS

Seminars are a popular source of academic, professional or technical instruction, presenting information to diverse audiences. They may be private or public, series or single, commercial or informative, lecture- or dialogue-based. They are less formal than academic lectures, allowing audience members to interrupt with opinions or discuss results.

Planning for a seminar should begin several months in advance by developing a theme. Is the seminar ground-breaking, **philosophical** or technically-orientated? Who is the target audience? Select the niche market carefully. When choosing a venue, remember that different seminar styles require different facilities. The higher the status of the seminar attendees, the more prestigious the venue must be. Additionally, the size of the location is dependent upon the estimated attendance figures.

Philosophical

Concerned with or given to thinking about the larger issues and deeper meanings in life and events

A seminar underway

Paid seminars typically attract more people than free seminars. This is because people believe that paid seminars present an image of academic integrity, educational value and increased expectations. Your organisation may be able to find sponsors as seminars are an effective method for organisations to promote their business. For instance, a car manufacturer's seminar has already assembled a niche market, so local car dealerships and garages have a guarantee of brand positioning.

COMMON MISTAKE

Don't assume a free seminar will attract more people than one they have to pay to attend.

DEALING WITH POTENTIAL PROBLEMS

Whatever type of event you are organising, it is important to consider the problems that might arise and the risks associated with these types of event. Contingency planning is a systematic approach to identifying what can go wrong in a situation. Rather than hoping that everything will turn out well you should try to identify what might go wrong and be prepared with plans, strategies and approaches for avoiding or coping.

Contingencies are problems anticipated by an organiser including low-probability difficulties that would have a major impact. The objective of contingency planning is not to identify and develop a plan for every possibility but to think about major risks and possible responses. Organisers who have given thought to contingencies and possible responses are more likely to achieve the client's objectives.

You need to consider:

- what may occur
- the worst case scenario
- what would cause the greatest disruption
- what happens if delays occur
- what happens if key people leave the organisation.

You will need to take into account the resources which will be required by the particular event, which may include:

- accommodation
- catering
- equipment
- car parking.

You will also need to consider any special requirements which attendees might have, such as wheelchair access, hearing induction loops or dietary restrictions.

You can then carry out a risk assessment for the event. Risk assessment will be unique to that event and will take into account the venue itself, the marketing and media attention attached to the event, any high risk attendees, and the size and location of the event.

Risk assessments should follow five steps:

1. Identify the hazard	2. Decide who might be harmed and how	3. Evaluate the risks and decide on precaution	4. Record your findings and implement them	5. Review your assessment and update if necessary

The risk assessment will also take into account all the potential risks at the event which may include:

- Fire – it will put checks in place regarding placement of chairs, aisles and access to emergency exits. It will also look at eliminating any potentially highly combustible material.
- Theft – large events are prime targets for theft. Unfortunately theft has to be a major concern to any event with crowds of people.
- Political activists/demonstrators – this may be anybody with a grudge against a company which is organising the event or participating in the event and may include ex-employees or current employees.

THE CITY & GUILDS TEXTBOOK

Identify risks associated with each activity and consider each of the following:

Physical risks	Injury, death, travel- or food-related illnesses, etc
Reputation risks	The reputation of the whole organisation, the reputation of the department responsible for the event
Emotional risks	Reactions of attendees, sensitive subject matter, potential controversy, etc
Financial risks	Cost reduction, proper budgeting, etc
Facilities risks	The safety of the facilities for your participants or attendees, the maintenance and clean-up of the facilities, etc

Assess each risk for the probability of it happening and the seriousness of the consequences. Make decisions about how to manage each risk identified. You can accept, modify, transfer, and/or eliminate each risk based on your assessment. Share your plans and risk management actions with your client and plan your event according to those decisions.

SHORTLISTED VENUES

When you have shortlisted venues that have the necessary facilities you will be in a position to compare costs. Ask each suitable venue for a quote, making sure that they provide information on whether the rate offered is a 24-hour, per-delegate rate or a room-hire rate plus accommodation. Ask whether prices are negotiable or if a discount is available if a certain number of attendees is involved.

When you receive the quotes, consider the following before choosing the lowest offer:

- whether a deposit is required and, if so, when
- what their policy is on cancellation refunds
- when final payment is required
- whether the total cost is within the budget you have agreed for the event.

Unless you have held similar events at a particular venue previously, do not make assumptions that the offered rooms will provide adequate facilities; check them out for yourself. There are a huge number of issues that you will want to be confident of before the date of the event; fire-fighting problems immediately before or even during the event is never satisfactory.

Perhaps the most important area of planning a venue is the availability of the most suitable layout for the event. Different types of layout are used for different types of event:

- theatre style layout
- classroom layout
- boardroom layout
- horseshoe layout
- banquet – cabaret layout.

Make sure the layout you require is available, and that rooms will be laid out in the required way before attendees arrive.

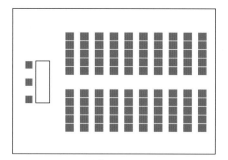
Theatre

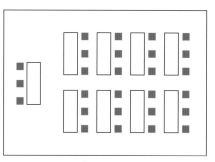
Classroom

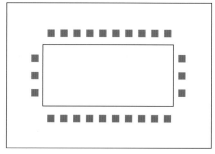
Boardroom

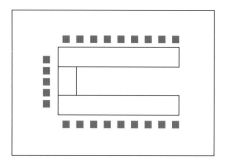
Horseshoe

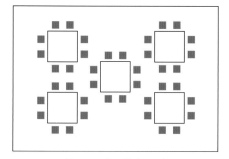
Banquet – Cabaret

CONSIDERATIONS AFTER VENUE SELECTION

When you have considered all the variables, you will be in a position to decide on the venue and start to arrange the event. While some types of event will require even longer, as explained above, most major events take up to 12 months to arrange, and you should put the following into your diary.

Twelve months before the event:

- confirm the venue
- invite speakers
- advise the venue of the estimated numbers.

Six months before the event:

- confirm the programme
- invite attendees
- agree catering requirements
- confirm room layouts
- confirm equipment requirements.

Two months before the event:

- acknowledge responses from attendees
- follow up unanswered invitations
- visit the venue
- send reminders to invited speakers.

One month before the event:

- assemble any resources required
- recheck arrangements.

Two weeks before the event:

- confirm the final details
- arrange pre-registration so attendees only have to give their name on arrival.

One week before the event:

- confirm final numbers to the venue
- work out seating plans.

You may be able to delegate some of these arrangements to other members of staff, but remember to monitor that they have been carried out correctly. When the day of the event arrives, it will be too late to find out that someone has forgotten to make sure there is somewhere for attendees to park.

> **HANDY HINT**
>
> If the venue you select is previously unknown to you, ask for the names of other organisations that have held similar events and check their experience of the venue. Finally, before committing yourself, visit the venue in person and check out the facilities offered and the level of customer service.

> **HANDY HINT**
>
> With the proper contacts, you can accomplish the different aspects of the event more easily and in less time

Check all the arrangements are in place before the event begins

SETTING UP AN EVENT

On the day of the event, arrive well before the start time so that you can check that all the arrangements are in place. You will need to liaise with the venue to make sure that all the client's requirements have been met.

Your responsibilities will involve checking that the catering has been organised for the agreed times. If a sit-down meal is included in the event, delegates may have been asked to indicate their choices for each course prior to the day. If not, you will need to confirm the deadline for providing this information to the catering staff and ensure that delegates are asked for their preferences in plenty of time.

If a buffet is to be provided, you will need to check where it is to be set out, and at what time, and that any special dietary requirements that you have been advised of have been catered for.

If the event is taking place at a venue that you are not familiar with, you will need to check where the toilets are and what provision there is for smokers. You will also need to know where fire exits are situated, where the assembly point is and whether there is a fire alarm test scheduled during the event.

You will want to reassure yourself that you know how to raise the alarm should an emergency arise, who to contact if first aid is required and where disabled access and exits are situated. Lastly, you'll want to check that all of the equipment and resources which have been requested for the event are in place and working.

You may be responsible for meeting and greeting delegates when they arrive

If there are guest speakers or presenters booked for the event, you will want to run through their arrangements with them. If they are providing resources of their own, such as computer disks or USB sticks containing their slides, make sure they are compatible with any hardware being provided by the organiser or the venue. This should have already been checked before the event, but it is well worth making sure that there will be no problems before it is too late to take any necessary action.

If delegates are staying overnight, check whether pre-registration has been organised so that arriving delegates have only to give their names to reception in order to receive their room key. If rooms are not ready at the time that delegates arrive, make sure there is locked storage available for their luggage. Delegates will not want to have to carry suitcases with them during the day if they have arrived by taxi.

You will need to carry out all of these checks before the first delegates arrive, as you will want to be available to greet them and welcome them to the event. You can check whether they have any questions or previously unstated requirements, show them where to sign in, where the cloakroom is, where they can find refreshments and where they need to go for the main event.

ACTIVITY

Attend an event and greet arrivals, directing them as necessary. Ask the event organiser for a witness testimony describing how you carried out the task.

If delegate packs are provided, you can direct the delegates to the area where they are being distributed, together with any identity badges and a seating plan. The actual handing out of packs and badges should have been delegated to another member of the team, leaving you free to deal with the delegates' needs on arrival.

When the event is underway, check the delegate list against the arrivals and follow up on non-arrivals that you have booked accommodation for. You will need to advise the venue as soon as you can of any accommodation that will no longer be needed, as the cancellation charge can be reduced if they are able to resell it.

This is also a good time to check whether all the contracted provision has been provided – both between you and the venue and between you and the client. If anything is missing, you will be able to investigate whether it can still be supplied or if there will be a need to adjust the payment to be made in line with the agreed **terms and conditions.**

Terms and conditions

The requirements laid down formally in an agreement or contract, or proposed by one side when negotiating an agreement

While the event is in progress, you need to be available to everybody. Your role is to handle any difficulties as they arise and, wherever possible, foresee them so they can be prevented. The delegates, and your client, are looking forward to an event that appears to proceed without any effort. It is your efforts that will make this happen.

Arrange with the reception area to advise you of late arrivals so that you can meet them and escort them into the event with a minimum of disruption. Keep at least one step ahead of each planned stage of the event. Check that refreshments will be available before they are due. Check that speakers have everything they need before their slot begins.

DEALING WITH PROBLEMS

Deal with any problems that arise quickly and efficiently. The list of potential problems is as long as the list of delegates, but the most likely, and the most serious, will include problems with catering. If refreshments and, even worse, meals are not provided on time and to the expected standard, this will have a major effect on the delegates' views of the whole event.

HANDY HINT

There will be countless calls on you – be patient and cheerful.

You will have been checking with the catering staff at regular intervals, so should be aware of any timing issues with enough notice to work around them. Quality issues, on the other hand, may not arise until the food is actually served. If the needs of a delegate with particular dietary requirements have not been met, you will have to use your initiative to make sure that they are adequately refreshed, and take the matter up with the caterers later. Check that their requirements had been made known to the caterers before laying the blame for the problem, however. You need the caterers' co-operation during the event and it will not help if you criticise them for failing to fulfil a requirement you had not made them aware of.

Another regular cause of problems will be equipment failure. Murphy's law states that 'anything that can go wrong will go wrong' and while this may be overly pessimistic, the fact is that you should always be prepared for equipment to fail, and for this to happen at the most inconvenient time. Wherever possible, have a standby piece of equipment available. If the equipment has been supplied by the venue as part of the contractual agreement, they should have a back-up available, but it is worth checking. Make sure you know who to contact at the venue if a problem such as a power cut should occur.

A problem that is difficult, if not impossible, to solve to everybody's satisfaction is the question of heating, lighting and ventilation. If you have 10 people in a room you will have 11 opinions on whether it is too hot, too cold, too bright, too dim, too stuffy or too airy. You can only provide facilities that meet the health and safety requirements and are working efficiently. In general, the more assertive delegates will get their way and others will put up with it.

The last problem that occurs regularly is the failure of speakers to arrive. This will usually be caused by transport problems. If they are travelling by public transport, delayed speakers will usually have the opportunity to warn you of their problems, so at least you have some time to deal with it, by rescheduling if possible.

Be prepared for problems occurring at the event, such as delayed speakers

Where speakers are travelling alone by car and are held up by unexpected delays, they may not be able to let you know, as they will not be in a position to use their mobile phones legally.

In these situations you can only apologise to delegates for their non-arrival and suggest moving on to the next item.

AFTER THE EVENT

Assessment criteria

This section covers assessment criteria 4.1 and 4.2

When the event is over, your work as event co-ordinator is far from finished. Your first task will be to clear and vacate the venue. Delegates who have stayed overnight will be checking out, and you need to be available to help resolve any issues. The joining instructions should have made it clear whether all, some of none of the delegates' expenses were being met by the organisers. If delegates leave without settling their accounts the venue may hold the organisation running the event responsible rather than the individual, as they are much easier to deal with.

Once all the delegates have left, deal with the equipment. If it has all been provided by the venue, check that there has been no damage caused to it during the event, to avoid any disputes later. If it has been hired from a separate supplier you will need to organise its safe return. If you have supplied it yourself you will need to pack it away safely. Confirm with your venue contact that everything is completed before leaving the site.

Your next task is to forward any papers, documents or activities resulting from the event to delegates. You may have received sales enquiries during the event which you will either deal with yourself or pass on to the sales department. These should receive priority. If records of activities which occurred during the event are to be circulated, consider whether people who were invited but unable to attend will need copies.

An important task will be to reconcile the accounts for the event to the original budget. You won't be able to finalise this until you have received all the invoices for the hire of the venue, the hire of equipment, catering, accommodation, speakers' fees and expenses. The true cost of the event will also include the cost of preparing for the event, postage costs, your travel costs and an amount for your time.

If your total costs exceed your budget, you will need to analyse the reasons in order to ensure that you can stay within budget for future events. Some of the areas to consider are:

- whether anything provided for the event was, in hindsight, unnecessary
- whether it is possible to introduce some form of sponsorship to cover some of the expenses
- whether an increase in the charge you make to the organisation putting on the event, or the individuals attending, is possible.

If your total costs were significantly below budget, you will want to look at the response the event received from the attendees before congratulating yourself on saving money. If you cut corners, the clients may decide to use someone else to put on future events so that they feel they have received value for money.

Your final task is to evaluate the event. Invite the client and the team responsible for delivering the event to a meeting to discuss what went well and what could have been improved. Organise this as soon after the event as possible, as other tasks and responsibilities will soon cloud people's memories. Have an agenda prepared so that the meeting can remain focused. Topics you will be seeking feedback on may include:

- venue
- entertainment
- food and beverages
- timeline for communications, invitations, etc
- invitations and other printed materials
- table arrangements
- staff assignments
- registration on arrival
- check-out on departure
- general event flow and timing
- opportunities for improvements
- successes and failures at the event.

Before the meeting, contact as many of the attendees as possible and ask for their feedback. This could be done most economically by email or, where small numbers are involved, a short telephone interview will gather important feedback. The questions you would like answers to may include:

- What did you like best about the event?
- What did you like least?
- Was the event too short, too long, or just right?
- How would you rate the food and beverages?
- Do you think the entertainment was appropriate for the event?

To complete the evaluation process, make files or binder sections for the materials you have created, including:

- financial report
- evaluation meeting minutes
- list of problems and possible solutions
- interview notes
- a copy of the survey to guests and a summary of the responses you received.

Organise them within the event files or binder you will be archiving. These will be important files to consider while making initial plans for future events. Be sure to back up any electronic files (including your software database) to a disk or flash drive.

HANDY HINT

Event evaluation can be challenging but is essential to future success. Using this process will give your next event a valuable boost.

ACTIVITY

Create a file containing all the necessary information on a completed event which will be useful for the organising of future events.

CASE STUDY
GLASTONBURY FESTIVAL

The extraordinary event that is the Glastonbury Festival takes place on Pilton Farm, near Glastonbury in Somerset. Most of the year it's farmland – but almost every summer a remarkable transformation takes place – it becomes a small temporary city the size of Oxford. More than 10 miles of pipes have been built beneath the fields over the years and another 15 miles are laid above ground in advance of the festival.

As the number of people staying at the festival site is about the same as the population of a small city, plenty of food and drink outlets are needed to meet their needs – along with around 3,000 toilets. Of course that number of people will produce a large amount of litter. Glastonbury Festival aims to recycle as much of the rubbish as possible. Renewable forms of energy are also used wherever they can be and people are encouraged to come to the festival by public transport.

Many stages are created for the performers. Large iconic ones such as the famous pyramid stage are erected as well as unusual one-off structures. Building the performing areas takes weeks: television camera towers, PA systems, support for videos screens and the actual stages themselves all have to be constructed. Over 50 people are involved in the logistics. It's a massive operation and has become known the world over.

UNIT 215 (B&A 27): TEST YOUR KNOWLEDGE

Learning outcome 1: Understand event organisation

1 Explain the role of the client in the organisation of an event.

2 Explain the purpose of team-building events.

3 Describe the five steps of a risk assessment.

4 Explain the security risks of an event.

5 Explain who you would report problems that you cannot solve to.

Learning outcome 2: Be able to carry out pre-event actions

1 Describe the venue requirements for a wedding.

2 Explain the reason that resources should be organised in a timely manner.

3 Describe the pre-event documentation that might be needed for an AGM.

4 Explain the importance of attendee responses.

5 State two potential needs of attendees.

Learning outcome 3: Be able to set up an event

1 List three types of layout for an event.

2 List two checks that should be made on equipment.

3 Explain why your behaviour during the event is important.

Learning outcome 4: Be able to carry out post-event actions

1 Explain the importance of restoring the venue to the required conditions.

2 Describe the follow-up actions to take after the event.

UNIT 227 (B&A 39) EMPLOYEE RIGHTS AND RESPONSIBILITIES

An employee has both rights and responsibilities in the workplace. An employer may not refuse an employee time off for legitimate reasons, but the employee must notify the employer immediately when requesting leave. Employers may not discriminate or harass employees, and employees may not discriminate or harass other employees. Employees have the right to be paid for any work they have carried out, but the employee must be honest when reporting the number of hours he has worked. The privacy of employees must be respected by an employer, unless the employer has justifiable reasoning for conducting a search.

In this unit you will cover the following learning outcomes:

1 understand the role of organisations and industries

2 understand employers' expectations and employees' rights and obligations.

Assessment criteria

This section covers assessment criteria
1.1, 1.2, 1.3, 1.4, 1.5 and 1.6

Sector

A component of an integrated system such
as an economy or a society

YOUR ROLE IN AN ORGANISATION AND INDUSTRY

Working in business administration, your occupation is not limited to one **sector**, but can be practised in all sectors across the economy. Business requires constant monitoring and informed decision-making in order to work at its best. Both the day-to-day operations and projects aimed at improving the business depend on the efforts of people with strong organisational skills. Business administrators are responsible for making sure that the details are taken care of.

It is important that you know:

- the type of organisation you work for, including the number of staff employed and the type of market in which they operate
- how your organisation is structured
- the way your organisation carries out different functions such as finance, operations, personnel, marketing and health and safety
- the different ways in which these tasks may be split between different people, departments and/or sites
- the changes that have taken place over recent years which have affected working practices and the way in which your organisation operates, and the impact that these changes have had on your organisation and the way in which your job role is carried out
- where to find out about the training and development opportunities within your organisation
- any issues of public concern that affect your organisation or industry.

The actual requirements of an individual job role are decided by the job holder's place within the organisation. However, there are several key functions that are found in most organisations. These include:

Planning	Involves a range of activities and may involve working out the sequence of steps for the development of a new product, or creating or updating critical software.
Budgeting	This means prioritising the financial needs of the company based upon the amount of money available. Invoices and salaries must be paid, supplies must be ordered and it is the job of the business administrator to make sure that every aspect of the business is funded while staying within appropriate financial boundaries.
Human resources	Part of most business administration careers. Every organisation needs the right mix of people in order to function, and it is often the responsibility of a business administrator to handle filling positions, providing training where necessary and even handling discipline and termination when needed.
Sales	Where a business administrator might lead a team of salespeople, co-ordinating sales routes to grow an existing customer base.

THE CITY & GUILDS TEXTBOOK

Business administrators can be found in the public sector as well, where they may be involved in the financial or personnel operations of local government, schools or other public organisations. Business administrators are found wherever a large number of details must be co-ordinated in order to ensure that the efforts of a group of people result in the most effective possible outcome. The organisational skills required in business administration are used to ensure that every aspect of the business has the people and supplies needed to accomplish their assigned tasks.

The directing of employees, issuing instructions and information so that everyone knows their role in the process and what is expected of them, can be the most challenging and rewarding part of a business administration job. No matter what product or service the organisation offers, quality control is necessary to detect and fix any problems or defects. Business administration jobs frequently include roles responsible for setting up quality control measures to ensure that the client or customer has their expectations met.

Because of the central role that the business administrator plays, they are most often found where business operations are happening. Whether the business is located in a factory, an office building or a construction site, business administrators will be found onsite, monitoring supply levels, equipment operation, the efficiency and well-being of employees and many other factors necessary to success. Being located near the core operations allows the business administrator to know what progress is being made and to respond quickly to any problems that arise.

In response to rising costs of travel and increasing traffic in major cities, many businesses now offer the option of **telecommuting**. Using internet-based communication tools, planning, organising, budgeting and other administrative tasks can be performed from

Telecommuting

Working from home on a computer linked to the workplace via a modem

COMMON MISTAKE

People think working from home is easier than going to the office – it can often be more stressful, with interruptions and temptations distracting you from getting the work done.

Many businesses now offer the option of telecommuting

nearly any location. Companies are discovering that full-time or part-time telecommuting can in many cases increase employee productivity and job satisfaction by reducing the stress associated with travelling. As roads and trains become more crowded and the cost of commuting increases, businesses may find that telecommuting is an effective option.

CAREER PATHWAYS

Career pathways in business administration will depend on the organisation and the industry you work in. As an example, people working in the public sector have several careers paths to choose from:

- The foreign service – people in foreign policy public administration jobs serve in embassies, consulates and other diplomatic missions. They analyse political and economic events and help UK citizens abroad.

- The security services – people working as administrators in national security help maintain a strong national defence by programming computers, updating and maintaining processes, etc.

- Planning – people working in planning departments help to develop plans that involve growth and renewal of urban, suburban and rural communities. Planners promote the best use of resources for residential, commercial, institutional and recreational purposes.

- Public administration jobs are also found in government agencies and public corporations, which have strict standards for the management of public resources. Public management careers require budgeting skills, personnel management, procurement and knowledge of regulations and policies.

- Public administration jobs in regulation and auditing suit people who possess technical knowledge about financial, public utility and transportation industries, the environment and/or technology. Their work includes conducting physical inspections, audits and investigations.

- Taxation – careers along the revenue and taxation pathway suit people who enjoy ensuring that governments receive revenues by collecting taxes, conducting audits, monitoring taxes payable and collecting overdue tax.

Another area where there are opportunities to follow a career pathway in business administration is in the healthcare industry. Healthcare administration career paths follow three levels:

- entry level positions
- middle management positions
- executive level positions.

Your first healthcare administration job will depend on your level of education and experience. People often start out in junior positions in larger organisations, but may obtain higher-level positions in some smaller organisations. People typically enter a career in healthcare administration by one of two paths: either they have just completed a degree and have little or no on-the-job experience or they began working in a related field and have sufficient career experience to move into a healthcare administration position.

Entry-level healthcare administration jobs include assistant administrative positions such as operating assistants, marketing assistants, insurance company representatives and accounting technicians. Graduates may obtain jobs as managers and supervisors in smaller organisations such as clinics and public health agencies.

Healthcare administration jobs at middle management level include department managers, case managers, marketing directors and contract negotiators. Positions at this level include chief financial officers, chief operating officers and chief executive officers. Healthcare administration executives often work 60 or more hours per week.

> **HANDY HINT**
>
> It may take as long as 10 years for healthcare administration managers to become senior level managers and executives.

INFORMATION AND ADVICE

When considering your career options, you will need to know who to go to for information and advice in your organisation. This may be your line manager or the human resources department, who can give advice on a range of topics related to:

- employment and personnel issues
- training
- additional learning support (ALS).

Additional learning support provides employees with the additional resources to access their learning. ALS requirements would normally be highlighted during the recruitment process and, following an initial assessment, would generally be discussed during induction.

Factors that may require ALS include:

- Asperger's and Autistic Spectrum Disorders (ASD)
- attention deficit hyper-activity disorder (adhd)
- dyslexia, dyspraxia or dyscalculia
- hearing or visual impairments
- mental health problems
- physical difficulties
- missed schooling or interrupted education.

Types of ALS include:

- needs assessments
- access to and/or the loan of specialist equipment and/or software
- information provided on a computer or through different printed formats, such as large print.

There are also external sources of information and advice and it is important that you know where to locate information outside your organisation. This can be obtained from a range of sources, including:

- Citizens Advice Bureau
- trade unions
- 'Access to Work' contact centres.

CODES OF PRACTICE AND PRINCIPLES OF CONDUCT

Organisations are regulated by legislation but in addition, many industries have specific codes of practice which can have an impact on the way they carry on business. A code of practice is a set of professional standards or written guidelines agreed on by members of a particular profession or written guidelines issued by an official body or a professional association to its members to help them comply with its ethical standards.

Codes of practice are normally considered when:

- government regulations are unlikely to occur or are inappropriate
- legislation exists and the objective is to assist in ensuring compliance
- there is need for, and commitment to, the development of controls to improve industry standards
- the objective is to provide customer-focused benefits beyond the minimum standards.

In some industries, principles of conduct are agreed which serve as models of **exemplary** conduct for organisations. In order to support the basic objectives of high levels of competence, performance and ethical conduct, all organisations are expected to understand and adhere to these principles of conduct.

An example of a set of principles of conduct is:

- In all professional, business or **fiduciary** relationships, an organisation shall act with honour and integrity in dealings with the public, employees, clients and other professionals.

Exemplary

So good or admirable that others would do well to copy it

Fiduciary

Adjective describing a legal or ethical relationship of trust between two or more parties

- An organisation shall continually strive to maintain and improve the knowledge, skills and competence needed for effective performance in their profession.

- An organisation shall apply care, skill, prudence and diligence.

- An organisation shall avoid any activity or conduct which constitutes a dishonest, deceitful, fraudulent or knowingly illegal act.

- An organisation shall maintain knowledge of and comply with the enforcement of laws, regulations and codes that foster the highest level of competence, performance and ethical conduct.

- An organisation shall respect confidential relationships that may arise in business or professional activities.

ISSUES OF PUBLIC CONCERN

Industries have become more concerned in recent years with demonstrating that they have practices in place to deal with issues of public concern that have faced different industries and different organisations.

Worries about corporate tax payments have replaced **remuneration** as the top public concern about business behaviour. According to a survey for the Institute of Business Ethics, 37% cited 'tax avoidance' as the main concern businesses needed to address, pushing remuneration out of top place. The ability of employees to speak out about company wrongdoing was rated the third most significant concern, at 22%, with business attitudes to the environment and human rights coming in at 16% and 15% respectively.

Remuneration

The paying or rewarding of somebody for their work or input

The survey also shows an increase in the proportion that think business as a whole is behaving ethically, as well as showing that people aged 55 and above are more likely to think that business is not behaving ethically than younger people. Tax is now clearly an issue of public concern and has risen very rapidly up the scale. The findings follow controversy over low tax bills paid by **multinationals** such as Amazon, Google and Starbucks, and a series of high-profile hearings by the Public Accounts Committee.

Multinational

A large company that operates or has investments in several different countries

REPRESENTATIVE BODIES

Within any industry there is a range of representative bodies that promote the views of a group of people with common interests. Representative bodies collect the views of their members and act as their voice in discussions with other groups on issues that affect them all. Representation occurs both within organisations and across sectors and industries, and can occur at both local and national levels.

It is important that you are aware of:

- any trade unions relevant to your occupation/industry and what membership can do for you
- any professional bodies relevant to your occupation/industry and what membership can do for you
- any regulatory bodies relevant to your industry and occupation, for example, the Chartered Institute of Legal Executives
- the name and role of the standard-setting organisation relevant to your occupation.

ACTIVITY

Find out which representative bodies operate in your organisation.

Assessment criteria

This section covers assessment criteria 2.1, 2.2, 2.3 and 2.4

Statutory

Covered by a permanent established rule or law, especially one involved in the running of a company or other organisation, and subject to the penalty laid down by that statute

EMPLOYEES' RIGHTS AND OBLIGATIONS

Your rights at work will depend on your **statutory** rights and your contract of employment. Your contract of employment cannot take away rights you have by law. So if, for example, you have a contract which states you are only entitled to two weeks' paid holiday per year when, by law, all full-time employees are entitled to 28 days' paid holiday per year, this part of your contract does not apply.

If your contract gives you greater rights than you have under law, for example, your contract gives you six weeks' paid holiday per year, then your contract applies. There are special rules about the employment of children and young people.

Statutory rights are legal rights based on laws passed by Parliament. Nearly all workers, however many hours per week they work, have certain legal rights. Some workers are not entitled to some statutory rights. They are:

- Anyone who is not an employee, for example an agency or freelance worker. However, most workers are entitled to certain rights such as the national minimum wage, limits on working time and other health and safety rights, the right not to be discriminated against and paid holiday.
- Employees who normally work outside the UK.
- Members of the police service. However, members of the police service are covered by discrimination law.

- Members of the armed forces. However, members of the armed forces are covered by discrimination law.
- Merchant seamen and share fishermen.
- Some workers in the transport industry are not entitled to paid holidays or limits on their working hours by law and have to rely on their contract.
- Trainee doctors are not entitled to paid holidays and have to rely on their employment contract. They are also limited to working a 58-hour week, rather than 48 hours.

Unless you are in the group of workers who are excluded, you will have the following statutory rights:

- A written statement of terms of employment within two months of starting work.
- An itemised payslip.
- To be paid at least the national minimum wage.
- Not to have illegal deductions made from pay.
- Paid holiday – full-time employees are entitled to at least 28 days a year.
- Paid time off to look for work if being made redundant. This applies once you have worked for two years for an employer.
- Time off for study or training for 16-17 year-olds.
- Paid time off for antenatal care.
- Paid maternity leave.
- Paid paternity leave.
- To ask for flexible working to care for children or adult dependants.
- Paid adoption leave.
- Unpaid parental leave for both men and women (if you have worked for the employer for one year) and the right to reasonable time off to look after dependants in an emergency.
- To work a maximum 48-hour working week.
- Weekly and daily rest breaks. There are special rules for night workers.
- Not to be discriminated against.
- To carry on working until you are at least 65.
- Notice of dismissal, provided you have worked for your employer for at least one calendar month.
- Written reasons for dismissal from your employer.
- To claim compensation if unfairly dismissed.

Employees have statutory rights, such as receiving an itemised payslip

- To claim redundancy pay if made redundant. In most cases you will have to have worked for two years to be able to claim redundancy pay.

- Not to suffer detriment or dismissal for 'blowing the whistle' on a matter of public concern (malpractice) at the workplace.

- The right of a part-time worker to the same contractual rights (pro rata) as a comparable full-time worker.

- The right of a fixed-term employee to the same contractual rights as a comparable permanent employee.

Note that sometimes an employee might only gain a right when you have been employed by your employer for a certain length of time as indicated in the list above where this is the case.

Your contract of employment is the agreement made between you and the employer. This could be in the form of a written agreement or what has been agreed verbally between you. It will also include 'custom and practice' agreements. These are how things are usually done in the workplace, for example if the employer always gives the employees a day's holiday in August. Even though this is not mentioned in the written contract this will form part of the contract of employment as it is the usual practice.

If the written contract says one thing, but in practice all the employees have been doing something else with the employer's knowledge and agreement, the 'custom and practice' would form the contract rather than the written statement.

A trade union may have negotiated an agreement with an employer about conditions at work. The negotiated agreement will often form part of a contract of employment, particularly if the conditions negotiated are more favourable than the previous ones.

All employees, regardless of the number of hours they work per week, are entitled to receive a written statement from their employer, within two months of starting work. The statement describes the main terms of the contract of employment.

The statement must give the following details:

- job title
- wages
- hours of work
- holiday entitlement
- sick pay
- pension schemes
- notice
- grievance, dismissal and disciplinary procedure.

HANDY HINT

You may have additional rights which may be set out in your contract of employment.

ACTIVITY

List any 'custom and practice' issues that you have in your workplace.

EMPLOYER'S EXPECTATIONS

While employees enjoy all the rights described above, they also have responsibilities to meet their employer's expectations in respect of their personal presentation, punctuality and behaviour. Employers will require employees to exhibit a range of personal attributes and behaviours including:

- Personal appearance – your clothes, hair, hands, nails, shoes, etc need to be clean and tidy and suitable for your job role.

- Positive attitude – you need to adopt a 'can do' approach to work.

- Approachability – customers and your colleagues need to feel that you are easy to talk to.

- Honesty – you may have access to stock and cash that belongs to the company. They will need to be able to trust you with it. Customers will also need to be able to believe information that you give them.

- Professional attitude – customers will look on you as the expert in the products and services you are providing. You shouldn't let any outside influences prevent you from doing your job to the best of your ability.

- Courtesy – customers and colleagues will expect to be treated with politeness.

- Helpful attitude – always try to be helpful to both customers and colleagues wherever possible.

You should also try to be punctual. If you aim to arrive at work 10 minutes before your start time, you will have a cushion against unexpected delays. If you arrive early, you can prepare yourself for the day's work, and be ready to start on time.

From time to time you may need to be absent from work. It is important that you inform your employer as soon as you realise you will not be at work when you should be. There will be a rule telling you who you have to inform and by what time; you may have to phone your supervisor before 10am, for instance.

From time to time you may need to be absent from work

When you return to work you may have an interview with your supervisor or someone from the human resources department. These can help identify short-term absence problems at an early stage. They also provide managers with an opportunity to talk to you about any issues which might be causing the absence.

The important thing is to remember that if you are not at work, someone else will have to do your work for you. If you are not happy when other people leave you to do their work, it is not fair if you take time off unnecessarily and leave your work to them.

Disciplinary procedures may be used to make it clear that inexcusable absence will not be accepted and that absence policies will be applied. The main causes of sickness absence are:

- minor illness including colds, flu, stomach upsets and headaches
- bone or muscle injuries
- back pain
- stress
- recurring medical conditions
- home or family responsibilities
- mental ill health, for example clinical depression and anxiety.

REGULATIONS

There are regulations to protect you from being unfairly treated. These include:

- The Employment Relations Act which covers among other things:
  - the recognition of trade unions
  - maternity/paternity leave and time off for dependants
  - the right to be accompanied at disciplinary and grievance hearings.
- The Employment Equality (Age) Regulations which make it illegal to treat an employee less favourably because of their age in:
  - recruitment
  - promotion
  - terms and conditions
  - redundancy and dismissal.
- The Employment Rights Act which includes sections on:
  - fair dismissal
  - complaints to a tribunal
  - reasonable notice
  - written contracts
  - rights to time off
  - flexible working
  - redundancy payments
  - compensation for lost earnings
  - time off for public duties, antenatal care and training
  - dismissals related to health and safety
  - protection against detriment caused by disclosing information.

- Working Time Regulations which impose an obligation on employers to ensure that employees:
  - work an average of no more than 48 hours per week calculated over a 17-week period including working lunches, job-related travel and time spent on business abroad
  - have an 11-hour continuous rest period between working days
  - have a continuous 24-hour period off work each week
  - have a break of 20 minutes if the day is more than six hours long.
- The Employment Act which includes sections on:
  - paternity leave and pay
  - maternity leave and pay
  - adoption leave and pay
  - dispute resolution.

Protection from unlawful discrimination is provided by the Equality Act in relation to the following protected characteristics:

- age
- disability
- gender reassignment
- marriage and civil partnership
- pregnancy and maternity
- race
- religion and belief
- sex
- sexual orientation.

The following pieces of legislation have been absorbed into the Equality Act:

- The Equal Pay Act which makes it illegal to offer different pay and conditions to men and women who perform the same type of work. This is defined as work of equal value in terms of effort and skills.
- The Race Relations Act which makes it illegal to treat employees differently because of their race, colour, nationality or ethnic origins.
- The Sex Discrimination Act which makes it illegal to treat employees differently because of their gender.
- The Disability Discrimination Act which makes it illegal to discriminate against disabled people in the areas of:
  - employment
  - access to goods, facilities and services
  - management, buying or renting land or property.

SOURCES OF INFORMATION

If you want any more information on your employment rights and responsibilities, you can try your line manager, your human resources department, your union representative, the intranet or external sources such as the Health and Safety Executive, the Department of Business, Innovation and Skills, professional associations such as the Chartered Institute of Personnel and Development (CIPD), the Trades Union Congress (TUC), the Advisory, Conciliation and Arbitration Service (ACAS), your trade union, the Citizens Advice Bureau, the internet, the public library or government agencies.

CASE STUDY
EMPLOYEE PROTECTION

Linda joined dental clinic Aspect Dentistry in June 2012, on a maternity leave contract. The 25 year-old had previously worked for the firm for 18 months before she left to have her daughter, Rachel, in 2009. She returned to work as a receptionist in 2012 and covered four morning shifts a week. Her contract was further extended by five weeks. Then Linda, who lives in Nantwich with her husband, Paul, a self-employed builder, told her boss that she was expecting her second child.

Linda told the practice manager her good news in February 2013, and the practice manager told the owner of the business. Everyone was happy for her. Then they took her aside at the beginning of March 2013 and said, 'we have no more work that we can give to you'. The owner said there were no hours available and that was that. The practice was really busy at the time, so Linda thought that it didn't add up. She took it further to her solicitor and he said it wasn't right.

Her employment was terminated and she left the business at the end of March, but she started legal proceedings and following a two-day employment tribunal held in Nantwich in December, a judge ruled in favour of Linda and she was awarded more than £7,000.

Her daughter, Sheila, was born on 6 August 2013.

UNIT 227 (B&A 39): TEST YOUR KNOWLEDGE

Learning outcome 1: Understand the role of organisations and industries

1 Explain the role of your organisation.

2 Describe a career pathway that you could follow.

3 State two sources of information and advice on training.

4 Explain what is meant by a code of practice.

5 List two issues of public concern that affect your organisation.

6 Describe the role of trade unions.

Learning outcome 2: Understand employers' expectations and employees' rights and obligations

1 State two statutory rights that you have in a workplace.

2 Explain what you must do if you are going to be absent from work.

3 List two pieces of legislation that protect the rights of employees.

4 List two external places you can obtain advice on your rights.

UNIT 101 (B&A 4) HEALTH AND SAFETY IN A BUSINESS ENVIRONMENT

The Health and Safety Executive (HSE) say that everyone is entitled to work in environments that are safe for them to do so, and that customers, visitors and contractors are entitled to be protected from any risk to their health and safety while they are on the premises. There are a number of regulations that impose responsibilities on both you and the employer in respect of health and safety. Your employer's basic responsibility is to provide safe and healthy conditions and processes for you to work in, while your responsibility is to behave in a safe and responsible way to protect yourself, your colleagues, customers and visitors from any harm.

In this unit you will cover the following learning outcomes:

1 understand health and safety responsibilities in a business environment

2 know how to work safely in a business environment

3 be able to comply with health and safety requirements in a business environment.

Assessment criteria

This section covers assessment criteria 1.1, 1.2, 1.3, 1.4, 1.5, 1.6 and 2.4

Interim

An interval of time between one event, process or period and another

WORKING SAFELY IN A BUSINESS ENVIRONMENT

It is extremely important that everyone in the organisation is working in a healthy and safe way. Monitoring and reporting are vital parts of an organisation's health and safety culture. Management systems must allow senior management to receive both specific (eg incident-led) and routine reports on the performance of health and safety policy. Much day-to-day health and safety information needs be reported only at the time of a formal review, but only a strong system of monitoring can ensure that the formal review can proceed as planned and that relevant events in the **interim** are brought to the management's attention.

EMPLOYER AND EMPLOYEE RESPONSIBILITIES

The organisation must ensure that:

- appropriate importance is given to reporting both preventive information, such as progress of training and maintenance programmes, and incident data such as accident and sickness absence rates

- audits of the effectiveness of management structures and risk controls for health and safety are carried out as often as necessary

- the impact of changes such as the introduction of new procedures, work processes or products, or any major health and safety failure is reported as soon as possible

- there are procedures to implement new and changed legal requirements and to consider other external developments and events.

Employees must ensure that they:

- take care of their own health and safety and that of others

- co-operate with their employer and co-workers

- do not interfere with safety equipment.

Effective monitoring of sickness absence and workplace health can alert the organisation to underlying problems that could seriously damage performance or result in accidents and long-term illness. The collection of workplace health and safety data can allow management to **benchmark** the organisation's performance against others in its sector. Appraisals of senior managers should include an assessment of their contribution to health and safety performance.

A regular review of health and safety performance is essential. It establishes whether the health and safety principles of strong and

Benchmark

To provide a standard against which something can be measured or assessed active leadership, worker involvement and assessment and review have been fixed in the organisation. It tells the organisation whether systems are effective in managing risk and protecting people.

Health and safety performance should be reviewed at least once a year. The review process should:

- examine whether the health and safety policy reflects the organisation's current priorities, plans and targets
- examine whether risk management and other health and safety systems have been effectively reporting
- report health and safety shortcomings, and the effect of all relevant management decisions
- decide actions to address any weaknesses and a system to monitor their implementation
- consider immediate reviews in the light of major shortcomings or events.

Larger public and private sector organisations need to have formal procedures for auditing and reporting health and safety performance. The board should ensure that any audit is seen as a positive management and boardroom tool. It should have unrestricted access to both external and internal auditors, keeping their cost effectiveness, independence and objectivity under review. Various codes and guides, many of them sector-specific, are available to help organisations report health and safety performance and risk management as part of good **governance**.

Performance on health and safety is increasingly being recorded in organisations' annual reports to investors and **stakeholders**. Management can make extra 'shop floor' visits to gather information for the formal review. Good health and safety performance can be celebrated at central and local level.

According to the Health and Safety Executive (HSE), sensible risk management is about:

- ensuring that workers and the public are properly protected
- providing overall benefit to society by balancing benefits and risks, with a focus on reducing real risks – both those which arise more often and those with serious consequences
- enabling innovation and learning, not stifling them
- ensuring that those who create risks manage them responsibly and understand that failure to manage real risks responsibly is likely to lead to robust action
- enabling individuals to understand that as well as the right to protection, they also have to exercise responsibility.

Stakeholder

A person or group with a direct interest, involvement or investment in something

Governance

The process of governing a country or organisation

Risks are acceptable when managed properly

Sensible risk management is not about:

- creating a totally risk-free society
- generating useless paperwork mountains
- scaring people by exaggerating or publicising trivial risks
- stopping important recreational and learning activities for individuals where the risks can be managed
- reducing protection of people from risks that cause real harm and suffering.

HEALTH AND SAFETY LEGISLATION

There is a wide range of legislation and regulation which affects health and safety in a business environment. The major piece of legislation is the Health and Safety at Work Act (HASAWA), which imposes duties on both employees and employers.

Employees must:	Employers must:
Work in a safe and sensible way	Provide a safe work area
Use equipment safely and correctly	Provide clearly defined procedures
Report potential risks	Ensure safe handling, storage and transport of items and substances

Employees must:	Employers must:
Help identify training needs	Train and supervise staff in health and safety matters
	Maintain safe entries and exits
	Provide adequate temperature, lighting, seating etc
	Ensure visitors are informed of any hazards

The Reporting of Injuries, Diseases and Dangerous Occurrences Regulations (RIDDOR) require employers to take action in the following circumstances:

- Death or major injury to an employee or member of the public – notify the enforcing authority without delay and complete an accident report form within 10 days.

- Accident causing an employee to be unable to work for more than seven days – submit a RIDDOR report form within ten days of the incident.

- Employee suffering a reportable work-related disease – complete a RIDDOR occupational disease report form.

- Something dangerous happens which does not cause a (significant) injury but clearly could have done – report immediately and complete an accident report form within 10 days.

> **HANDY HINT**
>
> The Health and Safety Executive supply a list of major injuries, dangerous occurrences and diseases that are reportable under RIDDOR.

The Management of Health and Safety at Work Regulations require employers of five or more employees to:

- carry out a risk assessment
- implement measures identified as necessary
- appoint competent people to implement the measures
- set up emergency procedures
- provide clear information and training
- work together with other employers sharing the same workplace.

The Workplace (Health, Safety and Welfare) Regulations 1999 aim to ensure that workplaces meet the needs of all members of a workforce and cover such topics as temperature, ventilation, lighting, space, passage ways, stairs, showers, wash basins, lavatories, workstations and maintenance among other things. The Equality Act requires that people with disabilities are fully included and not adversely affected by any workplace arrangements such as accessing and exiting the premises (particularly in an emergency), and accessing suitable sanitary and washroom facilities.

Where necessary, parts of the building – such as doorways – should be made accessible for people who are disabled

The Display Screen Equipment Regulations 1992 apply to all who regularly use computers in their work, and relate to work stations as well as equipment. They require employers to:

- assess all workstations for health and safety risks and lower the risks as much as possible
- plan work activities to incorporate rest breaks at regular intervals
- arrange and pay for eye tests and pay for spectacles or lenses if these are prescribed specifically for computer work
- provide health and safety training for users and retraining if the workstation is changed or modified
- provide users with information on all aspects of health and safety which apply to them and measures being taken to reduce risks to their health.

The Provision and Use of Work Equipment Regulations 1998 require that equipment provided for use at work is:

- suitable for the intended use
- safe for use, maintained in a safe condition and, in certain circumstances, inspected
- used only by people who have received adequate information, instruction and training
- accompanied by suitable safety measures eg protective devices, markings and warnings.

The Control of Substances Hazardous to Health Regulations (COSHH) 2002 requires employers to control any substances that may damage the health of staff or customers, for instance bleach, ammonia, acid, etc.

Employers must:

- assess the risk from hazardous substances
- decide how to prevent or at least reduce those risks
- assess the exposure to the risks
- ensure employees are properly informed, trained and supervised.

HAZARD, RISK AND YOUR JOB ROLE

Assessment criteria

This section covers assessment criteria 1.1, 1.2, 1.3, 1.4, 2.1, 2.2, 2.3, 2.4 and 3.4

All of these regulations will have some impact on your job role, as they will affect the way you carry out your tasks, the equipment you use and your working hours, breaks etc.

In order to understand what could pose possible health and safety risks in the workplace, the first thing to understand is the difference between a hazard and a risk.

A hazard is something that can cause harm, for example electricity, chemicals, working up a ladder, noise, a keyboard, a bully at work and stress. A risk is the chance, high or low, that any hazard will actually cause somebody harm. For example, working alone away from your office can be a hazard. The risk of personal danger may be high. Electric cabling is a hazard. If it has snagged on a sharp object, the exposed wiring places it in a 'high-risk' category.

There are a wide variety of hazards relevant to a business environment. For instance:

- Overuse or improper use of equipment, or poorly designed workstations or work environments may cause posture problems and pain, discomfort or injuries to the hands and arms.
- Poor lighting can cause headaches or sore eyes.
- Lack of control over timing and frequency of incoming calls or verbal abuse from customers could cause stress.
- High noise levels for long periods could cause hearing problems.
- Poor headset hygiene could cause hearing infections.
- Exposure to sudden loud sounds while using telephone equipment could cause shock.
- Call handlers may suffer voice problems including voice loss.
- Staff and visitors may be injured if they trip over objects or slip on spillages.
- Handling heavy or bulky objects may cause injuries or back pain.
- Falls from any height can cause bruising and fractures.
- Using faulty electrical equipment could cause electrical shocks or burns.
- Electrical faults can also lead to fires. If trapped, staff could suffer from smoke inhalation/burns.

There will be actions that can be taken in the case of identifying hazards such as those listed:

- Make sure you get breaks away from the screen.
- Report any pain suffered as a result of computer use.

ACTIVITY

Look around your workplace and make a list of any hazards. Give the list to the person responsible for health and safety policy in your workplace.

- Report if you feel unwell or uneasy about work issues.
- Access regular training on volume control.
- Modify working practices to minimise background noise.
- Maintain stocks of ear pads.
- Investigate any report of acoustic shock.
- Clean headset voice tubes regularly.
- Replace headset earpiece foam cover.
- Ensure spills are cleared up promptly.
- Use correct manual handling procedures.
- Use stepladders correctly.
- Check electrical installations regularly.

It is everybody's responsibility to identify hazards and risks resulting from:

- using machinery and equipment
- using materials and substances
- the way work is carried out
- unsafe behaviour
- breakages and spillages
- the environment.

If any risks are identified, they should be communicated to the person responsible for health and safety. Organisations will have at least one first aider or appointed person to be responsible for health and safety. Where the organisation has a health and safety officer, it is their responsibility to give advice and information on health and safety issues, ensure that training takes place and all necessary equipment and procedures are in place and followed. They are also responsible for carrying out risk assessments.

The majority of accidents in business environments are caused by slips, trips and falls. Untidiness around desks and in corridors can cause people to trip and fall. It is important that all shared areas, such as corridors, kitchens, photocopying areas and stairways are kept free from obstruction. An inspection should be carried out regularly to ensure that housekeeping standards are well maintained.

Fatalities in office accidents are usually caused by falls down staircases. It is easy to break an arm or leg or suffer a head injury from landing heavily. When carrying anything up or down stairs, one hand should be kept free to hold the handrail. Never use your mobile phone while walking up or down stairs.

The person nominated to take charge of health and safety must be a competent person, defined by the Management of Health and Safety at Work Regulations as someone with sufficient knowledge and experience to do the job properly.

ACTIVITY

Make a list of the first aiders in your workplace, including the person responsible for health and safety policy.

The Health and Safety Executive says, 'A risk assessment is nothing more than a careful examination of what, in your work, could cause harm to people.' Employers have a duty under the Management of Health and Safety at Work Regulations to carry out risk assessments to identify what hazards exist in a workplace, and how likely these hazards are to cause harm. They must then decide what prevention or control measures are needed. The frequency of scheduled risk audits will depend on:

- the level of risk
- legislation
- regulations
- organisation policy/procedures.

Employers are responsible for carrying out the assessment, and for any steps that they need to take to eliminate or control risk. They should not only walk around the workplace and inspect for any hazards, but consult you and your colleagues about the hazards you face.

It is everybody's resonsibility to identify hazards and risks

The HSE advises employers to follow five steps when carrying out a workplace risk assessment:

1 Identify hazards, that is to say anything that may cause harm – employers have a duty to assess the health and safety risks faced by the staff. They must systematically check for possible physical, mental, chemical and biological hazards. Common hazards can include:

   a Physical – lifting, awkward postures, slips and trips, noise, dust, machinery, computer equipment.

   b Mental – excess workload, long hours, working with high-need clients, bullying. These are also called 'psychosocial' hazards, affecting mental health and occurring within working relationships.

c Chemical – asbestos, cleaning fluids, aerosols.

d Biological – including tuberculosis, hepatitis and other infectious diseases faced by healthcare workers, homecare staff and other healthcare professionals.

2 Decide who may be harmed and how – identifying who is at risk starts with the organisation's staff but employers must also assess risks faced by agency and contract staff, visitors, clients and other members of the public on the premises. Employers must review work routines in all the different locations and situations where their staff are employed. For example in contact centres, workstation equipment must be adjusted to suit each employee. Employers have special duties towards the health and safety of young workers, disabled employees, night- or shift-workers and pregnant or breastfeeding women.

3 Assess the risks and take action – consider how likely it is that each hazard could cause harm. This will determine whether or not they should reduce the level of risk. Even after all precautions have been taken, some risk usually remains. Employers must decide for each remaining hazard whether the risk remains high, medium or low.

4 Make a record of the findings – organisations with five or more staff are required to record in writing the main findings of the risk assessment. This record should include details of any significant hazards noted in the risk assessment and action taken to reduce or eliminate risk. This record provides proof that the assessment was carried out, and the basis for a later review of working practices. The risk assessment is a working document. You should be able to read it. It should not be locked away in a cupboard.

5 Review the risk assessment to ensure that agreed safe working practices continue to be applied, for example that management's safety instructions are respected by supervisors and line managers and that they continue to take account of any new working practices, new machinery or more demanding work targets.

The basic rule is that employers must adapt the work to the worker. The key aims of risk assessment are to:

- Prioritise the risks – rank them in order of seriousness focusing on the significant rather than the trivial hazards.

- Make all risks small – there are two main options: to eliminate the hazard altogether, or, if this is not possible, control the risks so that harm is unlikely.

The management of Health and Safety at Work Regulations set out the following safety management guidance for employers for tackling risks. The basic approach is also known as a hierarchy of control:

Substitution
– try a risk-free
or less risky option

Prevention – for
example erect a
machine guard or add a
non-slip surface to a
pathway

Re-organise work to reduce exposure to a risk – a
basic rule is to adapt the work to the worker. Ensure
chairs and display screen equipment are adjustable
to the individual, and plan all work involving a
computer to include regular breaks. For monotonous
or routine work, introduce work variety and greater
control over work. For instance, in call centres
introduce work variety by providing work off the
phones, and varying the type of calls handled

As a last resort, issue personal protective
equipment to all staff at risk, and make sure they
are trained in when and how to use this
equipment, such as appropriate eye protection,
gloves, special clothing, footwear

- Provide training in safe working systems
- Provide information on likely hazards and how to avoid them
- Provide social and welfare facilities: for example washing facilities for the removal of contamination, toilet facilities

The HSE says risk should be assessed 'every time there are new machines, substances and procedures, which could lead to new hazards'. Also, if a new job brings in significant new hazards, then that job should be fully risk-assessed. If there is high staff turnover, then the way new staff do their work should be checked against the risk assessment and training provided in safe working practices if necessary.

Your organisation should have a procedure in place which explains your role in the case of a fire or other emergency. This procedure will cover:

- how you should raise the alarm
- how to evacuate the building
- where the fire exits are
- where to go when you have evacuated the building
- where to find fire extinguishers
- how and when to use them.

These will differ from organisation to organisation, but there are some basic things to know wherever you work. Make sure you have received adequate training in the procedures. Before an emergency happens, know the procedures above by heart, you will not have time to look for the instructions to refresh your memory.

What should you do if there is a fire in your workplace?

If you discover a fire, operate the nearest fire alarm. (If there isn't one, shouting 'fire, fire!' is usually pretty effective.) If and only if *you have been trained and the fire is small enough*, tackle the fire using the fire equipment available. Make sure you keep your escape route clear and know whose job it is to call the Fire Brigade. If it's yours, dial 999 and follow the instructions the emergency operator gives you. Direct customers and visitors to the nearest fire exit and shut doors and windows in any room where there is a fire

Of course, fire is not the only emergency you may come across. In most organisations, bomb threats are dealt with in a similar way to fires, but again find out what *your* company policy is, learn it and follow it.

There is also the possibility of a medical emergency involving staff, visitors or customers. The important thing in this situation is to know who the first aiders are and to get them to the patient as quickly as possible. You can do serious and possibly permanent damage trying to help when you have not had the proper training.

HANDY HINT

The basic rule in an emergency is 'Get out, call the emergency services out and stay out.' No personal belongings or property are worth losing your life for.

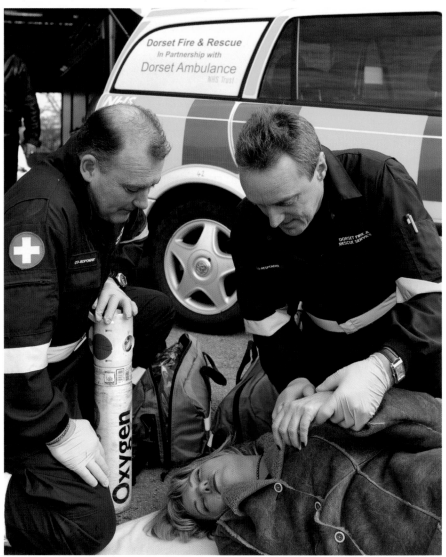

In a medical emergency, first call the first aider and then the paramedics if needed

SAFE MANUAL HANDLING

Assessment criteria

This section covers assessment criteria 3.1, 3.2 and 3.3

One of the greatest risks in a workplace is damage to your back from lifting items incorrectly. You should not attempt to lift or carry any heavy object until you have received training in manual handling. After training it is important that you use the correct techniques. Before lifting anything:

Plan the best way to carry it

↓

Assess the size and weight

↓

Ask for help if necessary

↓

Clear any obstructions from your path

↓

Consider lifting in two stages

Some practical tips for safe manual handling:

- Keep the load close to the body for as long as possible while lifting. Keep the heaviest side of the load next to the body. If a close approach is not possible, try to slide it towards the body before attempting to lift it.

- Your feet should be apart with one leg slightly forward to maintain balance (alongside the load if it is on the ground). You should be prepared to move your feet during the lift to maintain stability.

- Where possible the load should be hugged as close as possible to your body. This may be better than gripping it tightly with hands only.

- At the start of the lift, slight bending of the back, hips and knees is preferable to fully flexing the back (stooping) or fully flexing the hips and knees (squatting).

- Don't flex your back any further while lifting. This can happen if the legs begin to straighten before starting to raise the load.

- Avoid twisting your back or leaning sideways, especially while your back is bent. Your shoulders should be kept level and facing in the same direction as your hips. Turning by moving the feet is better than twisting and lifting at the same time.

- Keep your head up and look ahead, not down at the load, once it has been held securely.

- The load should not be **jerked** or **snatched** as this can make it harder to keep control and increase the risk of injury.

- There is a difference between what you can lift and what you can safely lift. If in doubt, seek advice or get help.

- If precise positioning of the load is necessary, put it down first, then slide it into the desired position.

Where the guidelines are exceeded it will be necessary to get help to handle the item.

Jerked

Pulled with a sudden strong movement

Snatched

Grabbed or grasped hastily

Take care when lifting heavy objects

It is important when using any piece of equipment or tools that you follow the manufacturer's instructions. Before you use any equipment for the first time, you should read through the manual and familiarise yourself with the features and operating systems to fully understand the hazards and safety requirements. The most important reason for following this is to ensure the safety of yourself and your colleagues. Some equipment may have blades which could seriously injure people if not used properly. Another reason is to avoid damaging the equipment. If you damage equipment through failing to follow the manufacturer's instructions, you will **invalidate** the guarantee and your organisation will have to pay for the repairs.

Organisations have policies and procedures on health and safety to ensure the well-being of staff, visitors and customers. It is important

Invalidate

To deprive something of its legal force or value, for instance by failing to comply with some terms and conditions

that you know and understand your organisation's policies and procedures in order to maintain a safe environment. Follow the legislation and carry out any responsibilities and specific policies that relate to your job role.

Everybody is responsible for minimising the risks to health and safety in the workplace. The factors to be taken into account when identifying health and safety risks include:

- legislation
- regulations
- organisational policy and procedures.

Following health and safety procedures correctly will help to minimise risk. So will good housekeeping. This means keeping the workplace clean and tidy, and removing and disposing of waste. All areas need to be kept clean as illness can spread by dirty conditions. The premises need to be kept tidy or there will be risk of falling over items left in aisles or spillages that are not dealt with immediately.

HANDY HINT

All equipment should have an instruction manual, although these may be difficult to find. Inserting the make and model of the piece of equipment into a search engine should give you what you are looking for.

Untidy premises can cause health and safety risks

HEALTH AND SAFETY OFFICERS

People with different responsibilities for the health and safety in the workplace will have different information and advice needs. Employees will need to know and understand the policies and procedures, their own responsibilities and how to assess their own risks. The health and safety officer will need to understand the legislation and regulations, government guidelines, how to carry out risk assessments, the reporting procedures, how health and safety is monitored, internal communication methods and the management of the health and safety policy.

The organisation as a whole must understand the legislation and regulations, the importance of risk assessments, the reporting procedures and the resources required to carry out any actions to reduce risks. To communicate information on health and safety, the golden rule is not to use a single method of communication but to use multiple channels including:

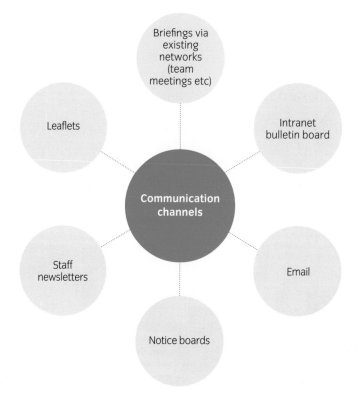

CASE STUDY
HEALTH AND SAFETY

A truck manufacturer in the north east wanted to take advantage of the knowledge of their workers in managing noise and vibration issues, but management were aware that a project to tackle hand-arm vibration issues was only going to work if they could gain workers' trust and co-operation. This was not going to be easily achieved when workers were asked to keep a record of what tools they used and for how long, and after the first week only four forms from a workforce of 78 were returned.

From the poor response rate, management quickly realised that the staff were suspicious of the reasons they were being asked to record the information requested. Workers' trust was vital before they could really get them involved in what they were trying to do, so they arranged for training to raise awareness of the health issues involved when using vibrating hand tools and explained that they couldn't fully address the situation without their workers' help.

By talking to the workers and involving them in solving the problem, the company found out that workers become 'attached' to their hand tools. If the tools did the job well, the workers would continue to use them, no matter how old the tools were or how much vibration they caused. A tool amnesty was held, production lines were retooled with efficient, low-vibration equipment and workers were told about the risk and how to avoid it.

The company have also set up a suggestion scheme, complete with boards around the production line where staff can raise any issue they like. Every week, teams now check the boards, note any suggestions that come under their area of responsibility and consider what action they can take. A staff member's suggestion card remains on the board until they are happy it's been acted on, only they can remove it.

As a result, they've had hundreds of suggestions in the six months the boards have been up, and made dozens of improvements.

UNIT 101 (B&A 4): TEST YOUR KNOWLEDGE

Learning outcome 1: Understand health and safety responsibilities in a business environment

1 Describe an employer's responsibilities in a business environment.

2 Describe an employee's responsibilities in a business environment.

3 Name the legislation which affects the use of computer screens.

4 Describe why it is important to work safely.

Learning outcome 2: Know how to work safely in a business environment

1 List two possible health and safety risks in the workplace.

2 List two ways of avoiding accidents in the workplace.

3 State two reasons for reporting hazards and accidents in the workplace.

4 Describe your organisation's emergency procedures.

Learning outcome 3: Be able to comply with health and safety requirements in a business environment

1 Describe why it is important to use approved techniques when lifting heavy objects.

2 Describe how an employee's personal conduct relating to health and safety procedures could endanger others.

3 Explain why it is important to follow manufacturers' instructions in the use of equipment.

4 Explain the importance of complying with organisational policies on health and safety.

SUGGESTED ANSWERS TO TEST YOUR KNOWLEDGE QUESTIONS

Communication in a business environment

Learning outcome 1
Understand the requirements of written and verbal business communication

1 Different methods of communication include written communication, verbal communication and non-verbal communication. Each will be used in different circumstances. More formal communication is likely to need written communication while verbal communication will often be appropriate to informal situations. Non-verbal communication is, of course, always in use whenever two or more people are together.

2 The purpose of communicating in a business environment is to send a message to an individual or group of people in order to request action, inform, teach, persuade, motivate or inspire.

3 The answer to this question will be personal to the learner.

4 Verbal communication would be appropriate to pass on a message, to seek information, to ask for advice, to place an order, to promote products or make an enquiry.

5 Written communication would be appropriate when more formal communication is needed, for instance when a record is needed for future reference, such as purchase orders, invoices, or disciplinary or grievance situations.

Learning outcome 2
Be able to produce written business communications

1 Written communication must be checked before it is sent so it is error-free and also presented accurately in order to create a positive impression of the organisation and to avoid confusion and misunderstanding.

2 The appropriate tone in responding to a customer complaint is professional and business-like, while acknowledging that the

customer has not been satisfied with the product or service your organisation has provided.

3 Accurate grammar, spelling and punctuation are important in order to ensure that the desired message is delivered clearly and unequivocally, and also to present a professional image.

4 The use of plain English will allow the receiver to understand exactly what you mean. Plain English is written clearly and concisely so the reader can take the required action.

5 It is important to meet deadlines because communication is pointless if it is produced after the usefulness of the information is past.

Learning outcome 3
Be able to communicate verbally in business environments

1 Active listening is important to ensure that the message is received. Active listening means:

   a looking at the speaker

   b being interested in what they say

   c asking questions

   d not interrupting

   e not planning your response while listening

   f summarising.

2 It is important to summarise verbal communication to ensure that the listener has understood the main points of the message.

3 Varying the tone, volume, pace, pitch, rhythm and inflection of your voice will avoid you being boring, dull and monotonous, and therefore losing your audience.

4 Information must be presented clearly so that the message is received and not misunderstood.

5 It is important to check that the audience has understood the message to avoid misunderstandings and allow you to clarify anything that has not been understood.

CHAPTER 2 UNIT 224 (B&A 36)

Principles of providing administrative services

Learning outcome 1
Understand the organisation and administration of meetings

1 Two differences between formal and informal meetings are:

  a formal meetings are more likely to require minutes

  b informal meetings require less documentation.

2 It is necessary to plan for meetings so that the object of the meeting is met.

3 Two procedures involved in organising meetings are:

  a informing attendees of the date, time and place

  b agreeing an agenda.

Learning outcome 2
Understand the organisation of travel and accommodation

1 Three types of travel are:

  a rail

  b road

  c air.

2 It is important to confirm instructions to avoid costly mistakes.

3 Two reasons to keep records of business travel are to:

  a account for costs incurred and paid for directly by the organisation for auditing purposes

  b meet expense claims from the traveller for costs incurred and paid for by them.

Learning outcome 3
Understand how to manage diary systems

1 Advantages of:

  a a paper-based diary are:

  - it can be taken with you
  - it can be locked away for confidentiality.

  Disadvantages are:

  - it can be lost or misplaced
  - only one person can make entries.

   b an electronic diary system are:

   - increased security through the use of passwords or encryption
   - information can be downloaded
   - different people can access them simultaneously.
   - it is not always easy to take with you
   - it requires some it skills to use
   - information can be deleted accidentally.

2 Information essential to record a meeting in a diary system includes:

   - date
   - time
   - duration
   - location
   - purpose
   - people involved
   - resources required.

3 Changes to arrangements may be made verbally, by telephone or by email, depending on the person's location and the available timescale.

Learning outcome 4
Understand how to use office equipment

1 Getting quotations enables you to check you are getting the best deal.

2 The answer to this question will be personal to the learner.

3 Two uses of a telephone are to make and receive calls.

4 The equipment to be used would be a photocopier and a binding machine. The photocopier would be the most efficient way to produce multiple copies, double-sided in colour and collated. The binding machine would be the most efficient way to bind the copies.

Learning outcome 5
Understand the use of mail services in a business context

1 Some organisations do not like the mail clerk to open mail marked:

   a for the attention of

   b personal

   c confidential

   d private.

2 There is urgency for dispatching mail because outgoing mail may contain items that are being waited for by customers, clients or suppliers.

3 A courier service may be used to deliver mail if they are considered cheaper or more efficient than Royal Mail or if Royal Mail has size restrictions on a large parcel which the courier does not.

Learning outcome 6
Understand customer service in a business environment

1 An external customer is one that does not work for the organisation providing the product or service.

2 The answer to this question will be personal to the learner.

3 It is important to meet or exceed the expectations of the customer so that they return and use the services of the organisation again.

4 The answer to this question will be personal to the learner.

CHAPTER 3 UNIT 225 (B&A 37)

Principles of business document production and information management

Learning outcome 1
Understand how to prepare business documents

1 Types of document that may be produced in a business environment include stationery such as letterheads, compliment slips, business cards and memos, promotional material such as catalogues, brochures and leaflets, and forms, which are essentially documents requiring information to be filled in.

2 Text and non-text can be integrated by inserting pictures, graphs and clip art. There are a variety of different features that can be used in programs such as Microsoft Word. Other applications such as Excel and PowerPoint help with integrating text and non-text in spreadsheets and slides.

3 It is important to agree and meet deadlines because a document, however well produced, is pointless if it is produced after its usefulness is past.

4 Version control clearly identifies the development of the document. It allows you for example to retain and identify the:
- first draft which was submitted to someone for comment
- draft which was created as a result of comments
- versions that went back and forward for further comment
- final version which was signed off.

5 The Data Protection Act enforces the correct storage, use and disclosure of personal information held electronically, on paper or on voice recordings.

6 A completed document is checked for accuracy by:

a looking through it yourself

b asking someone else to look through it

c using spell-checking tools

d proofreading for spelling, punctuation and grammar.

Learning outcome 2
Understand the distribution of business documents

1 It is important to maintain confidentiality because there may be information which is commercially sensitive in documentation which will be available to people outside the organisation. Any document must comply with the principles of the Data Protection Act, the Copyright, Designs and Patents Act and intellectual property rights, which include copyright, trademarks, patents, industrial design rights, trade dress and trade secrets.

2 The answer to this question will be personal to the learner.

Learning outcome 3
Understand how information is managed in business organisations

1 It is important to agree objectives and deadlines before researching information so that only the required information is researched and the parameters to be used can be agreed and so that the information is produced and delivered on time while it is still useful.

2 Files should be retained in archives using the same system as is used in the live filing system because it makes them easier to find if necessary, and makes the activity of archiving quicker and simpler.

3

Types of record	Types of confidential information
Human Resource records	Staff names, addresses, national insurance numbers, salaries, disciplinary information
Accounts records	Customer financial information, discounts, terms and conditions, overdue accounts, bank details
Telephone directories	None – these are public records

Types of record	Types of confidential information
Register Office records	None – this is public information
Medical records	Personal information relating to medical histories
Search engine information	None – these are public records

CHAPTER 4 UNIT 226 (B&A 38)

Understand employer organisations

Learning outcome 1
Understand organisational structures

1 Two differences between organisations in the private sector and those in the public sector are:

    a private sector organisations are set up to make a profit

    b public sector organisations are owned by local or national government.

2 The difference between a partnership and a corporation is that a partnership is owned by a number of named individuals, while a corporation is owned by shareholders, who can buy and sell their shares.

Learning outcome 2
Understand the organisational environment

1 The answer to this question is personal to the learner.

2 A SWOT analysis is an examination of strengths, weaknesses, opportunities and threats of an organisation.

3 Change is important because any organisation that is not moving forward and improving is moving backwards compared with its peers.

CHAPTER 5 UNIT 239 (M&L 1)

Manage personal performance and development

Learning outcome 1
Be able to manage personal performance

1 The purpose of continuously improving performance is to make you secure in your present employment and to improve the team's overall performance. Benefits are greater efficiency, increased motivation, increased job security, opportunities for progression.

2 It is important to accept responsibility for your own work because this shows a mature attitude and a willingness to improve.

3 In order that the problem can be resolved by someone with the appropriate level of authority.

Learning outcome 2
Be able to manage own time and workload

1 Your work–life balance is how you organise your days, how many hours you spend at work, and how much time you spend with friends or doing other extracurricular activities.

2 The answer to this question will be personal to the learner.

3 The answer to this question will be personal to the learner.

Learning outcome 3
Be able to identify own development needs

1 Benefits of:

a encouraging feedback include showing a willingness to listen and learn, and commitment to self-improvement

b accepting feedback from others include knowing where you need to improve and reassurance that you are working to an acceptable standard.

2 The answer to this question will be personal to the learner.

3 The answer to this question will be personal to the learner.

Learning outcome 4
Be able to fulfil a personal development plan

1 Learning and development can:

a Improve you own work by:

- increasing your skills and levels of knowledge
- increasing your self-confidence

b Benefit your organisation by:

- improving your levels of performance
- assisting in succession planning

c Identify career options:

- gaining qualifications and needed for progression
- making you aware of opportunities.

2 Purposes of a performance appraisal include:

- measuring your performance against expectations
- discussing gaps between performance and expectations
- identifying goals and objectives
- identifying targets
- identifying opportunities for learning and development.

3 Headings that would be found in a learning plan:

- objective
- timescales
- resources needed
- measure of achievement.

CHAPTER 6 UNIT 240 (M&L 2)

Develop working relationships with colleagues

Learning outcome 1
Understand the principles of effective team working

1 The benefits of effective team working are that teams offer support, promote shared working and provide efficiency.

2 Any two of:

- Plant – this team member is the creative member of the team, solving problems in unconventional ways.
- Monitor evaluator – this team member is logical and considers options dispassionately.
- Co-ordinator – this team member concentrates on objectives and delegating work.
- Implementer – this team member plans a strategy and ways of carrying it out.
- Completer finisher – this team member checks for errors.
- Teamworker – this team member helps the team to come together and is able to identify the work required to complete the task.

- Shaper – this team member provides the drive to keep the team moving forward.
- Specialist – this team member has an in-depth knowledge of a particular area of the team's objectives.

3 Constructive feedback explains what should have been done as well as what should not have been in order to assist learning for the future.

4 Compromise is useful when time is short and the issue is too complex for a simple right or wrong answer.

Learning outcome 2
Be able to maintain effective working relationships with colleagues

1 It is important to acknowledge the contribution of individuals to the achievement of team objectives to provide encouragement and because the purpose of forming a team is to benefit from the various qualities of its members.

2 It is important to treat colleagues with respect because they deserve it and because they will perform better.

3 Two benefits of fulfilling agreements made with colleagues are:

a your colleagues will be satisfied

b if you make and keep promises, your colleagues will sing your praises and recommend you for other tasks. (If you fail to fulfil a commitment, the story is likely to follow you.)

4 Change that is done to us is most likely to meet resistance because no one likes being told what to do and we don't feel in control.

Learning outcome 3
Be able to collaborate with colleagues to resolve problems

1 Taking others' viewpoints into account in decision-making helps to build the team's commitment and confidence, create opportunities for the team to excel and create a vision which the team can share.

2 Taking ownership of a problem means accepting responsibility for finding and implementing a solution.

3 It is important to minimise disruption to business activities as this can lead to customer dissatisfaction, lost sales and lost profit.

4 You should resolve only problems within your level of authority because there may be implications that you are unaware of if you attempt to resolve problems that are beyond your authority.

CHAPTER 7 UNIT 203 (B&A 15)

Collate and report data

Learning outcome 1
Understand how to collate and report data

1 Different ways of organising information include:
- in flat-file databases
- in relational databases
- in paper form.

2 Different ways of reporting information include:
- written reports
- statistical reports
- verbal reports.

3 It is important to present information in the agreed format to meet the requirements of the person requesting the information.

4 Reports present information in a concise and easily understood way.

5 The Copyright, Designs and Patents Act 1988.

Learning outcome 2
Be able to collate data

1 It is important that information is complete, accurate and up to date to meet the requirements of the person presenting the information.

2 Research information can be validated by checking the sources of the information and the credibility if its author.

3 Information can be organised into tables, charts or graphs such as scatter graphs, pie charts, bar or column charts, line graphs, radar or spider charts.

4 It is important to present information within the agreed timescale to maintain efficiency and give a positive impression.

Learning outcome 3
Be able to report data

1 House style is a set of rules concerning spellings, typography and other conventions observed in a particular organisation.

2 It is important that reports are distributed only to authorised readers in order to maintain confidentiality.

CHAPTER 8 UNIT 204 (B&A 16)

Store and retrieve information

Learning outcome 1
Understand information storage and retrieval

1 Unsuccessful job applications must be retained for six months after notification.

2 Files should be retained in archives using the same system as live files because this makes them easier to find and easier to archive.

3

Types of record	Types of confidential information
Human Resource records	Staff names, addresses, national insurance numbers, salaries, disciplinary information
Accounts records	Customer financial information, discounts, terms and conditions, overdue accounts, bank details
Telephone directories	None – these are public records
Register Office records	None – this is public information
Medical records	Personal information relating to medical histories
Search engine information	None – these are public records

4 Answers are:

a false – unless there is inadequate protection

b true.

5 The most effective ways of storing each are:

a Purchase invoice – alphabetically/chronologically. You are most likely to look for them under the name of the supplier and the date of the order.

b National insurance numbers – alpha-numerically because they consist of letters and numbers.

c Vehicle registrations – alpha-numerically because they consist of letters and numbers.

Learning outcome 2
Be able to gather and store information

1 Confidential information must be disposed of in a way that makes it impossible to retrieve. Paper records should be shredded, electronic records must be deleted in a way that cannot be recovered.

2 The answer will depend on the organisation the learner works for.

3 The answer to this question will be personal to the learner.

Learning outcome 3
Be able to retrieve information

1 The answer to this question will be personal to the learner.

2 The answer to this question will be personal to the learner.

CHAPTER 9 UNIT 205 (B&A 17)

Produce minutes of meetings

Learning outcome 1
Understand how to take minutes of meetings

1 It is important that minutes are accurate as they are a record of events, discussions and decisions taken at a meeting. Inaccuracy can lead to disputes or incorrect decisions. It is important they are grammatical because poor grammar can lead to confusion or misunderstanding.

2 At some meetings there is a legal requirement under the Freedom of Information Act to make a record. At board meetings there may be a requirement under the Companies Act.

3 See the glossary of useful terms at the end of this chapter – any of these terms could be explained in answer to this question.

4 The role of the chairperson is to:
- start the meeting on time
- clarify roles and responsibilities
- establish ground rules and guidelines
- participate as an attendee
- follow the agenda and keep the meeting focused on agenda items
- retain the power to stop what's happening and change the format
- encourage accountability
- summarise key decisions and actions

- record recommendations and allocate responsibilities for specific tasks
- make the most of the experience present – ask questions to draw out people with experience
- allow time to hear experts' points of view but allocate time with clear directions
- for important issues, when time is limited, set up a sub-committee to collect facts, review the situation, and prepare recommendations to be considered at the next meeting
- close the meeting on time
- agree the items to be included on the agenda
- follow agenda items in sequence and inform the minute-taker of any departures from the agreed agenda
- summarise specific points, decisions or courses of action agreed for each specific agenda item before moving on to the next item
- provide specific guidance to the minute-taker on what to record for a particular agenda item where lengthy discussion has occurred or a complex issue has been discussed
- take time to review the minutes when they are drafted.

5 It is important to work in partnership with the chairperson so that the meeting is as effective as possible.

Learning outcome 2
Be able to take notes of meetings

1 Verbatim minutes would be taken in parliamentary and courtroom proceedings.

2 Allocated responsibilities must be recorded to allow follow-up actions to be taken before or at subsequent meetings.

Learning outcome 3
Be able to produce minutes of meetings

1 Notes would record the discussion so that minutes can give a precise account. You should leave a line between each line of the notes to allow further comments to be added in if necessary.

2 If you required clarification you should address your question directly to the chairperson.

3 Active listening means:

- looking at the speaker
- being interested in what they say
- asking questions
- not interrupting

- not planning your response while listening
- summarising.

4 Professional language is used in minute-taking because the minutes may be viewed by senior members of the organisation and other important people.

CHAPTER 10 UNIT 207 (B&A 19)

Provide reception services

Learning outcome 1
Understanding reception services

1 The receptionist is usually the first person that a visitor sees on arrival at the premises. The impression given by the receptionist is the impression the visitor will take of the organisation. Therefore, the presentation and attitude of the receptionist is important in helping to portray the organisation positively.

2 The receptionist can create a positive impression of themselves by being well-presented, well-spoken and having a good working knowledge of the organisation and the surrounding area, and a generally professional attitude.

3 The purpose of suggesting improvements to a reception area is to improve the impression given to visitors and the efficiency, health, safety and security of the organisation.

4 The answer to this question will be personal to the learner.

5 The answer to this question will be personal to the learner.

Learning outcome 2
Be able to provide a reception service

1 The role of the receptionist in the event of an emergency evacuation is to:
- make sure visitors understand the procedure
- confirm visitors have left the building with the person they had come to meet
- contact colleagues to ensure safe evacuation of visitors
- close the doors on leaving the building
- take the visitors' book and staff signing-in records to the person responsible for checking everyone is accounted for.

2 Entry procedures are in place to ensure that only authorised people are in the building and that there is a record of those on the premises in case of emergencies. Departure procedures are in place so that security checks can be carried out if necessary and to

avoid the risk of someone being thought to be unaccounted for in an emergency when they have actually left the premises.

3 Health and safety hazards typically found in a reception area include:

- slippery floors
- damaged floors
- holes in carpets
- wet floors
- patterned floors
- trailing cables
- damaged cables
- hot liquids
- electrical sockets
- obstructions
- discarded rubbish.

4 Problems that may be encountered with visitors include:

- aggression
- not recording their departure
- not being aware of safety and security procedures.

5 Additional duties may include:

- answering the phone
- dealing with post
- photocopying
- data entry.

CHAPTER 11 UNIT 211 (B&A 23)

Understand the use of research in business

Learning outcome 1
Understand the research process

1 It is important to agree objectives and deadlines before researching information so that only the required information is researched and the parameters to be used can be agreed.

2 Information should be recorded and stored in ways that allow it to be retrieved easily if needed again.

3 It is necessary to record the sources of information in case you need to go back to the source for confirmation or clarification. Also in case any issues of copyright arise.

4   It is important to check the reliability of sources of information because internet content, in particular, is unregulated. Repeating information that is inaccurate will lead to further errors.

5   The internet is often easier to access than paper-based sources of information. However, paper-based sources are more reliable, as the author is usually known.

Learning outcome 2
Understand how to use research in business

1   The answer to this question will be personal to the learner.

2   Research information can be validated by checking the sources of the information and the credibility of its author.

3   Legislation which affects the publication of research findings includes the Copyright, Designs and Patents Act, the Copyright (Computer Programs) Regulations and the Data Protection Act.

4   Personal and organisation-specific ethics can affect research through their need to ensure honesty, objectivity, carefulness, openness, confidentiality and respect for intellectual property.

CHAPTER 12 UNIT 215 (B&A 27)

Contribute to the organisation of an event

Learning outcome 1
Understand event organisation

1   The client's role is to state their requirements and set the budget.

2   Team-building events increase overall employee performance, promote co-operation among team members and across teams, improve job satisfaction and help to broaden the understanding of organisational goals and objectives.

3   Risk assessments should follow five steps:

   a   identify the hazard

   b   decide who might be harmed and how

   c   evaluate the risks and decide on precaution

   d   record your findings and implement them

   e   review your assessment and update if necessary.

4   The security risks at an event include fire, theft and demonstrations.

5   The answer to this question will be personal to the learner.

Learning outcome 2
Be able to carry out pre-event actions

1 The venue requirements for a wedding include catering, entertainment and accommodation

2 Resources should be organised in a timely manner so that the event runs to plan and satisfies the needs of the attendees

3 Pre-event documentation for an AGM would include information on date, time and venue, notice of motions to be voted on, voting forms and forms to indicate intention to attend

4 Attendee responses help to plan for the number of attendees when booking catering and accommodation

5 Potential needs of attendees include dietary requirements, transport for those who need it, directions to the event and translators/interpreters.

Learning outcome 3
Be able to set up an event

1 Different types of layout for an event are:
 - theatre style layout
 - classroom layout
 - cabaret layout
 - horseshoe layout
 - boardroom layout
 - banquet layout.

2 Two checks that should be made on equipment are

 a that it is suitable

 b that it is working.

3 Your behaviour during the event is important because it reflects on the organisation that you represent.

Learning outcome 4
Be able to carry out post-event actions

1 It is important to return the venue to the required conditions because it will be part of the venue's terms and conditions and because the next user will expect to find it in a useable condition.

2 The follow-up actions will depend on the event plan and any agreements made during the event but are likely to involve evaluating the event in various respects.

CHAPTER 13 UNIT 227 (B&A 39)

Employee rights and responsibilities

Learning outcome 1
Understand the role of organisations and industries

1 The answer to this question will be personal to the learner.

2 The answer to this question will be personal to the learner.

3 Two sources of information on training are the human resources department and the relevant trade union.

4 A code of practice is a set of professional standards or written guidelines agreed on by members of a particular profession, or written guidelines issued by an official body or a professional association to its members to help them comply with its ethical standards.

5 The answer to this question will be personal to the learner.

6 The role of trade unions is to achieve common goals such as protecting the integrity of their trade, achieving higher pay, increasing the number of employees an employer hires and better working conditions.

Learning outcome 2
Understand employers' expectations and employees' rights and obligations

1 Statutory rights that you have in a workplace could be any of:

- A written statement of terms of employment within two months of starting work.
- An itemised payslip.
- To be paid at least the national minimum wage.
- Not to have illegal deductions made from pay.
- Paid holiday – full-time employees are entitled to at least 28 days a year.
- Paid time off to look for work if being made redundant. This applies once you have worked for two years for an employer.
- Time off for study or training for 16-17 year-olds.
- Paid time off for antenatal care.
- Paid maternity leave.
- Paid paternity leave.
- To ask for flexible working to care for children or adult dependants.
- Paid adoption leave.

- Unpaid parental leave for both men and women (if you have worked for the employer for one year) and the right to reasonable time off to look after dependants in an emergency.
- To work a maximum 48-hour working week.
- Weekly and daily rest breaks. There are special rules for night workers.
- Not to be discriminated against.
- To carry on working until you are at least 65.
- Notice of dismissal, provided you have worked for your employer for at least one calendar month.
- Written reasons for dismissal from your employer.
- To claim compensation if unfairly dismissed.
- To claim redundancy pay if made redundant. In most cases you will have to have worked for two years to be able to claim redundancy pay.
- Not to suffer detriment or dismissal for 'blowing the whistle' on a matter of public concern (malpractice) at the workplace.
- The right of a part-time worker to the same contractual rights (pro rata) as a comparable full-time worker.
- The right of a fixed-term employee to the same contractual rights as a comparable permanent employee.

2 The answer to this question will be personal to the learner.

3 Two pieces of legislation that protect the rights of the employee are:
- the Equality Act
- the Working Time Directive.

4 Advice on rights can be obtained from:
- Health and Safety Executive
- Department of Business, Innovation and Skills
- Chartered Institute of Personnel and Development (CIPD)
- Trades Union Congress (TUC)
- Advisory, Conciliation and Arbitration Service (ACAS)
- your trade union
- Citizens Advice Bureau
- the internet
- public library
- government agencies.

CHAPTER 14 UNIT 101 (B&A 4)

Learning outcome 1
Understand health and safety responsibilities in a business environment

1 An employer's responsibilities are to:
   a provide a safe work area
   b provide clearly defined procedures
   c ensure safe handling, transport and storage of items and substances
   d train and supervise staff in health and safety matters
   e maintain safe entries and exits
   f provide adequate temperature, lighting, seating, etc
   g ensure visitors are informed of any hazards.

2 An employee's responsibilities are to:
   a work in a safe and sensible way
   b co-operate with employers
   c not interfere with safety equipment
   d use equipment safely and correctly
   e report potential risks
   f help identify training needs

3 The Display Screen Equipment Regulations.

4 It is important to work safely to protect yourself and others from harm.

Learning outcome 2
Know how to work safely in a business environment

1 The answer to this question will be personal to the learner.

2 Ways to avoid accidents in the workplace include:
   - keeping all shared areas, such as corridors, kitchens, photocopying areas and stairways free from obstruction
   - carrying out an inspection regularly to ensure that housekeeping standards are well maintained
   - when carrying anything up or down stairs, one hand should be kept free to hold the handrail
   - never use your mobile phone while walking up or down stairs.

3 It is important to report hazards and accidents in the workplace to:
   - order to comply with RIDDOR
   - reduce the risk of further accidents.

4 The answer to this question will be personal to the learner.

Learning outcome 3
Be able to comply with health and safety requirements in a business environment

1 It is important to use approved techniques when lifting heavy objects to prevent strain and injury.

2 If an employee does not follow the health and safety policy and procedures, they could put themselves and others at risk.

3 It is important to follow manufacturer's instructions in the use of equipment, materials and products because failure to do so could cause damage to the equipment, cause risk to people, and invalidate the guarantee.

4 It is important to adhere to health and safety policies to avoid harm to yourself and others.

GLOSSARY

A

Accountability Responsibility to somebody or for something

Acquisition An action in which a company buys most, if not all, of another company's assets in order to assume control

Ad hoc Meaning literally 'for this' or 'for this situation' so for a particular purpose, for example, when a sub-committee is set up especially to organise a works outing

Adjourn To hold a meeting over until a later date

Adopt minutes Minutes are 'adopted' when accepted by members and signed by the chairperson

Advisory Providing advice or suggestion, not taking action

Agenda A schedule of items drawn up for discussion at a meeting

Altruism An attitude or way of behaving marked by unselfish concern for the welfare of others

Ambassador An official representative of an organisation

Amendment An addition or alteration to a motion

Anecdotal Consisting of or based on second-hand accounts rather than first-hand knowledge, experience or scientific investigation

Apologies Excuses given in advance for inability to attend a meeting

Archive A collection of documents such as documents or computer records, kept for future reference

Articles of association Rules required by company law which govern a company's activities

Articulate To express thoughts, ideas, or feelings coherently

Attendance list In some meetings a list is passed round to be signed as a record of attendance

Authority The right to act in certain ways designated by the organisation and to directly influence the actions of others through instructions

B

Belbin Meredith Belbin measured preference for team roles which he had identified

Benchmark To provide a standard against which something can be measured or assessed

Bibliography A list of referenced books and articles which appears at the end of a book or other text

Broadsheet newspaper that is printed in a large format and is associated with serious journalism

Bureau de change An office, often found in a bank, which allows consumers to exchange one currency for another. The bureau de change charges a commission for the currency exchange service.

Business case The business justification for initiating a task or project

Bye-laws Rules regulating an organisation's activities

C

Capital expense Money spent on assets that have a useful life of more than one year

Cascade Pass information on in a downward flow or direction within an organisation

Cash flow The cash flow of a business is the movement of money into and out of it. Also used to describe the funds in a company's bank account that allow them to carry out their day-to -day business operations such as payment for supplies and staff salaries.

Casting vote An extra vote that a chairperson may use to reach a decision if votes are equally divided

Chairperson The person nominated/given authority to run a meeting

Chairperson's agenda Based upon the meeting agenda but containing explanatory notes

Classify To assign things or people to categories

Cohesion The state or condition of joining or working together to form a united whole, or the tendency to do this

Collaborative Working together towards a common end

Collective responsibility A convention by which all meeting members agree to abide by a majority decision

Commercially sensitive Information that an organisation would not like to be in the public domain as it may give an advantage to a competitor

Committee A group of people usually elected or appointed who meet to conduct agreed business and report to a senior body

Communal Used or owned by all members of a group or organisation

Competence The ability of an individual to carry out a task properly to the required standard

Complementary Combining with something else in a way that enhances it or emphasises its qualities

Comprehensive Including everything, so as to be complete

Conflict The internal or external discord that occurs as a result of differences in ideas, values or beliefs of two or more people

Consensus Agreement by general consent, no formal vote being taken

Constitution Set of rules governing activities of voluntary bodies

Constructive feedback Feedback which involves telling the person what you think they can improve on and then providing an example or a suggestion

Consulate The office of a government official living in a foreign city to promote the commercial interests of the official's own state and protect its citizens

Consumables Items that are intended to be discarded after use

Contrary Not at all in agreement with something

Convene To call a meeting

Conventions The customary way in which things are done within a group or organisation

Convey To communicate or express something

Correlation A relationship in which two or more things are mutual or complementary, or one is caused by another

Cross-contamination The passing of bacteria or other harmful substances indirectly from one person to another

Cross-referencing A reference from one part of a file to another part containing related information

Customised Altered to fit somebody's requirements

D

Data controller The person who decides the purpose for which personal data is to be processed

Database An organised collection of data.

Daunting Likely to discourage, intimidate, or frighten somebody

Decision matrix A matrix used by teams to evaluate possible solutions to problems. Each solution is listed. Criteria are selected and listed on the top row to rate the possible solutions. Each possible solution is rated on a scale from 1 to 5 for each criterion and the rating recorded in the corresponding grid. The ratings of all the criteria for each possible solution are added to determine each solution's score. The scores are then used to help decide which solution deserves the most attention.

Decision minutes Resolution minutes are sometimes called 'decision minutes'

Decision tree A decision tree is a graph that uses a branching method to illustrate every possible outcome of a decision

Delegate Give authority to somebody else to act, make decisions or allocate resources on one's behalf

Differentiate To establish a difference between two things or among several things

Digitise Convert an image, graph, or other data into digital form for processing on a computer

Diplomacy Skill and tact in dealing with other people

Disconcerting Making somebody feel ill at ease, slightly confused, or taken aback

Discretion The power to make decisions sensitively on the basis of one's knowledge and the ability to keep sensitive information secret

Domain names The name of the website as it appears in the address bar (followed by a suffix such as .com, .edu etc and often preceded by www.)

Dumbing down The deliberate diminishment of the intellectual level of the content of schooling and education, of literature and cinema, and of news

Eject Remove someone (by force if necessary) from a meeting

Empathy The ability to identify and understand another's situation, feelings and viewpoints, and to put yourself in the other person's shoes

Empowerment Giving somebody a greater sense of confidence or self-esteem

Encapsulate To enclose something completely

Encryption The conversion of computer data and messages into something incomprehensible using a key, so that only a holder of the matching key can reconvert them

Engagement The feeling of being involved in a particular activity

Enhancement The increase of the clarity, degree of detail, or another quality of an electronic image by using a computer program

Ergonomic Designed for maximum comfort, efficiency, safety and ease of use, especially in the workplace

Ethical Consistent with agreed principles of correct moral conduct

Ex officio Given powers or rights by reason of office

Executive Having the power to act upon taken decisions

Exemplary So good or admirable that others would do well to copy it

Exemption Permission or entitlement not to do something that others are obliged to do

Expenditure The amount of money spent

Extroversion Interest in and involvement with people and things outside yourself

F

Fiduciary Adjective describing a legal or ethical relationship of trust between two or more parties

Fight or flight A reaction that occurs in response to a perceived harmful event, attack, or threat to survival

Flexi-time A variable work schedule, in contrast to traditional work arrangements, requiring employees to work a standard 9am to 5pm day

G

Generic Relating to or suitable for a range or class of similar things

Governance The process of governing a country or organisation

Guillotine Cut short a debate – usually in parliament

H

Hierarchical Relating to or arranged in a formally ranked order

Honorary post A duty performed without payment, eg Honorary Secretary

House style A set of rules concerning spellings, typography, etc

Hybrid A system made up of a mixture of paper and electronic systems

Hypocrite Somebody who pretends to have admirable principles, beliefs, or feelings but behaves otherwise

I

Illegible Impossible or very difficult to read

Improvised explosive device (IED) A simple bomb that someone, especially a terrorist or guerrilla, has made themselves

Indices Scales that express the price, value or level of something in relation to something else or to a base number

Inflection A change in the pitch or tone of the voice

Initiate To cause something, especially an important event or process, to begin

Innovation A new invention or way of doing something

Integral Part of something larger and not separate from it

Intelligence Services An organisation that gathers information about the secret plans or activities of an adversary or potential adversary

Interactions Communication between or joint activity involving two or more people

Interim An interval of time between one event, process or period and another

Intra vires Within the power of the committee or meeting to discuss and carry out

Invalidate To deprive something of its legal force or value, for instance by failing to comply with some terms and conditions.

Itinerary A plan for a journey listing different places in the order in which they are to be visited

J

Jargon Language that is used by a group or profession, especially words and phrases which are not understood or used by other people

Jerked Pulled with a sudden strong movement

L

Lie on the table Leave item to be considered instead at the next meeting (see 'table')

Lobbying A practice of seeking members' support before a meeting

Lucid Clear and easily understood

M

Merger The combining of two or more independent corporations under a single ownership

Missive A letter or other written communication, often formal or legal communication

Motion The name for a 'proposal' put forward for discussion at a meeting

Motivate To make somebody feel enthusiastic, interested, and committed to something

Mover One who speaks on behalf of a motion

Multinational A large company that operates or has investments in several different countries

N

Narrative Narrative minutes are a summary of the meeting including discussions and conclusions

Nem con From the Latin 'nemine contradicente', literally 'no one speaking against' so with no one dissenting, unanimous

Neutral Belonging to, favouring, or assisting no side in a dispute, contest, or controversy

O

Objective Based on facts rather than thoughts or opinions, free of any bias or prejudice caused by personal feelings

Opposer One who speaks against a motion

Optical An instrument or device that is sensitive to light

Optimise Make something such as a method or process as good or as effective as possible

Other business Either items left over from a previous meeting, or items discussed after the main business of a meeting

P

Parameter A fact or circumstance that restricts how something is done or what can be done

Peripheral Externally related or connected, for example, a device linked to a computer to provide communication (as input and output) or auxiliary functions (such as additional storage)

Philosophical Concerned with or given to thinking about the larger issues and deeper meanings in life and events

Point of information The drawing of attention in a meeting to a relevant item of fact

Point of order Querying or drawing attention to a breach of rules or procedures –proceedings may be interrupted on a 'point of order' if procedures or rules are not being kept to in a meeting

Pre-existing Something that already existed

Price differential A difference in the prices of two products or of the same product in different places

Profit The difference between sales and expenses

Proposal The name given to a submitted item for discussion (usually written) before a meeting takes place

Proxy This means 'on behalf of another person' – a proxy vote signifies that one person is authorised to vote on behalf of another person who may be absent

Punitive Causing great difficulty or hardship

Q

Qualified buyer An individual or company who is in the market and displays some evidence of being financially able to buy

Qualitative Relating to or based on the quality or character of something, often as opposed to its size or quantity

Quality standard A document that provides requirements, specifications, guidelines or characteristics that can be used consistently to ensure that materials, products, processes and services are fit for their purpose

Qualitative Relating to or based on the quality or character of something, often as opposed to its size or quantity

Quantitative Relating to, concerning, or based on the amount or number of something; capable of being measured or expressed in numerical terms

Quorum The minimum number of people needed to be in attendance for a meeting to be legitimate and so commence

R

Read-only tag Users are unable to change the content without saving the file with a new title

Refer back To pass an item back for further consideration

Remuneration The paying or rewarding of somebody for their work or input

Repetitive strain injury (RSI) An injury of the musculoskeletal and nervous systems that may be caused by repetitive tasks, forceful exertions, vibrations, pressing against hard surfaces and sustained or awkward positions

Resolution A firm decision to do something or in meeting terms, the name given to a 'motion' which has been passed or carried, used after the decision has been reached

Router A piece of equipment or software that finds the best way of sending information between any two networks

S

Search engine A website designed to search for information on the World Wide Web

Seconder One who supports the 'proposer' of a motion or proposal by 'seconding' it

Secret ballot A system of voting in secret

Secretary Committee official responsible for the internal and external administration of a committee

Sector A component of an integrated system such as an economy or a society

Shelve To drop a motion which has no support

Simultaneously Done, happening, or existing at the same time

Sine die From Latin, literally, 'without a day', that is to say indefinitely, eg 'adjourned sine die'

Snatched Grabbed or grasped hastily

Spam An unsolicited, often commercial, message transmitted through the internet as a mass mailing to a large number of recipients

Stakeholder A person or group with a direct interest, involvement or investment in something

Standing committee A committee which has an indefinite term of office

Standing orders Rules of procedure governing public sector meetings

Statutory Covered by a permanent established rule or law, especially one involved in the running of a company or other organisation, and subject to the penalty laid down by that statute

Sterling The currency in pounds and pence used in the United Kingdom

Swipe cards A card inserted into a reader to allow access

SWOT analysis SWOT analysis is a structured planning method used to evaluate the 'strengths', 'weaknesses', 'opportunities' and 'threats' involved in a project or in a business venture

Synergy The working together of two or more people, organizations, or things, especially when the result is greater than the sum of their individual effects or capabilities

Succinct Expressed with brevity and clarity, with no wasted words

T

Table To introduce a paper or schedule for noting

Tabloid A small-format popular newspaper with a simple style, many photographs, and sometimes an emphasis on sensational stories

Taken as read To save time, it is assumed the members have already read the minutes

Team dynamics The unconscious, psychological forces that influence the direction of a team's behaviour and performance

Telecommuting Working from home on a computer linked to the workplace via modem

Terms and conditions The requirements laid down formally in an agreement or contract, or proposed by one side when negotiating an agreement

Transcribe To write out an exact copy of something heard such as a discussion or audio recording

Treasurer Committee official responsible for its financial records and transactions

U

Ultra vires Beyond the authority of the meeting to consider

Unanimous All being in favour

USB Universal serial bus: a way of connecting a printer, keyboard, or other piece of equipment to a computer using a special cable and without having to turn the computer off and on again

V

Validity Having binding force in law

Varifocal Spectacles with composite lenses for distant, intermediate, and near vision

Visa An official endorsement in a passport authorising the bearer to enter or leave, and travel in or through, a specific country or region

INDEX